Frederick S.
& Stephen W. Weston

Contemporary Threat Management

A PRACTICAL GUIDE FOR IDENTIFYING, ASSESSING AND MANAGING INDIVIDUALS OF VIOLENT INTENT

A Practical Guide Series
By Specialized Training Services

San Diego, California

Published by Specialized Training Services
(An imprint of Specialized Training Services, Inc.)
9606 Tierra Grande, Suite 105
San Diego, CA 92126

Edited by Drew Leavens

Printed in the United States of America

Library of Congress Cataloging-in-Publication Data

Calhoun, Frederick S. & Weston, Stephen W.
Contemporary Threat Management /
Frederick S. Calhoun & Stephen W. Weston
p. 280
ISBN 0-9703189-3-6

Library of Congress Control Number: 2003111268

The Specialized Training Services Practical Guide Series:

Contemporary Threat Management
Frederick S. Calhoun & Stephen W. Weston

Children Who Witness Homicide and Other Violent Crimes
Tascha Boychuk-Spears, Ph.D., R.N.

School Violence Threat Management
Kris Mohandie, Ph.D.

Violence Risk and Threat Assessment
J. Reid Meloy, Ph.D.

For information on these and other books, tapes, videos and training offered by Specialized Training Services, contact:

Specialized Training Services, Inc.
9606 Tierra Grande, Suite 105
San Diego, CA 92126
(858) 695-1313, (858) 695-6599 (fax)
or visit our website at: www.specializedtraining.com

TABLE OF CONTENTS

Dedication

This book is dedicated to every person who has suffered from acts of intended violence and to each professional who is committed to preventing future violence.

PART I. CONTEMPORARY THREAT MANAGEMENT

CHAPTER ONE

Contemporary Threat Management

Threat management has come of age. It now offers the best hope of identifying, investigating, and managing individuals of violent intent. Formerly, most law enforcement officers felt powerless to do anything about an individual's potential for violence unless that individual broke the law. Too often, of course, that meant waiting too late to prevent any violence. Now, however, law enforcement agencies, human resource departments, school administrators, social service providers, mental health professionals, and members of a host of other professions involving human interactions cannot afford to ignore the lessons being drawn from contemporary threat management. The research has grown too extensive and the practical experiences too many and too frequent for anyone to hide behind claims of ignorance.

Newspapers across the country report instances of intended violence daily. They occur in workplaces large and small; at schools and universities; churches and synagogues; social gathering places; and against intimates, public figures, government officials, and social outriggers. Indeed, the problem has become so endemic that we can now draw a conceptual link connecting these seemingly disparate instances of murder and mayhem. Contemporary threat management provides the bridge. It postulates that individuals intending to commit an act of violence must engage in specific *attack-related* behaviors. Although this applies equally to an array of criminal activities, we confine our conception to any act of violence for its own sake, undiluted by other base criminal aspirations, such as armed robbery, rape, or extortion. Contemporary threat management deals with assassinations, planned acts of domestic violence; premeditated attacks at schools, universities, churches or workplaces; and other instances in which the perpetrator specifically targets other individuals because of who they are, how they are related to the perpetrator, or what they symbolize.

In developing the concept of contemporary threat management, we drew on the research and case experiences of a rather disparate group of law enforcement and private agencies having security responsibilities. In studying how these agencies managed their cases, we noticed more similarities than differences, despite the fact that the various agencies' clientele ranged from presidents to public officials to jurists to public figures to schools and workplaces to battered spouses to the helpless and forlorn. The pudding, then, provided the proof. If the same threat management techniques apply to so many different and disparate victims, some link must exist. The link lay not in the various targets, but in the fact that the perpetrators all clearly intended violence against those targets.[1]

Establishing the Need for the Threat Management Process

We propose a simple test any law enforcement agency, security department, mental health care provider, or government agency can use to determine if its organization needs to establish a threat management process to enhance the security it provides. Take a moment to visit with anyone in your organization or clientele that routinely receives communications or reports from within the organization or from outsiders. Ask the following four simple questions:

1. Have you ever seen communications or contacts that struck you as inappropriate for the setting in which the communication or contact occurred?

2. Have you ever received a letter, phone call, or visit that you considered strange, unusually angry, too personal, or too emotional?

3. In the course of doing your job, have you ever felt scared or concerned for your personal safety?

4. If you find yourself in an unnerving situation on the job, do you know who to call or report the circumstances to?

Invariably, seasoned employees answer these questions the same. "Yes, we get strange letters, calls, and visits all the time. Other than '911,' we don't know who to call to report them." Frequently, the receptionist, clerk, administrative assistant, or social worker will point to a box in the corner or a bottom file drawer where he or she has been keeping all the "nut" mail over the years.

Case Study:

Sweethearts

A threat manager gave a briefing on inappropriate communications and contacts to the staff of the Chief Executive Officer (CEO) of an internationally known corporation. Afterward, one of the staff members pulled open a file drawer. Inside were crammed hundreds of letters from various individuals addressed over the years to succeeding CEOs. Some letters were threatening, some were delusional ramblings, others contained vulgar hand-drawings, and some expressed unrequited love for the CEO.

"We call this the sweetheart file," the staff member explained.

By opening lines of communication, threat managers will get reports on subjects making inappropriate communications or contacts to offices and employees within the threat manager's jurisdiction.

SOURCE: Authors' personal knowledge.

Other key employees will no doubt disclose that strange people regularly approach perimeter security, only to be turned away. Involved individuals will readily confess their suspicions and fears once asked, but rarely does anyone ask if they are worried. In workplaces, schools, government offices, or other places, individuals working, studying, or visiting frequently make ominous comments or gestures. Those who overhear those comments or see the gestures wonder *to themselves* if this subject might "go off" soon. The blind concessionaire in a government building hears a lot of outraged mumblings, but does not know who to tell about them. A school secretary feels discomfited whenever a certain teacher comes to the front office, but she worries that reporting her discomfort will make her look weak or foolish. The security officer at a large factory thinks the homeless man who camps out near the public entrance has been acting stranger than normal lately, but he is not sure who he should tell about it. The administrative assistant at an abortion clinic notices that one of the regular protestors has become more brazen whenever the assistant enters or leaves the clinic, but he does not know if that change in behavior should be reported to the local police. A wife involved in a contested divorce suspects that her estranged husband may try to take their children, but she cannot articulate her suspicions beyond just a feeling, nothing more specific than that. Who will listen to her, indeed, to any of them?

Case Study:

Geometry of Love

Robert Wissman's co-workers and friends noticed a definite change in his behavior over several days. But since they could explain its cause, they thought little of it. Wissman, they knew, was involved in a "love triangle" involving two other workers at the Nu-Wood Decorative Millwork plant in Goshen, Indiana. Wissman, who also ran a firearm's dealership out of his house, had sought bankruptcy protection in 1998. Three years later, his friends reasoned, Wissman's financial woes were compounded by the emotional stress of the triangle. No wonder he behaved differently.

On the morning of December 6, 2001, Wissman erupted. He got into an argument with the other man in the triangle and threatened him. Greg Oswald, the plant manager, either fired Wissman on the spot or told him he would be fired. Since neither Wissman nor the manager survived the day, Wissman's employment status remains unknown. Witnesses did report that Oswald and a supervisor escorted Wissman out of the plant. Wissman allegedly threatened to return to work with a gun. Shortly before noon, Oswald briefed the remaining employee's that Wissman "was not himself." He instructed the plant workers to lock all the doors except the front entrance and to call for help if they saw Wissman.

According to Oswald's wife, who had lunch with him that day, Oswald also called the Goshen police. He told his wife that the police could not do anything unless Oswald got a restraining order. The police had no record of the call.

Wissman made true on his threat. He returned to the plant about 2:30 in the afternoon, entering through the front door. He began shooting a .12 gauge shotgun, wounding half a dozen of his former colleagues and killing Oswald. Wissman then shot himself with the shotgun four times in the head and chest before dying.

Individuals of violent intent often let their intentions be known, but only trained threat managers may be able to recognize the warning signs and implement measures to defuse the risk.

SOURCE: Associated Press, December 6 & 7, 2001; New York Times, December 6 & 7, 2001; Washington Post, December 6 & 7, 2001.

The test will show that many things are going on that need to be attended to, but no one yet attends to them. Take the case of Robert Wissman, whose fellow employees noticed changes in his behavior several days prior to his attack, who fought with his romantic rival and got fired, and who threatened to come back to the plant with a gun. The plant manager feared enough to warn his employees and to lock the doors and, possibly, to call the police. But no one knew how to manage Wissman away from the violence he clearly intended. An alert, well-trained threat manager would quickly have recognized Wissman's financial problems, compounded by his emotional distress over the triangle, and exacerbated further by losing his job. The collapse of those inhibitors, combined with the intimacy of his relationship with his co-worker, gave great credence to his threats.

Consequently, the first step in establishing a threat management process is to identify someone with the right aptitude, attitude, and interest to serve as the lead for identifying, assessing, investigating, and managing threat management cases. The aptitude requires patience and the ability to empathize. Attitude should include an insatiable curiosity and the ability to find imaginative solutions. But most of all, the candidate should want to get involved in non-traditional law enforcement or security cases.

Once those individuals are selected, this book will help them understand and apply the contemporary threat management process. It will also point them to other research monographs, professional associations, and other sources they can use to further educate themselves in whatever area of threat management for which they take responsibility.

Scope of the Book

We divided the book into three sections. The first section introduces contemporary threat management and shows how it applies to combating acts of intended violence. That, of course, requires us to first define the concept of intended violence and show how it serves as a conceptual link connecting the different venues in which such violence occurs. That definition and discussion makes up the next chapter. Although it may strike some readers as more philosophical than they need, we believe it a necessary exercise. For too long now, various researchers and practitioners have tried to apply the lessons of contemporary threat management across the different venues without articulating the underpinnings that connect those venues. By trying such an articulation, we argue that such a connection exists.

In the third chapter, we briefly summarize the most practical applications drawn from the now quite voluminous research on intended violence. First, we wholly adopt psychiatrist James Gilligan's conclusion that all violence seeks justice. From this precept, we deduce that intended violence first and always begins with the perpetrator believing that the violence will achieve the end he or she seeks. In other words, individuals of violent intent always have a grievance. Second, we review the research on threats as indicators of future violence. This leads to our definition of the *Intimacy Effect*, which asserts that the more personal or intimate the relationship between the subject and target, the greater the validity of threats. Finally, we discuss a number of studies that tried, but failed miserably, to profile individuals of violent intent. The relevant research clearly shows that any such profiling misleads far more than it helps.

Chapter four makes the connection among the various venues of intended violence explicit and practical. It depicts the several milestones along the path to intended violence. These are the specific *attack-related* behaviors in which anyone intending to commit an act of violence must engage. First, the subject must have some grievance or purpose that violence will assuage. From that grievance, the subject must next settle upon the idea that violence and violence alone will resolve or avenge the issue. The idea leads next to figuring out how to commit the violence by researching the target and the setting for the violence and planning how to do it. The research and planning leads to preparations, such as obtaining a weapon, arranging to deliver that weapon to use against the target, putting personal affairs in order, or arranging an escape. Once prepared, the subject must breach whatever security measures surround the target. Finally, the breach allows the actual assault, but that must be buttressed with the boldness to do it.

The second section describes in detail the contemporary threat management process. Throughout the five chapters composing this section, we emphasize practical measures any threat manager can use to identify, assess, investigate, and manage individuals of violent intent. In the fifth chapter, we define Inappropriate Communications and Contacts (IC&Cs). The definition encompasses the *attack-related* behaviors composing the path to intended violence. Threat managers can use IC&Cs to train anyone on what to report. This puts the burden of initially identifying individuals of violent intent on the potential targets, their staffs, or families. Unfortunately, threat managers do not control the burden. Subjects focus their *attack-related* behaviors on their targets, not on threat managers. Hence, only the target is in a position to notice the IC&Cs.

Chapter six provides several tools threat managers can use to assess the risk that the subject poses to the target. These tools include evaluating the circumstances and context of the IC&C in particular and the situation in general. In addition, we describe ways the threat manager can evaluate what the subject considers to be at stake and how important those stakes are to the subject. This includes determining how many things, both tangible and intangible, the subject values. These are called inhibitors. Threat assessments must measure how many inhibitors the subject has or lacks. Finally, we recommend that in each case, the threat manager ask two opposite questions. First, has the subject been acting like a Hunter; that is, like individuals act as they proceed down the path to intended violence. Second, has the subject been acting like a Howler; that is, like individuals act who have no desire for proceeding down the path to intended violence. By balancing behaviors associated with hunting against behaviors associated with howling, the threat manager can gain better insight into the subject's true intentions.

The seventh chapter outlines practical ways threat managers can use to investigate subjects suspected of harboring violent intentions. Essentially, we recommend proceeding methodically, moving from thoroughly investigating the circumstances and context of the IC&C to finding out what has been happening to the target to what has been happening to the subject to actually interviewing the subject. Although subject interviews contain their own risks, including officer safety, we believe they are so important that we give an extended discussion of how, when, and where they should be held. But we emphasize, too, that threat managers should not attempt them until all other investigative leads and areas have been thoroughly investigated. Subject interviews are too important and too risky to be rushed.

Chapters eight and nine describe in great detail the eight threat management strategies available to threat managers. Chapter eight focuses on the four non-confrontational strategies, chapter nine on the confrontational ones. For each strategy, we describe what it entails, then offer a detailed description of the advantages and disadvantages of each. In addition, we make several observations on when and when not to attempt each strategy. We also point out the relative effectiveness of each strategy within the different venues of intended violence. Throughout, our goal is to provide threat managers with practical tools they can use to manage subjects of violent intent away from violence.

The third section addresses setting up a threat management process. Chapter 10 gives specific suggestions for training someone in threat management. In addition, the chapter discusses ways in which threat managers can manage their caseloads. We recommend designating these type cases as either active, chronic or habitual, long term, or inactive. Experienced law enforcement officers will immediately notice the difference here from criminal investigations, which usually are designated open, cleared, or on-going. Threat management cases cannot be so easily arranged. Many subjects engage in behaviors that suggest some potential for risk, but it remains at such a low level that the threat manager has little choice but to continue monitoring the subject, sometimes for years. Other subjects may engage in IC&Cs, then become quiescent for extended periods of time, only to resurface periodically. Still other subjects seem to derive some personal benefit or emotional kick by habitually or chronically engaging in certain types of IC&Cs without escalating their behaviors to move farther along the path to intended violence. Managing threat management cases is infinitely complicated by the infinite variations of the subjects.

Design of the Book

Throughout the book, our emphasis has been on providing pragmatic advice and techniques for threat managers to use. As part of this strategy, we have designed the book in such a format that it can be read in one of two ways. Obviously, it can be read cover to cover with great practical benefit. But throughout, we have inserted numerous *case studies* and *case illustrations* that provide brief, straightforward, and interesting examples of a particular point. Essentially, these are war stories we use to illuminate particular points that we deal with more extensively in the text. These cases, we think, lend themselves to skimming through the text. If a case study or illustration catches the reader's eye, we guarantee the reader will learn at least one thing by reading the case. If that arouses further curiosity, then the reader can sate it by reading the text immediately surrounding the case study. Either way, our purpose has been to put practical tools and concepts into the hands of anyone interested in applying the process of contemporary threat management.

---

[1] We use *subject* to refer to any individual who has come to law enforcement attention as potentially capable of violence. *Potential target* or *target* refers to those individuals who may be the potential recipients of the violence. Unfortunately, target carries with it an implication that the subject has a violent intent, but we could find no neutral term that fit. Object, for example, plays well against subject, but makes no sense within this context. Protectee refers too specifically to officials and public figures who already have protective details. Consequently, we ask the reader to accept the term target without negative connotation and only as a neutral term for individuals potentially at risk.

CHAPTER TWO

Intended Violence

Charles J. Whitman did not sleep the night before he died. Busy, he relied on dexedrine to keep him going. Early in the evening, he began typing out a note explaining himself as a "victim of very unusual and irrational thoughts." Interrupted by a visit from friends, Whitman did not get back to his writing until early the next morning. "3 a.m.," he then wrote, "Both dead."

Shortly after midnight, Whitman killed his mother at her new apartment. She had moved from Florida to Austin, Texas, the month before after separating from her husband. Whitman well understood why. He, too, had been the victim of his father's physical abuse. But his mother's presence near his home also reminded him how like his father he was. As he confessed to a university psychiatrist several months earlier, he, too, had found occasion to beat his wife. Whitman could not abide his fear that he would become his father. "I have just taken my mother's life," he wrote after first strangling her, then bludgeoning the back of her head. "I am very upset over having done it. . . . This is the only way I could see to relieve her sufferings but I think it was best." With his first chore accomplished, Whitman returned to his apartment. He still had much to do.

When he arrived home, Whitman approached his sleeping wife. This time, he did not beat her. Instead, he stabbed her five times in the chest with a hunting knife. He could not imagine that she would want to live past this day, given what he was planning. "At this time though, the prominent reason in my mind is that I truly do not consider the world worth living in and am prepared to die and I do not want to have her to suffer," his note said. In Whitman's mind, killing his mother and wife spared them the pain and humiliation he was about to rain down upon his father. Murdering them was an act of generosity. His next murders would not be so generous.

Whitman had a plan. He had been thinking about it, plotting it, for months. Five months earlier, he had told a University of Texas psychiatrist that he had been "thinking about going up on the tower with a deer rifle and start shooting people." The psychiatrist shrugged off the statement as a manifestation of the frustrations Whitman felt over his parents' separation and his own self-perceived failures to surpass his father's achievements. Unfortunately, Whitman did not follow up with the psychiatrist. He did not keep their second appointment.[1]

Instead, his thoughts became plans, the plans led to preparations, and the preparations brought him to the early morning hours of the last day of his life. He spent the time finishing his written explanation. He left the note beside his wife's body. When the stores opened Monday morning, he went shopping. After returning home, he packed his Marine footlocker with his purchases: two rifles, one equipped with a scope; a carbine; a shotgun; three pistols; 700 rounds of ammunition; water; food; and sundry supplies. He used a rented dolly to carry the footlocker to his car. After loading it, he drove onto the University of Texas Austin campus. The clock tower dominated the skyline, beckoning him. Parking the car, he hauled his footlocker to the tower, then up the elevator.

He killed the receptionist on the 28th floor, but let a husband and wife take the elevator down. When two families tried to enter the top floor, Whitman fired on them with his newly sawed-off shotgun. He then went out on the observation deck where he used the dolly to jam the door. From there, he had a clear view of the campus and bordering streets, a sniper's view of the students, faculty, staff, and business patrons hustling about as the clock struck noon.

Whitman began shooting one of the rifles. While in the Marine Corps, he had earned a "sharp-shooter" rating on the rifle. He was especially proficient at rapid fire from long distances and particularly accurate against moving targets. He put that training to use for just over an hour and a half, firing indiscriminately at anyone who came within his sights. All told, Whitman killed 14 (including his wife and mother) and wounded 31 before three policemen stormed the observation deck and killed him. The date was August 1, 1966.*

Although Whitman was not the first person to engage in rampage-style killings – in this or any other country – his sniping at the campus after murdering his loved ones neatly ties together a number of different types of violence which law enforcement

*On November 15, 2001, David Gunby died of wounds he suffered from Whitman's shooting, thus becoming Whitman's fifteenth victim.

specialists and researchers have lately begun to categorize. The decade of the sixties witnessed not only Whitman's murders, but also several political assassinations and other prominent acts of violence. So much violence of this sort occurred that President Lyndon Johnson appointed a presidential commission to study violence in general, assassinations in particular.[2]

Over the next three decades, research and – sadly – practical experience greatly informed our understanding of the kinds of violence in which Whitman engaged. For example, law enforcement and researchers would now describe Whitman's actions as a particularly vicious combination of domestic violence, workplace violence, school shooting, and suicide by cop. Beyond Whitman, they have also defined other discrete types of similar violence, such as public-figure attacks and hate or ideological crimes against houses of worship, abortion providers, gays, or other social outriggers. As scholars surveyed these disparate types of violence, there seemed to be an inchoate sense – little better formed than wishful thinking – that each of these types of violence was conceptually more similar than different. Lessons learned from one type could be applied to other types. Despite such wishing, however, no conceptual synthesis connecting them all has yet been successfully proffered.

Fortunately, that has not stopped a practical linking. Researchers at the Secret Service's National Threat Assessment Center (NTAC) recently concluded their "Exceptional Case Study Project" (ECSP), an analysis of some 83 assassins and attempted assassins. They then shifted their attention to 37 specific school shooting incidents, modeling their research after the approach taken in the ECSP. In addition, NTAC occasionally offered a three-and-a-half day threat assessment seminar that covers such disparate types of violence as public-figure attacks, violence against women, and workplace violence. The findings of the ECSP heavily influenced each block of instruction.

Similarly, the Federal Bureau of Investigation's (FBI) National Center for the Analysis of Violent Crime normally focuses on serial killers and rapists, as well as others of uncommon violent bent. Nonetheless, agents assigned there also published an analysis of recent school shootings. Currently, FBI agents are preparing a study of workplace violence. The security firm Gavin de Becker, Incorporated, routinely conducts threat assessments for public figures, corporations, domestic relationships, and schools. The assessments rely on the same methodological approach [3]

Clearly, most of those working in this field, by their actions and their research, certainly imply that some conceptual connection exists. There seems to be great faith that, in fact, more similarities than differences connect these various types of violence. Yet, precisely because so much research has been done across so many different types of violence, the field has reached the point where some conceptual synthesis is desperately needed. It is time to define what exactly it is we are studying.

Secret Service researchers made an initial stab at forming such a definition. They coined the concept of *targeted violence*, which they initially defined as "situations in which there is an identified (or identifiable) target and an identified (or identifiable) perpetrator." Subsequently, they added to this definition the proviso that both perpetrator and target be identifiable prior to the violence. Further, according to their concept, the target could be a specific individual or an institution or a facility. "But each case," they explained, "would be an instance of targeted violence if a target was known – or was knowable – prior to the incident."

Yet, having staked a claim to a conceptual synthesis, the Secret Service researchers immediately abandoned it. In a footnote, they confessed that they left their definition "intentionally vague." They did not intend it as "an operational research definition" (which is precisely what is needed). Instead, they tossed it out as "a conceptual heuristic to stimulate thinking." Unfortunately, what the field needs now to further advance the research is a precise operational research definition.[4]

Perhaps it is just as well. The concept of targeted violence, though sound in certain circumstances, does not stretch very far. The Secret Service originally derived its definition from the study of assassins, who do indeed target a specific public figure for assassination. But the concept becomes mired in its own definitional quagmire if we then try to apply it to other types of assaults. Clearly, Whitman targeted his mother and wife for violence, but he did not specifically target any other particular individuals. When he fired from atop the clock tower, he was not shooting at the University of Texas as an institution or at the campus grounds as a facility. Rather, he shot randomly at anyone he could sight, on and off campus. He did not pick the clock tower because of its symbolic association with the university. Rather, as he had occasionally said to friends when they passed by the tower, it was a perfect sniper's nest. Whitman chose the tower for its practical, not institutional, attributes. Randomness has no place in any commonsense definition of targeted. The concept works for public-figure assassinations, even some domestic violence cases. But the term targeted violence is stretched too far when applied to the clock-tower massacre, Columbine and similar school shootings where the victims are selected by chance. Even most cases of workplace violence involve some degree of random victim selection.

Where, then, is the conceptual link? Domestic violence involves assaults on intimates, but how can that possibly relate to an assassination of a president? What conceptual connection can there be between killing a judge and killing classmates? Anti-abortionists use violence – both arson and assassination – to express their opposition to abortion, but how is that linked to workplace violence?

The conceptual mistake, made blatant by these questions, is to try to forge the link through the victims, not the perpetrators. There is no conceptual connection between presidents and abused spouses, nor between classmates and abortion providers, jurists and co-workers. The victims, whether specifically targeted or randomly selected, have nothing in common beyond their victimization. The conceptual link must lie elsewhere.

Several school shooters first killed their parents before randomly attacking their classmates. Workplace violence frequently stems from domestic disputes. In 1983, Michael Perry first killed his family in Louisiana before traveling to Washington, D.C., in hope of attacking Justice Sandra Day O'Connor. Other attacks on public figures frequently include plans for suicide by cop. The perpetrators, then, frequently link the several types of violence simply by committing more than one type in a series of violent acts. But how can that actual connection be translated into a conceptual one?[5]

Clearly, any synthesis ultimately developed will not rest on choice of target. Nor can it rest on the degree of specificity of the target. Whitman targeted specific individuals (his mother and wife) but, once atop the tower, he fired randomly at any target of opportunity. Similarly, in 1998, Kip Kinkel first killed his parents, then fired at any students who happened to be lunching in his high school cafeteria. Rachele Shannon launched her career of violence by burning half a dozen or more abortion clinics. She ended it attempting to kill an abortion doctor. On December 31, 2003, Nevia Abraham kidnapped a female postal worker. With his gun to her neck, he forced her to drive her mail truck through a residential community 20 miles north of Miami, Florida, with police in hot pursuit. Abraham intended to use the postal woman as a ruse to gain entry to his former girlfriend's house so he could kidnap the couple's two children. Abraham finally surrendered after a two-hour standoff. These types of violence – however ultimately labeled or defined – can be very specific in its target selection or very random, or both.[6]

In addition, each category results in a crime, but the perpetrators do not act like the typical criminal with whom most law enforcement officers are familiar. Whitman, for example, sought no bounty or profit and had no thought of escaping. His actions were coldly calculated, not spurred by some uncontrolled, spontaneous, emotional outburst. He knew and had full command of what he was doing. Finally, whether he knew his victims or not, he clearly intended his violence to kill or maim them, not frighten, rob, or bend them to his will. In these respects, Whitman very much resembles what research tells us about those who engage in school shootings, workplace violence, public-figure attacks, and hate crimes. In all, the perpetrator intends well beforehand to act violently; is not motivated by profit or blinding passion; and plans to damage, injure, or kill.

These three elements, it seems to us, point us toward a conceptual synthesis connecting what is now called domestic violence, workplace violence, school shootings, public-figure assaults, and hate crimes. We think they can best be linked by the concept of *intended violence.*

Intended Violence

We stress all three elements – intent, lack of profit or unbridled passion in the motive, and plans to damage, injure, or kill – to distinguish this type violence from more commonly understood crimes of profit or passion. Although armed robberies are intended acts of violence, their purpose is to profit the robber. The violence is ancillary to the goal of profit. Similarly, in crimes of passion, violence frequently erupts from the heat of clashing emotions. Yet, it does so spontaneously and without premeditation or clear intent.

As a result, the defense against for-profit violence focuses on making the profit inaccessible to the perpetrator or at such a high cost in terms of punishment as to deter the attempt. The defense against passion-inspired violence requires the victim to escape or defuse the emotion. Thwarting intended violence relies on another strategy entirely. It requires identifying the potential aggressor, assessing the risk, and managing the individual away from violence. Those tactics apply to all the various types of intended violence, thus confirming the conceptual link.

Acts of intended violence serve different purposes than monetary gain or emotional release. Indeed, one of the distinguishing features of intended violence is the disparate range of their causes. Crimes for profit have a singular aim – to gain a monetary benefit. Crimes of passion soothe volatile emotions through violent release. Acts of intended violence, however, are not generated by a single dominating purpose. Rather, they range the gamut from achieving some ideological goal to acting out delusions, from gaining notoriety to slaking revenge, from killing individual classmates to slaughtering fellow workers – or any combination of these or other causes. Indeed, they are best defined by the two things they are not: crimes of profit or passion.

With crimes of profit or passion, the motive drives everything. With acts of intended violence, reasons can be telling, but they are not necessarily precisely focused or centered on one objective. In the next chapter, we cite James Gilligan's view that all violence is a search for justice. That general claim works best when understood as an umbrella concept reminding the threat manager that individuals of violent intent arrive at that intent from some sense of being wronged. They have a grievance. Understanding that their grievance motivates them – rather than a desire for profit or booty – will help the threat manager identify, assess, and manage these individuals.

What links acts of intended violence is the very intent itself. Violence among humans can generally be divided into two types. Reid Meloy describes them as predatory or affective. We prefer the terms intended and impromptu. Predatory seems too inflammatory and affective too obtuse. Nonetheless, the definitions are essentially the same. Intended or predatory violence is planned and premeditated. Impromptu or affective is a spontaneous outburst sparked by the circumstances of the moment.[7]

With intended violence, the perpetrator is somehow, for whatever reason, inspired to engage in violence. Once he or she develops the idea, the next step is to devise plans and preparations, then attack. These activities require specific, noticeable actions. The actions are common to all types of intended violence (as well as violence for profit), regardless of the victim or the specificity in victim selection.

As with any criminal endeavor, intended violence occurs across a range of venues. It can target public figures or intimate partners, specific individuals, or victims of opportunity. As defined by victim selection, intended violence can be characterized into two categories which, unfortunately, are not mutually exclusive. *Targeted* violence is very specific in the choice of victim. *Opportunistic* violence is quite the opposite. It is very general in the selection of victims.

We define targeted violence as an act of intended violence directed at a specific individual or symbolic physical structure empty of people. (The importance of the structure being empty is explained below.) Public officials, public figures, fellow workers, domestic partners, empty courthouses, empty schools, empty churches and synagogues, and empty abortion clinics have all been targets of intended violence. Targeted violence should be understood as intended, profitless violence directed at a specific entity, whether empty place or individual. This definition makes the specificity in victim selection its most distinguishing feature. It is a planned attack against a particular person or structure.

Case Study:

Death-Bed Confession

In mid-June 1955, 17-year-old Edward V. Dobek hid in a tree along the path through the park leading to the high school. He waited there for two particular girls to pass by on their way home from school. Dobek did not want to flirt with them or eavesdrop on their chatter. Rather, he intended to kill them both. For that purpose, Dobek had with him a .22 caliber semi-automatic rifle.

A few days before, the girls had teased him about something. Dobek never gave more details than that. Yet, whatever the girls did, it was enough for him to begin thinking of killing them, then planning how and where. He chose their route home from school at a relatively secluded part of the county park.

As the girls passed his hiding place, Dobek opened fire. He

squeezed off 17 rounds, killing both girls. He left them in the park and stole his way home.

The police were stumped. No arrests were ever made for the murders. Dobek was never suspected. Forty-five years later, Dobek summoned his sister to his deathbed. He confessed, providing enough details that the police were able to confirm the truth – but he was already dead.

Dobek deliberately plotted to ambush two particular girls who had incurred his wrath.

SOURCE: Washington Post, June 15, 2000.

The other form of intended violence is best described as opportunistic. Rather than target a specific victim, opportunistic violence selects its human targets randomly, usually by the place they happen to be at the time the attack is launched. Take, for example, one of the most infamous acts of opportunistic violence in recent times. On April 20, 1999, Eric Harris and Dylan Klebold shot their way into Columbine High School seeking to kill as many students and teachers as they could. They did not seek out specific individuals for assassination. Instead, they shot their victims as they found them: in the cafeteria, the hallways, and the library. Their true objective was a large body count, not any specific bodies. They simply killed indiscriminately. Indeed, they intended, but failed, to explode several large bombs to increase the carnage.[8]

In the fall of 1999, Buford Furrow decided to attack Jews. The first two sites he surveilled appeared to him to have too much security, making an attack difficult and dangerous. He settled on a Jewish community center, which doubled as a day care center. Shooting young children seemed safe enough. Furrow did not care who he shot, only that they happened to be present at the Jewish facility.[9]

Hence the importance of stressing empty structures as targeted for violence, but peopled structures as opportunities for slaughter. Once people are known to be in the building, the intended violence becomes opportunistic. With opportunistic violence, the attacker goes to a particular place where people, usually people sharing something in common, happen to be. It is the place, not the individual people, which attracts the assailant. One of the hallmarks of opportunistic violence is precisely the fact that the perpetrator intends to kill the victims, but not because of who they are, but where they are and what they are – students, Jews, gays, co-workers, court officials, or some other grouping. The perpetrator kills them because by their presence at that location, their murder represents something symbolic, if only to the attacker. After Whitman killed his mother and wife, his remaining victims meant nothing to him. They simply happened to be within range from the clock tower. Killing anyone who came into his sights served his purpose of tallying a large body count.

In September 2000, Ronald Gay finally had enough of all the jokes about his last name. He announced in a crowded Roanoke, Virginia, bar that he was going to kill some homosexuals. He asked for directions to the local gay hangout. Once there, he order a drink. After a few minutes, Gay pulled a gun and began firing. He killed one person and wounded six. Gay was not interested in who his victims were as individuals, only that they happened to be at a so-called "gay" bar. Victims of opportunistic violence literally find themselves in the wrong place at the wrong time.[10]

Case Study:

The Irate Garnishee

In March 2000, Michael McDermott began working at a computer consulting company just outside Boston. He brought with him troubles with the Internal Revenue Service. By December, the IRS was deducting from his wages. The forced withdrawals outraged McDermott. He directed his wrath at the company accounting department. Shortly before Christmas, he began yelling at the accountants for taking his money for IRS.

The day after Christmas, McDermott went to work heavily armed, the weapons hidden in a duffle bag. For his mid-morning coffee break, McDermott took an AK-47, a shotgun, and a pistol from his cubicle and walked toward the accounting department. He began killing people in the reception area, then in accounting. A total of seven died, most from gunshots to the head.

When he killed as many as he could, McDermott went back to the reception lobby and waited for the police. When they arrived, he briefly resisted, but the police subdued him.

A search of his office cubicle uncovered numerous weapons. At his house, police found bomb-making equipment.

Rather than seek out specific individuals who had somehow offended him, McDermott selected his victims randomly, simple targets of opportunity who happened to be – for him – in the right place at the right time.

SOURCE: Washington Post, December 26, 27, 2000.

In the worst form of intended violence, the subject combines targeted with opportunistic violence. Workplace and domestic disputes frequently involve attacks on specific individuals – former supervisor or ex-spouse – but also assaults on whomever happens to be around, such as former co-workers or ex-in-laws. In July 1999, Mark Barton murdered his wife and hid her body in a closet. The next day, he killed his two children. These were clearly acts of targeted violence in a domestic setting. On the third day, Barton drove to Atlanta, Georgia, to the two day-trading stock brokerages where he had lost a large sum of money. In at least one of the firms, he searched for the office supervisor, another example of targeted violence. However, at both firms, Barton walked through the offices shooting at anyone who came into his view, any victim of opportunity. After killing nine people, Barton fled the scene, eventually killing himself once the police caught up with him. Far from being mutually exclusive concepts, the worst form of intended violence combines targeted with opportunistic.[11]

The principal difference between opportunistic and targeted violence is that the latter focuses on individuals, opportunistic violence centers on places the target group is believed or happens to be. To assassinate a public official, the assassin has to go wherever that official is. The place only becomes important to the degree to which it complicates the kill. Whitman, for example, had to go to his mother's apartment to find and kill her. Afterward, he returned to his own apartment where he found his wife asleep. Assailants determined on attacking particular individuals must find their targets wherever they happen to be.

The principal venues for opportunistic violence are geographic settings: clock towers; workplaces; and identifiable-group locations such as gay bars, religious facilities, schools, courthouses, or abortion clinics. To kill gays or random co-workers or random individuals, the killer has to go to the bar, workplace, or best sniper's nest – like the clock tower. Assailants determined on attacking groupings of people must find their victims at the place they group.

With targeted violence, the victim is mobile. With opportunistic violence, the targets are tied to a geographic place. In the example of Mark Barton's assault on the two day-trading brokerages, his search for the office supervisor proved fruitless. The manager had gone to lunch and thus survived. Barton looked no farther nor did he wait for the man to return. He started shooting. Targets are mobile; opportunities fleeting.

The challenges to law enforcement in thwarting acts of intended violence are formidable. Heightened security measures, disengaging behaviors, and non-provocations offer little defense against intended violence precisely because it is planned beforehand. The planning can take the security measures into account and devise some tactics – however primitive – to subvert them. On August 5, 1993, Jack Gary McKnight was scheduled to be sentenced to ten years in a federal penitentiary for possession of marijuana with intent to sell, compounded by possession of semi-automatic weapons. Out on bond, McKnight instead shot his way into the federal courthouse in Topeka, Kansas. He killed one court security officer, who was manning the magnetometer and x-ray machines, and wounded two civilians. Neither the guard nor the machines prevented McKnight from forcing his way in. He knew they were there and came up with a crude, albeit effective, way to get past them. He simply shot his way through.[12]

Nonetheless, the security devices did the job they were designed to do. They raised the alarm that someone was bringing contraband weapons into the courthouse. Because McKnight fully intended to act violently, the alarms neither dissuaded nor stopped him. The officer he shot never had a chance.

McKnight's example, confirmed by similar cases (such as when Russell Weston shot his way into the U.S. Capitol building in July 1998), offers a simple but crucial lesson about security screening. For those intent on violence at any screened facility, the presence and placement of the screening equipment essentially determines the precise location where the gunfight will begin. The equipment signals the gunman that this is where he or she will have to reveal the weapon. It may also convine the attacker that the violence should take place on the other side of the equipment, that is, away from the entrance such as in the parking lot. The point, of course, is simple. Security measures should never create the illusion in anyone's mind, especially those charged with protective responsibilities, that they are impregnable. Screening equipment is essentially a sophisticated alarm sounding danger. It does not deflect that danger.

Intended violence, then, is characterized by premeditation, some motive other than profit or spontaneous passion, and a clear purpose to injure or kill. To this point, the choice of victim does not matter. The definition provides a conceptual link connecting assassinations, workplace and domestic violence, and hate or ideological assaults. Going farther, the degree of victim specificity, whether specifically targeted, randomly selected, or worse, both, helps further refine the concept. But what is most crucial to the concept, both as a conceptual link to varied types of violence and a practical way to thwart them, is the fact that it is premeditated and therefore planned and prepared for. That planning and preparing require certain actions and behaviors which law enforcement can notice and to which it can respond.

Contemporary Threat Management

The best defense against any act of intended violence is to employ the principles and methods of contemporary threat management. Like any such violence, Whitman's intent led him to think about it, plan it, prepare for it, and then launch the attack. Typically, too, he talked about it beforehand. Friends and acquaintances later remembered several occasions when he described the tower as a good sniper's nest. He confessed to the psychiatrist five months earlier that he had been thinking about going up there armed with a deer rifle.

Throughout that thinking, planning, preparing, and talking, Whitman engaged in behaviors that were noticeable. Had those who noticed them reported them to the proper law enforcement authorities, and had those authorities been properly trained in twenty-first century contemporary threat management practices, police might have averted the tragedy. But, of course, he was not reported and the authorities over three decades ago could not have been trained in a method that did not yet exist.

Research and practical case experience since 1966 have significantly advanced law enforcement's ability to identify, assess, and manage individuals who, like Whitman, pose a risk of intended violence. These three elements – identification, assessment, and management – are the principle elements defining contemporary threat management. The pioneering work of Gavin de Becker, the Los Angeles Police Department Threat Management Unit, and the California Highway Patrol Special Investigations Unit, bolstered by the research of James Clarke, Park Dietz and his associates, Reid Meloy, Kris Mohandie, Frederick S. Calhoun, and the United States Secret Service, have shed a veritable floodlight on the behaviors and actions of individuals who pose a risk of engaging in this type of violence. Contemporary threat management is not some slapdash theory nor some hair-brained conjecture. It has been formed and molded from practical case experience with violent individuals as well as detailed, scholarly research into violence and threatened violence.

And it works. Thirty years after Whitman climbed the clock tower, a man with a large head shaped like a pumpkin entered the governor's office in another western state and took a seat. For several minutes, he stared at the receptionist, neither talking nor moving. Uncomfortable with the man's demeanor, the receptionist pressed the silent alarm to summon security.

When the officers approached, Pumpkin Head blurted out, "Do you know that once you've been committed to a mental hospital, you can't own a gun for five years." The officers briefly interviewed him, noted his name and address, and escorted him out with a warning not to come back unless he had some legitimate business.

Two days later, Pumpkin Head returned. The officers recognized him and stopped him. When they asked his business there, he replied that he was just testing security. A week later, the midnight shift stopped Pumpkin Head as he slowly circled the capitol in his car. In the backseat, the officers found a detailed, hand-drawn floor plan of the building and a Marine Corps snipers manual. They questioned him, then released him.

At this point, the police reports came to the attention of the unit trained in contemporary threat management. The officers noted the unusual behavior and comments, as well as the repeated visits. Their training alerted them to a potential problem. After circulating Pumpkin Head's Department of Motor Vehicle picture, the threat managers learned that one of their officers had seen Pumpkin Head at a local gun store. The officer remembered him staring at the long rifles as though absolutely fascinated. A check of nearby gun stores revealed that Pumpkin Head frequently visited them, either to stare at the long guns or to read the rifle magazines.

The investigation further revealed that, several years earlier, Pumpkin Head had been committed to a mental hospital for paranoid schizophrenia. His five-year ban on owning a gun was due to expire in two weeks. Based on his fixation with the capitol and his obvious obsession with rifles, the threat managers concluded that Pumpkin Head clearly posed a risk of violence. Using his behaviors and proof that he had fallen off his medication, as well as their knowledge of contemporary threat management, the threat managers convinced Pumpkin Head's doctors to recommit him.

Contemporary threat managers must identify the risk, assess its potential, conduct a protective investigation, then implement appropriate management strategies to defuse it. This book is a manual of how to do just that.

If the goal of contemporary threat management is to avert violence altogether – and that very much is the objective – then law enforcement must change from reacting to violent episodes to somehow identifying their potential occurrence and then taking steps to defuse the risk. We are not talking here about *predicting* violence. Predictions are the province of angels and fools. Instead, we advocate establishing procedures that enable the threat manager to identify potential problems, assess their seriousness, investigate the circumstances, and then devise the most appropriate strategies for managing the case. We call this process contemporary threat management.

Contemporary threat management is not like traditional law enforcement, so traditional ways of thinking often hinder more than help. Although the tools and talents of a good criminal investigator are necessary in combating this form of violence, the law itself may help too late. In these type cases, by the time a law is broken someone may be dead or injured. Lee Harvey Oswald committed no crime against President John F. Kennedy until he pulled the trigger of his rifle. Although James Earl Ray had a history of petty crimes, he committed none that would have linked him to Martin Luther King, Jr., until Ray assassinated him. George Lott, who fired on a crowded courtroom in Texas, violated no laws until he opened fire and killed two attorneys and wounded two judges. Intended violence frequently entails no criminal activity linking the assailant to the target until the actual act of violence begins.[13]

As a result, the normal law enforcement response of arresting the perpetrator of some illegal act does little good in defusing the risk, however effective it is in punishing the guilty. Applying traditional law enforcement strategies to stop the violence can be quite ineffective. Other means and methods need come into play. Knowing what those other strategies are and, most importantly, using them effectively requires a new approach and a new way of thinking.

This new way of thinking is best described by the concept contemporary threat management. The idea of managing the case is crucial to embracing the concept. What we are trying to do is avert any violence. That requires a proactive, innovative approach. Once the threat manager identifies the potential subject – understanding that such identification is itself a mean trick – the threat manager cannot wait for the subject to act. The subject's next step might be violence. Rather, the threat manager has to assess the degree of risk, then devise some intervention strategy best suited to defusing that risk. And that is what contemporary threat management is all about – finding the best way to keep the subject from acting out violently.

Threat management depends on three distinct but interrelated steps. First, the threat manager must be able to identify that a potential risk exists before it becomes an actual risk. Second, the threat manager must be able to assess – accurately and continuously – the exact level of risk at any point in time throughout the duration of the case. Finally, the threat manager must manage the subject away from violence. This requires conducting a thorough protective investigation and then choosing the best combination of threat management strategies most suited to ensuring the safety of the potential target. Contemporary threat management requires a distinctive approach and focus. In many cases, there may be no crime until too late. The threat manager who waits for a crime risks waiting too long. In many cases, there may be no ready solution to diverting the subject away from his or her intended violence. The threat manager who pines for some easy way out risks letting the subject solve things. In many cases, the solution may involve long-term management and oversight of the subject. The threat manager who expects the subject to behave like a criminal risks losing sight of other ways to manage the case. Such customary law enforcement responses as arrests, restraining orders, or mental health commitments may, in these situations, be merely stopgaps, temporary respites from long-term problems, if indeed they can be employed at all. With no quick or ready solutions, contemporary threat management cases may linger open for months, even years. They are not easily resolved.

Nor is there any straight definition or standard for clearing the case. Unlike criminal investigations, which clear automatically with a judicial conviction, threat management cases rarely have such simple or straightforward endings. The subject can continue to pose a risk for years with little to be done beyond monitoring him or her. Arrests, though helpful, are not resolutions. Some individuals behind bars continue to pose a danger to the target. In other cases, the subject may simply disappear in relation to the target. For example, someone may complain inappropriately, even threateningly, about some action taken by the mayor, then never be heard from again. When can such a case be closed?

The difference between traditional criminal investigations and contemporary threat management emerges most clearly by understanding the different focus of each. Criminal investigations first determine if a crime has occurred, then center on bringing the criminal to justice. The purpose is to punish criminals for crimes already committed. The essential element of a criminal investigation is discovering a criminal act; its purpose is to bring the perpetrator to justice.

Conversely, threat management focuses on prevention rather than punishment. Its purpose is to ensure no harm comes to the potential victim. That is, it seeks to prevent the act of violence – the crime – from ever taking place. If the starting point for a criminal investigation is the occurrence of the crime, the starting point for threat management is the initial suspicion that a crime *may* take place at some future time. Pumpkin Head committed no crime, but he clearly appeared to be contemplating one. Consequently, threat management first identifies a potential threat, then assesses and investigates the seriousness of the risk, then develops the appropriate management strategies. Throughout the course of the case, that assessment and management must be constantly reevaluated and fine-tuned, with the safety of the target kept always at the forefront.

Criminal investigations deal with *what happened*; threat management confronts *what might happen.* Between the two lies a world of separation. In order to succeed, the threat manager must fully recognize and internalize the difference between punishing and preventing. Defusing the risk is the only measure of success. In the case of the Pumpkin Head man, the ultimate solution – re-commitment to a mental hospital – seemed clear enough. Convincing the doctors, however, became the challenge. Although the police recognized him as a serious risk, they had to prove to his doctors that he was. In the realm of threat management, punishing the subject can mean failure. Preventing the crime means victory.

Nor can the police rest easy having committed him again. After all, he had been in a mental institution before. Whatever crime the threat managers prevented this time, they may well have to prevent it again once Pumpkin Head is released back into the community.

Summary

We suggest that intended violence differs from other forms of human violence because it is premeditated, not motivated by hope of profit or release of passion, and entails plans to damage, injure, or kill. This definition provides a conceptual link to different venues in which intended violence is acted out. Assaults on public figures, domestic disputes, hate crimes, and workplace violence differ greatly in target definition, but the violence against them follows the same process.

Intended violence can take two forms, or a combination of both. It can target specific individuals or it can target opportunities for wreaking havoc. The first focuses on particular people, the second on places people congregate. Both targeted and opportunistic violence are planned and therefore follow the process inherent in intended violence.

The contemporary threat management approach identifies, assesses, and manages individuals of violent intent. Criminal investigations aim to punish crimes that have already occurred. Contemporary threat management aims to prevent a crime – homicide – from taking place. Hence, contemporary threat management requires a different way of thinking and a different law enforcement approach. The remaining chapters provide detailed, practical specifics on that thinking and that approach.

Notes to Chapter 2

[1] New York Times, "Text of Psychiatrist's Notes on Sniper," August 3, 1966.

[2] Friedman, Leon, ed. *Violence in America: Final Report of the National Commission on the Causes and Prevention of Violence*, 16 vols. (NY: Chelsea House, 1983).

[3] Robert Fein and Bryan Vossekuil, "Assassination in the United States: An Operational Study of Recent Assassins, Attackers, and Near-Lethal Approachers," *Journal of Forensic Science*, March 1999, 321-33;. Fein, et al., "Threat Assessment in Schools: A Guide to Managing Threatening Situations and to Creating Safe School Climates," United States Secret Service and United States Department of Education, Washington, D.C., May 2002; Gavin de Becker, *The Gift of Fear: Survival Signals that Protect Us from Violence* (NY: Little, Brown, 1997).

[4] Fein and Vossekuil, "Assassination in the United States," 332.

[5] De Becker, *Gift of Fear*, 261-76.

[6] New York *Times*, April 20, 2000; Chicago Sun-Times, October 15, 2000; New York *Times*, August 20, 21, 22, 1993; Associated Press, January 31, 2003, February 6, 2003.

[7] J. Reid Meloy, *Violence Risk and Threat Assessment: A Practical Guide for Mental Health and Criminal Justice Professionals* (San Diego, CA: Specialized Training Services, 2000), 87-98.

[8] Gavin de Becker, "What the Columbine Report Didn't Tell You: The Threat Assessment Challenge Facing Schools," May 19, 2000, http://www.APBNews.com. ; William H. Erickson, et al., *The Report of Governor Bill Owens' Columbine Review Commission*, May 2001, http://www.state.co.us/columbine, 25-32.

[9] Report on Buford Furrow at www.wired.com/news/story/21210.html August 10, 30, 1999; "Shooter Surrenders," August 10, 1999, Wired Digital, Inc., http://www.wired.com/news/story/21210.html; "L.A Shooting Subject to Enter Plea," August 30, 1999, Lycos.com, http://www.lycos.com/news/flash/jewishcentershooting.html.

[10] Washington *Post*, September 24 and 26, 2000.

[11] New York *Times*, July 29, 1999; Atlanta Journal-Constitution, July 30 and 31, 1999; "Atlanta Slayings," http://www.wired.com/news/news/story/21022html.

[12] Frederick S. Calhoun, *Hunters and Howlers: Threats and Assaults Against Federal Judicial Officials in the United States, 1789-1993*, (Arlington, VA: United States Marshals Service, 1998), xvii-xix.

[13]Linda Laucella, *Assassination: The Politics of Murder* (Los Angeles, CA: Lowell House, 1998), 230-262; 295-304; James Garbarino, *Lost Boys: Why Our Sons Turn Violent and How We Can Save Them* (NY: Free Press, 1999), 3.

CHAPTER THREE

Applying the Practical Applications of Research on Violence

Without question, the research on intended violence deserves its own Dewey decimal library classification. The volumes devoted to the various acts of intended violence would, if grouped together, fill dozens of bookshelves. The subject has long attracted attention from numerous perspectives. Sigmund Freud addressed the issue from a psychological view in his classic study *Civilization and Its Discontents* (1938). Konrad Lorenz devised an anthropological explanation in *On Aggression* (1966). Oftentimes, violent events inspired more studies. The 1963 assassination of President John F. Kennedy spawned its own small library. That card catalogue reads like a who's who of conspiracy theorists, assassination buffs, and the occasional movie producer.[1]

The riotous 1960s, compounded by several political assassinations and attempted assassinations, induced both scholarly and governmental interest on various aspects of intended violence. President Lyndon Johnson sponsored a National Commission on the Causes and Prevention of Violence that produced a sixteen-volume report. The studies "included a historical study of violence in America; studies of group violence, individual violence, and political assassinations; an analysis of firearms ownership and control; a report on violence in the media; and a special reconsideration of law and order." The Commission pessimistically concluded that "special features and pressures of American society would continue to produce individual acts of violence." Depressingly, in the more than thirty years since the report's publication, that projection proved amply born out.[2]

Throughout the 1970s, scholarly interest in intended violence centered largely on the psychology of public-figure assassins. Not surprisingly, a consensus quickly emerged that public-figure assassins were – one way or another – mentally disturbed. "In every case of assassination or attempted assassination but one (the politically motivated attempt on the life of President Harry S. Truman by supporters of the Puerto Rican nationalist movement in 1950)," Richard Restak timidly concluded, "the evidence suggests the conclusion that the perpetrator was at least temporarily deranged." Sidney Slomich and Robert Kantor used bolder language. They described assassins as "marginal, anomic men from estranged strata of society." Unfortunately, none of the research provided much practical advice in the way of recognizing the derangements, much less the anomie, prior to the violent act.[3]

The lack of practical advice remained a problem as more studies came out during the 1980s and into the 1990s. Most of the findings offered little of use to law enforcement officers caught in the grip of identifying, assessing, and managing individuals of violent intent. The impracticality of the research hardly improved after researchers broadened their interests from political violence to other venues. Research on domestic disputes and co-worker violence focused on the mental twists of the perpetrators, but gave little direction on how law enforcement could get into the mind of any suspects.

For example, one expert noted that one sign for recognizing a domestic abuser was that such abusers frequently took hostages. However true that observation may be, from a law enforcement perspective waiting to see if a spouse will take a hostage means waiting way too late. A list of abuser-traits published by the American Judges Association also included after-the-fact actions. The list contained such evidence of abuse as pushing, shoving, kicking, beating, and "assault with a weapon" – all evidence that the abuse had already occurred, not that it may be about to take place. A summary of traits related to co-worker violence included such immeasurables as psychoses, "impaired neurological functioning," and personality disorders. Unfortunately, those diagnoses usually occurred after the violent incident, only seldom, if ever, before it.[4]

But the lack of practical advice in the research on intended violence simplifies achieving our purpose here. Rather than attempting to summarize the voluminous number of studies published over the last half century, we will pick and choose those findings that offer the most promise of arming a threat manager with the most useful tools pertinent to contemporary threat management. This is not to dismiss out of hand the vast scholarship on intended violence. Understanding the psychological, sociological, and even anthropological attributes of individuals of violent intent helps fill out a contextual background within which threat managers operate. Each threat manager needs to dig into the literature on intended violence in order to build that background. Any easy summary constructs but a partial context.

Our purpose here is the very limited one of arming threat managers with the best and most practical tools to use in identifying, assessing, and managing individuals of violent intent. We dispense with the more theoretical studies not from any lack of interest or respect, but only in the interest of maintaining our focus on practicality over theory.

The practical lessons of the research can be grouped into four interrelated, but distinct findings. These pertain to the overarching motive prompting acts of intended violence, the nature of threats, the discounting of perpetrator profiles, and the process of violence. The research on motive strongly suggests that, however unique each individual act of violence certainly is, every such act shares a common motive. Understanding that motive helps the threat investigator identify individuals of violent intent. The research on threats sharply divides the various venues of intended violence. The findings suggest that threats are strong pre-incident indicators in certain venues, but practically meaningless in other venues. Understanding how to distinguish when threats have value and when they do not helps the threat investigator assess individuals of violent intent. The current move away from perpetrator profiles helps remove investigative blinders, thus allowing the threat investigator to identify and assess all the clues and circumstances generated in any case. Finally, the discovery that violent acts result from a process of behaviors reunites the various venues because the behaviors and the process of engaging in them applies to all acts of intended violence, regardless of victim or place. Understanding the behaviors making up that process is the single most important tool a threat manager can use to identify, assess, and manage individuals of violent intent.

In this chapter, we take up each of these practical findings in turn, with the exception of the process of violence. That process we explore in great detail in the next chapter. Its singular importance to threat management warrants the extra attention.

The Mother of All Motives

"*All violence,*" psychiatrist James Gilligan determined, "*is an attempt to achieve justice.*" He reached that remarkable conclusion after spending a twenty-five-year career providing psychiatric services throughout the Massachusetts state prison system. Gilligan treated the most depraved and violent inmates. Yet, he consistently found that the prisoners resorted to violence – both in and out of prison – because of a profound sense that he or she was treated unfairly. The justice each sought, he continued, was not based on some standard set by society, but derived from

> what the violent person perceives as justice, for himself or for whomever it is on whose behalf he is being violent, so as to receive whatever retribution or compensation the violent person feels is "due" him or "owed" to him, or to those on whose behalf he is acting, whatever he or they are "entitled" to or have a "right" to; or so as to prevent those whom one loves or identifies with from being subjected to injustice. *Thus, the attempt to achieve and maintain justice, or to undo or prevent injustice, is the one and only universal cause of violence.*

Gilligan based his understanding of violence as the pursuit of justice on the attitude and actions of those sent to prison for violating society's system of justice.[5]

Gilligan's view derived from a subjective, personal interaction with violent individuals, a very micro-view of the subject. Interestingly, Harvard historian Crane Brinton reached practically the same conclusion, but from a much larger perspective. Brinton dissected the American, French, and Russian Revolutions in *The Anatomy of Revolution.* "Men revolt," he concluded, "not when they are hungry, but when they are wronged." Perceived injustices perpetrated by the ruling classes against those whom they rule fueled all three revolutions. The widespread belief that each government and ruling class ruled unfairly outraged the ruled. They then rose in violent revolt.[6]

Ironically, the pursuit of justice linked the violent felon to the revolutionary patriot. Each sought a just existence, a life that seemed fair to them. In the end, perhaps all that separated the felon from the patriot was not the specific justice each demanded, but the degree to which each succeeded in obtaining it.

But how does the research on various venues of intended violence support the conclusions Gilligan and Brinton reached after coming from such opposite directions? Resoundingly well. In a study of over three thousand threats and assaults against federal judicial officials, one conclusion emerged with startling clarity: "Whether voluntarily or in chains, as long as men and women bring their troubles before the federal bar with their own sense of justice and their own definition of what is fair and right, some of them will always be disappointed and angered by the decisions handed down. That disappointment and anger can easily ferment into danger." As the study further explained:

> Those who besiege the judiciary are the beseechers, both the innocent and the damned. They are drawn to the courts in great expectation of exoneration and affirmation. They do not seek justice, but agreement. When Charles Koster carried his daughter's suit to the Southern District of New York, he expected Judge Richard Daronco to sustain her. When Walter LeRoy Moody appealed to the Eleventh Circuit, he expected Judge Robert Vance to affirm his pleadings. When the courts rejected the suits, both men lashed back violently.

Each man, one with bullets, one with bombs, brutally assassinated the judge who denied him the self-defined justice each sought. It was not in any way the justice courts dispense, but the highly selfish, personalized justice each man defined for himself. They pursued their justice through revenge because each felt wronged by the courts.[7]

Case Study:

Revenge Served Cold

In 1966, Theobalt Magnini obtained a summons against his neighbor for "maintaining a vicious dog." Municipal Court Judge James N. Colasonto dismissed the complaint because the evidence against the dog did not support the charge. Instead, he explained to Magnini, the more appropriate complaint would be the dog was running loose in the neighborhood. The judge suggested Magnini file on those grounds.

But Magnini did not pursue the matter further. Instead, he brooded over his failed attempt to get the justice he sought against that pesky dog. He turned his anger from the dog to the judge who denied his claim. Time did nothing to diminish Magnini's outrage – and his desire for retribution.

Just before 7:00 a.m. on November 24, 1970 – nearly five years after bringing his complaint before Judge Colasonto – Magnini went to the judge's home and rang the doorbell. When the judge opened the door, Magnini fired five times.

A few hours later, Magnini called a local newsman. He explained that he had held a grudge against the judge ever since Colasonto dismissed his complaint. Now he had avenged himself.

When the police began converging on his house, Magnini used his gun one last time to kill himself. Two days later, Judge Colasonto died of his gunshot wounds.

Those of violent bent are relentless pursuers of their own kind of justice. Time does little to assuage them.

SOURCE: Washington Post and New York Times, November 25, 26, and 27, 1970.

Perhaps it comes as no surprise that those who lose their case before the courts feel denied the justice they believed due them. After all, every court case has two sides, one of which, at the least, loses. The losers rarely feel justly treated.

Yet, the concept that the pursuit of justice motivates acts of violence finds support from the research on other venues of intended violence. Even the most cursory review of school shootings turns up complaints from the shooters about being teased or tormented by fellow students. For example, researchers associated with the Secret Service studied about three dozen recent school shootings. They found that "many attackers felt bullied, persecuted, or injured by others prior to the attack." The student – sometimes students – lashed back at the persecution (though not always at their actual persecutors) in revenge, which was just another way of seeking justice.[8]

The official inquiry into the April 1999 shooting rampage at Columbine High School concluded that the two perpetrators, Dylan Kliebold and Eric Harris, "were manifestly embittered" about a previous arrest for breaking into a car. The report added that both boys "expressed clear hatred for society in general and, beyond that, for all humankind." Psychologists James McGee and Caren R. DeBernardo researched sixteen recent non-inner-city school shootings, including the Columbine incident. They described the shooters as "Classroom Avengers" because each was motivated by some sense of being treated wrongly. According to their research, the critical motive driving Classroom Avengers was vengeance over "discipline by parents or authorities and/or rejection, bullying or humiliation by peers or girlfriends." Interestingly, McGee and DeBernardo drew inspiration for their model from a similar study of workplace violence incidents that styled the perpetrators as "Workplace Avengers."[9]

Case Study:

A School Boy's Torment

Just about everybody, it seemed, loved to pick on sixteen-year-old Toby R. Sincino. All the bullies and want-to-be bullies at Blackville-Hilda High School in Blackville, South Carolina, made Sincino their target of choice. Since he was under five feet tall, they could – and frequently did – cram him into any hall locker. They had just as much fun dunking him head first into the hallway trash cans.

Sincino compounded this persecution by becoming a discipline problem himself. Consequently, school authorities added to his sense of being persecuted. During the 1994-95 school year, he was expelled, but readmitted the following fall. In early October 1995, he made an obscene gesture, thus incurring a school suspension. Based on his previous record, that suspension required another expulsion. He told his school principal that he did not expect to live to twenty-one.

He was right.

On October 12, 1995, at 8:45 in the morning, Sincino went one last time to school, this time considerably increasing his stature by carrying a gun. Although banned from the campus by his suspension, no one stopped him. His first shot struck a math teacher in the hallway. He proceeded past two classrooms, then entered the third where a math class was being held. He shot and wounded the teacher. Standing at the front of the class in full view of his former fellows, Sincino put the pistol to his right temple and pulled the trigger.

Young or old, individuals of violent intent believe themselves exonerated by the violence.

SOURCE: United Press International, October 12, 1995

Research on co-worker violence also found that the perpetrators considered themselves unfairly treated, usually by being fired, passed over for promotion, dunned, or disrespected. T. Stanley Duncan, writing in the Federal Bureau of Investigation's *Law Enforcement Bulletin,* remarked that those who engaged in violence against co-workers and supervisors had "unfounded grievances and complaints" and viewed themselves "as a 'victim.'" He considered co-worker violence as "crimes of revenge, committed only to victimize the target and emotionally appease the perpetrator." Steve Kaufer and Jurge Mattman agreed. "The single largest trigger of rampage-type attacks in the workplace by employees is termination," they advised. Similarly, Chris E. McGoey observed that "common workplace triggers that might instigate violence are terminations, layoffs, bad performance evaluations, and believing they were passed over for promotion." As with school shootings and attacks on judicial officials, co-worker violence culminated a misplaced search for justice.[10]

Domestic violence also involved the pursuit of a self-defined justice. "When a batterer believes that he is about to lose or has permanently lost his partner, if he cannot envision life without her or if the separation causes him great despair or rage, he may choose to kill," advised the Danvers, Massachusetts, police department after reviewing dozens of studies on spousal abuse. Study after study on intimate partner violence pointed to the abuser's need to control and dominate the partner. Violence occurred when the partner acted against the domination, thus denying the abuser the control he or she sought.[11]

In a national survey focused on violence against women, researchers at the National Institute of Justice found that:

> Violence perpetrated against women by intimates is often accompanied by emotionally abusive and controlling behavior. The survey found that women whose partners were jealous, controlling, or verbally abusive were significantly more likely to report being raped, physically assaulted, and/or stalked by their partners even when other sociodemographic and relationship characteristics were controlled. Indeed, having a verbally abusive partner was the variable most likely to predict that a woman would be victimized by an intimate partner. These findings support the theory that violence perpetrated against women by intimates is often part of a systematic pattern of dominance and control.

Abusers believe they have the right to control their partner. They then become wronged by the partner when the partner does something that challenges that control. The abuser then feels aggrieved and seeks to alleviate that grievance by physically re-imposing the domination.[12]

Case Study:

Controlling Lives

John Lisowski waited until he was out of the country on business before e-mailing his wife of 20 years to tell her he had met someone else and wanted a divorce. A few days later, in September 2002, Sungnam Lisowski applied to the state of Illinois for a firearm owner's identification card.

Two months later, she received the gun owner's card. A month after that, she bought a handgun. That same day, she went to a shooting range for target practice.

Five days later, on Christmas morning, she shot her husband in the back of the head while he sat in front of the computer where she had read the e-mail. She then went upstairs and shot their two daughters. She shot one daughter five times, the other daughter three times. Police believed she reloaded the pistol three times. Miraculously, both girls survived.

After shooting her daughters, Sungnam Lisowski then went into another bedroom and shot herself twice in the chest. She, too, survived.

Domestic abusers use violence to gain what they consider just.

SOURCE: Chicago Tribune, January 9, 2003

Finally, the research on public-figure assassins supports the premise that the pursuit of justice motivates acts of intended violence. Mark David Chapman, who killed John Lennon, felt disenchanted because phonies succeeded where he did not. He decided, then, to shoot the one he considered the phoniest of them all. John Hinckley could find no other way to link himself with the object of his love obsession than to assassinate the president – and what could be more unjust than unrequited love? Often, especially in the United States, assassins seek to gain infamy by killing someone famous. Unable to win fame on their own, they essentially steal it from their famous victims.

We have hammered home the point enough. We seek here merely to establish the concept that intended violence first and always begins with the perpetrator believing that the violence will achieve the end he or she seeks. That end is a very personal, self-righteous search for a self-defined justice. The pursuit is relentless.

For the threat manager, the practical application of this finding is the recognition that individuals of violent intent are driven to their act by some sense of being wronged. They have a grievance. Identifying that grievance, that sense of injustice, will go a long way toward helping the threat manager identify, assess, and manage those of violent intent.

On the Nature of Threats

In 1991, a team of researchers led by Park Dietz published two articles based on their study of inappropriate communications sent to Hollywood celebrities and similar letters mailed to members of Congress. Both studies led Dietz and his colleagues to a startling conclusion. They found that explicit threats of physical harm had little bearing – even an opposite bearing – on the actual behavior of the person uttering the threat. For Hollywood celebrities, Dietz et al. found "no association between threatening and approaching." It followed, then, that "the presence or absence of a threat in the communication is no indication whatsoever of whether a subject is going to pursue an encounter." Their initial conclusion ran against common sense and traditional practice, both of which held that threateners were the most dangerous individuals.[13]

The finding that emerged from the team's study of communications to members of Congress was even more pronounced. "Subjects," the research team wrote, "who sent threats to a member of Congress were significantly *less* likely to pursue a face-to-face encounter with him or her." The team elaborated:

> The finding regarding threats was particularly robust. Each of the following aspects of threats, taken alone, was significantly associated with not approaching: threatening any kind of harm toward any public figure; threatening to kill any public figure or those around a public figure; indicating that a threat would be executed by the subject or his agent; indicating that a threat would be executed by someone other than the subject or his agent; making any direct threat; making any veiled threat; making any conditional threat; and making any implausible threat.

From this finding, Dietz et al. concluded that waiting for a threat before contacting law enforcement, or law enforcement waiting for an explicit threat before opening an investigation or taking measures to thwart "dangerous encounters" would be a serious mistake.[14]

Subsequent research on public-figure attacks confirmed the Dietz team's finding. Secret Service researchers analyzed 83 attackers and near attackers of presidents, celebrities, jurists, and other public figures. Like Dietz and his colleagues, the Secret Service researchers concluded that "persons who *pose* threats most often do not make threats, especially explicit threats." Fewer than a tenth of the 83 attackers and near-attackers communicated a threat. More tellingly, none of the 43 individuals in the study who actually attacked a public figure ever made an explicit threat to the target.[15]

A study of threats and assaults against federal judicial officials by Frederick S. Calhoun drew a distinction between attackers, who he called hunters, and threateners, who he called howlers. Between the two, Calhoun concluded,

> lies a world of difference. They are extremes: one an actor, one a talker: one a doer, one a writer. Between them is a huge chasm, a clear distinction. The hunters hunt and rarely howl; the howlers howl and only rarely hunt.

Based on this fundamental difference between hunters and howlers, the study identified distinctive characteristics of each. Howlers communicated with their targets in writing, over the telephone, or through informants. Hunters engaged in face-to-face confrontations and suspicious activities, including physical assaults.[16]

Based on a career providing security services to public figures in the United States, Gavin de Becker fully embraced what the research told him. As he explained in *The Gift of Fear*:

> It is a tenacious myth that those who threaten public figures are the ones most likely to harm them. In fact, those who make direct threats to public figures are far less likely to harm them than those who communicate in other inappropriate ways (lovesickness, exaggerated adoration, themes of rejection, the belief that a relationship "is meant to be," plans to travel or meet, the belief that the media figure owes them something, etc.). Direct threats are not a reliable pre-incident indicator for assassination in America, as demonstrated by the fact that not one successful public-figure attacker in the history of the media age directly threatened his victim first.

The demythologization of threats as indicators of future action led the United States Marshals Service, the California Highway Patrol, and other law enforcement agencies charged with protective responsibilities to shift away from waiting anxiously for a threat. Instead, they began broadening their investigations to include inappropriate communications or contacts between the targets and those who might cause them harm. These agencies taught their targets to report inappropriate communications or contacts even if they lacked explicit expressions of an intent to cause harm. In effect, the focus shifted from what individuals said to what they did. Actions indeed spoke louder than words.[17]

Case Study:

Hunters vs. Howlers

Kansas police arrested Jack Gary McKnight for growing marijuana on his farm. The U.S. Attorneys' office took the case because the police also found weapons in McKnight's home. McKnight pled guilty knowing he would receive a ten-year sentence without hope of probation or parole.

But McKnight also knew he would not be going to jail. Instead, he spent his last months of freedom on bail quietly building two-dozen pipe bombs. On the day before his scheduled sentencing, he bought three handguns. He took the guns and bombs to court the next day, using them to kill a court security officer, wound a civilian, damage the courthouse interior, and then kill himself. McKnight never threatened anyone, told anyone of his plans. He made his preparations in secret. McKnight was a hunter.

Unlike McKnight, the L.oneA.ryanW.arrior (LAW), or so he styled himself, wrote letters to public officials throughout the country threatening that his movement would soon overthrow the government and torture all its former officials. The LAW had a slight problem. Confined to the Tennessee Colony prison in Texas, his ability to carry out his revolution seemed questionable at best. However, for those officials who did not know of his status, his threats caused some fear and discomfort, despite the lack of physical intimidation.

Hunters and howlers behave in entirely different ways – the former acts, the latter talks.

SOURCE: Frederick S. Calhoun, Hunters and Howlers: Threats and Assaults Against Federal Judicial Officials in the United States, 1789-1993, (Arlington, VA: United States Marshals Service, 1998), xvii – xix.

Then the research shifted from public-figure assassins to other venues of intended violence. Suddenly, threats made a comeback. In several venues, especially domestic disputes, co-worker violence, and school shootings, the attackers threatened their victims, often repeatedly, then actually attacked. School shooters frequently discussed their plans with their friends, even received encouragement from cronies to act out violently. In a number of instances of co-worker violence, the attacker warned his intended victims that he would be back and then there would be trouble.

Despite the research discounting threats toward public figures, for years local law enforcement well understood the importance of threats as pre-incident indicators of domestic violence. The Danvers, Massachusetts, Police Department put threats of homicide or suicide at the top of its list of various warning signs of potential domestic homicide. Similarly, the Metro Nashville, Tennessee, Police Department emphasized the importance of taking intimidation and threats against a domestic partner seriously. In a study of criminal justice strategies toward intimate partner violence, Kerry Healey and Christine Smith reported that "prior threats to kill" and suicide threats were among the most important warning signs of potential domestic abuse. The Department of Justice's National Violence Against Women Survey found that "women who were physically assaulted by an intimate partner were significantly more likely to be injured if their perpetrator threatened to harm or kill them or someone close to them." Clearly, threats within domestic contexts are an important pre-incident indicator of violence. Howlers, apparently, are quite capable of attacking those they love.[18]

Case Study:

From Threat to Action

For 16 years, Steve and Janice Lancaster enjoyed a happy marriage living in Southern Maryland. High school sweethearts, they had two children, a boy and a girl. But things changed. Steve took a mistress, yet refused to give Janice a divorce. Beatings began. Janice had him arrested, then dropped the charges, then had him arrested again. In February 1999, Steve told Janice that he would kill her and himself.

Janice hired an attorney and instituted divorce proceedings, but she knew her husband well. A hunter, he owned several weapons. He had been raised in a violent household himself. His father went to prison for seven years for abusing his wife. Only 33, Janice wrote out instructions for her funeral: "When I die bury me in my long white dress. I want a pretty blue coffin." She, too, had begun to think about, and fear, an escalation in the violence.

In August 1999, Steve told his children that he was "going to kill your mother stone dead." The abuse continued, but the physical injuries were always relatively minor. Steve never served more than a few days in jail. In the fall of 1999, he wrote a letter: "Janice, I don't have anything left so don't keep pushing me to the limit. . . . Be very careful with me. . . . I'm right on the edge. . . . I know what I got to do to settle all of this . . . one way only and you know what I'm talking about. . . . I'm ready to go any time to lay my body to rest and [I am] not going to be the only one." Clearly, Steve had moved beyond the impromptu assaults he had been committing and now was contemplating something much more horrific.

On December 28, 1999, the Maryland court issued a protection order compelling Steve to move out of their house and keep away from his wife. On January 3, 2000, Steve parked a mile from his wife's house just before dawn. Dressed in dark clothes and a stocking cap, he walked to the house carrying a shotgun. He killed Janice, then himself.

Their son heard the shotgun blasts while waiting at his school bus stop. "I think that came from my house," he said.

In domestic situations, threats carry great weight.

SOURCE: Washington Post, August 27, 2000.

The same held true in cases of co-worker violence. The U.S. Government Office of Personnel Management listed "direct or veiled threats of harm" among the warning signs of potential co-worker violence. The Workplace Violence Research Institute advised employers in 1998 that "one of the most important elements in any prevention program is a zero tolerance policy for threats, harassment, intimidation and weapons possession." Jurg W. Mattman analyzed over 200 incidents of workplace violence. He found that co-worker violence was associated with any individual who "threatens or verbally abuses co-workers and supervisors."[19]

Case Study:

Threats and Violence in the Workplace

Richard Farley worked at ESL, a high-tech Silicon Valley company. Laura Black also worked there and soon Farley became smitten with her. She, however, wanted nothing to do with him. After rejecting several of his advances, Farley began threatening her and their co-workers.

When Farley's supervisors threatened to fire him, Farley again indicated he would turn violent. "Are you saying that if you are fired you will kill me?" one of them asked him. "Not just you," Farley replied.

The company fired Farley and prohibited him from the office. The ban, however, had little effect on the shotguns and other weapons he brought back. He shot his way into the building, then proceeded to shoot everyone he encountered as he prowled about the building. He shot Laura Black once, then left her bleeding but alive. In all, Farley killed seven co-workers and wounded three.

In co-worker violence situations, threats carry great weight.

SOURCE: Gavin de Becker, The Gift of Fear: Survival Signals That Protect Us From Violence (New York: Little, Brown and Company, 1997), pp. 141-2.

Research on school shootings also suggests that threats frequently precede the violence. Harris and Kliebold, according to the governor's final report on the Columbine shooting, threatened one particular fellow student and posted their plans for havoc on an Internet site. An FBI report on non-inner city school shootings highly recommended that schools establish a threat assessment procedure "managed by properly trained staff." In a study of selected school shootings, Secret Service researchers found many instances in which the eventual school shooter discussed his plans with friends. Similarly, the U.S. Department of Education compiled a list of "early warning signs" for school violence. The list included "expression of violence in writings and drawings" and "serious threats of violence" as behaviors school officials should be on the look out for.[20]

Case Study:

The Chatty School Shooter

Evan Ramsay felt tormented at the Bethel, Alaska, high school he attended. Classmates picked on him, teachers disapproved of his poor performance. Only a few close friends seemed to understand him. When he mentioned one day that he ought to take a gun to school and kill his worst tormentors, his friends applauded the plan. One friend even showed him how to load the shotgun he took from his house.

Word spread among the students. On the appointed day, a small crowd of students began gathering on the balcony overlooking the front lobby. One student brought a video camera to record the events, but in the excitement of the shootings he forgot to turn it on.

Ramsay arrived with the shotgun hidden in his pant leg. He killed the school principal and one of the schools' star athletes before surrendering.

In school situations, talk of violence carries great weight.

SOURCE: Bryan Vossekuil, et al., "The Final Report and Findings of the Safe School Initiative: Implications for the Prevention of School Attacks in the United States," U.S. Secret Service and U.S. Department of Education, 2002, p. 25.

How, then, can the threat manager reconcile the contradictory research on threats and their importance as pre-incident indicators? Gavin de Becker first pointed to a way out of the confusion in *The Gift of Fear.* As a practical matter, de Becker strongly recommended assessing threats in the context in which they were uttered. He noted that "in interpersonal situations (neighbor, friend, spouse) a threat tends to actually increase the likelihood of violence by eroding the quality of communication and increasing frustration, but the very same threat conveyed to a public figure does not portend violence at all." Reid Meloy also noted the difference between threats to public figures and threats to people the threatener knows personally. Yet, the full implications of this difference and how it applies to threat management has eluded most researchers working in this field.[21]

We suggest that the interpersonal aspect of the context in which the threat is made is crucial to assessing the seriousness of a specific threat of violence. The best way to conceptualize this context is to place it along the continuum we call the *Intimacy Effect.* The intimacy effect simply postulates that the more intimate the relationship between the threatener and the target, the more likely the threat will serve as a pre-incident indicator of future violence. Although researchers have not fully explored this aspect of threats, the evidence suggests that the degree of intimacy within the relationship has a direct bearing on the validity of threatening statements. Simply put, the more intimate the relationship, the more likely threats will be carried out.

For example, in cases of domestic violence – obviously, the most intimate of any kind of relationship – threats are frequently carried out. They fit into a pattern of escalating emotion and action. Similarly, in workplace and school settings – in which the intimacy is more social than physical – threats also gain in value because the co-workers and fellow students know each other and work with each other daily. But the importance of threats begins to diminish as the intimacy of the relationship recedes. Threats to public figures – whether presidents, celebrities, jurists, or abortion providers – have not been shown to have a strong relationship to ultimate violence.

Consequently, threats should be assessed within the *social* setting in which they are uttered. The assessment, as de Becker urges, needs to account for the context of the situation. The most important element of that context is determining just how well the threatener and his or her potential victim know each other. On an intimacy scale, threats increase in importance the more the context falls at the intimate end of the continuum. They decrease as the relationship moves toward the other end where threatener and target are strangers to each other.

Actuarial Profiles

Insurance companies earn their stock in trade by playing the odds. They ease their gamble by building sophisticated profiles of their clientele. They call these profiles actuarial tables. The tables tell them, with considerable accuracy, that individuals of a certain age, race, weight, and personal habit – *when grouped with similar individuals* – will die at around a certain age. Because insurance companies deal in groupings, their profiles work well enough for most companies to turn a profit. They always have to deal with a few individuals who die out of turn, but that is usually off set by about the same number who take longer to die. Done well, with constant monitoring of changes in the characteristics of the herd, insurance companies can go years successfully gambling on how high to set their rates.

Law enforcement longs for its own actuarial tables. Some years ago, the FBI established a Behavioral Science Unit that specialized in profiling criminals. Though the unit has long since changed its name, it continues to work with other law enforcement agencies by providing expert advice based on its studies and composites of criminal behavior. Some of the unit's early members have retired into private practice, splitting their time writing books and consulting, but always profiling.

Unfortunately, profiling criminals works on the same basis as actuarial tables. It deals in statistical trends based on large numbers. Threat management works in specifics, on a literal case-by-case basis. Threat managers have no business trading in the generalities of criminal profiles. Putting one's faith in a general profile ensures blinding oneself to important evidence and information simply because it goes against the expectations built into the profile.

Perhaps no other case proved the danger of profiling than the Fall, 2002, sniper shootings in the Washington, D.C., metropolitan area. Media pundits, several of them retired members of the FBI's Behavioral Science Unit, assured the anxious public that the sniper would, when eventually caught, be a lone white male in his thirties who could not maintain steady relationships with women, had a military background, and had been fired from Michael's craft store. When eventually caught, the sniper turned out to be two black males of widely different ages who had nothing to do with craft stores other than occasionally preferring their large parking lots as locales for their crimes. One of them had a military background, but he, apparently, did not do the actual shootings in most of the attacks. The older of the two was in his 40s, the younger only 17.[22]

Still, the temptation to build profiles on small sample sizes (microcosmic compared to insurance actuarial tables), has long attracted researchers in the field of intended violence. President Johnson's National Commission on the Causes and Prevention of Violence reviewed the eight known presidential assassination attempts from Andrew Jackson to John F. Kennedy. That small actuarial table led the commission to the following profile:

> Although we cannot unravel the significance of the similarities between the assassins, we could make this statement: we could predict after President Kennedy's assassination that the next assassin would probably be short and slight of build, foreign born, and from a broken family – most probably with the father either absent or unresponsive to the child. He would be a loner, unmarried, with no steady female friends, and have a history of good work terminated from one to three years before the assassination attempt by a seeming listlessness and irascibility. He would identify with a political or religious movement. Although identifying with the cause, the assassin would not in fact be part of or able to contribute to the movement. Not every presidential assassin has had every one of the foregoing traits, but some combination of the above characterized them all.

With the perspective of forty years and nearly a half dozen attacks on presidents after this profile was written, its robust confidence seems now sadly quaint.[23]

Since the commission compiled its actuarial table, there have been more than half again as many presidential assassination attempts. Only one of the assassins – Sirhan Sirhan, who killed Robert F. Kennedy – was foreign born. The rest were homegrown Americans. Two were women. They came, too, in different sizes: some small, some heavy, some tall, some short. All, no doubt, were in some shape or form mentally disturbed or unbalanced, but their insanity did not prevent them from functioning well enough to actually get a shot off at the president.[24]

The Secret Service now acknowledges that any profile of a public-figure assassin is a "myth." After researching more than eighty public-figure attackers, Secret Service researchers concluded that "attackers and near-lethal approachers do not fit any one descriptive or demographic profile (or even several descriptive or demographic profiles)." Even the not-so-surprising conclusion that assassins are, almost by definition, mentally ill did not hold up in the study. "In most cases, however, mental illness does not appear to be a primary cause of assassination behavior," the study observed, "Attacks on prominent persons are the actions of persons who see assassination as a way to achieve their goals or solve problems, which requires a fairly rational process." In sum, public-figure attackers do not make up an actuarial table from which threat managers can gamble their target's lives.[25]

Still, the temptation remains. After a series of non-inner city school shootings in the mid-1990s, psychologists James P. McGee and Caren R. DeBernardo profiled the shooters and labled them "Classroom Avengers." The profile included such characteristics as white males who were a student at the school, loners, and seeking revenge. Their actuarial table consisted of 16 cases.[26]

However, Kris Mohandie, another psychologist, took a more comprehensive approach to school shootings. He looked beyond the non-inner city, mid-1990s school shootings. His research uncovered shooters who were female, Black and Hispanic, and non-students. Rather than developing some all encompassing profile, Mohandie grouped the shootings into three very general types:

> *Type I* events involve perpetrators who have no relationship to the school and choose to attack the school for their own idiosyncratic reasons. *Type II* events involve perpetrators who are customers of the school, including students, former students, and family members of students. *Type III* events involve perpetrators who have an employment-related relationship with the school.

Researchers who focus exclusively on incidents or perpetrators of most interest to them may well find characteristics that fit into a profile, but their methodology blinds them to incidents in the same venue but well outside their actuarial table.[27]

Others have compiled profiling lists of domestic abusers and

"Workplace Avengers." We scoff at such efforts not because they are ludicrous, but because they are so dangerous. Threat managers who turn to profiles and checklist characteristics willfully close their eyes to the specific evidence pertaining to the case they have before them. Insurance companies have to profile because, in the end, all their customers eventually die. Threat managers cannot afford to profile because, in the end, their targets deserve to live another day.

Case Study:

I Know the Man

In 1999, Lynn Milam of Ernando, Mississippi, nearly died of acute bouts of diarrhea and vomiting. Medical tests determined that the arsenic levels in her body were 100 times above normal. Police immediately suspected foul play. Their profile of domestic abusers pointed them to her husband, Tom. "They said someone was trying to kill me, and they were almost 100 percent sure it was Tom," Milam remembered.

But she didn't believe the police assessment for a second. Further testing showed that his body had even more arsenic than hers. The investigation then turned to the building materials the couple was using to construct an A-frame cabin. The arsenic came from the wood preservative used to treat the cabin's lumber.

But how was Milam so sure that she was not the victim of some criminal plot of her husband's? "I know the man," she said, "If he were going to kill me, he'd just shoot me."

Profiles describe populations at a very general level; individuals operate at a very specific level.

SOURCE: New York Times, June 26, 2002.

Summary

In this chapter, we have not attempted to summarize the voluminous research on intended violence. Rather, we extracted the three most practical lessons of that research which we believe every threat manager should keep constantly in mind. First, no matter how bizarre or irrational, every individual of violent intent is driven to that violence by a highly personalized grievance. Intended violence is not spontaneous, impulsive, or motiveless. It is embarked upon for a specific reason which can be generally described as the relentless pursuit of justice. Second, in no circumstances should threats of physical harm be ignored or discounted. Instead, they should be assessed against the *Intimacy Effect* and within the social context in which they were uttered. Third, threat management has no room for profiles or checklist characteristics. Each case is unique and needs its own unique assessment and management. In the remaining chapters of this book, we offer specific, practical strategies and tactics the threat manager can apply to every case of potential intended violence, regardless of venue.

Notes to Chapter 3

[1] Sigmund Freud, *Civilization and Its Discontents*, (Garden City, NY: Doubleday, 1958). *The Warren Commission Report: The Official Report of the President's Commission on the Assassination of President John F. Kennedy*, (Stamford, CT : Longmeadow Press, 1993). We do not have the space here for even a partial listing of the Kennedy-conspiracy books.

[2] Leon Friedman, ed., *Final Report of the National Commission on the Causes and Prevention of Violence*, 16 vols., (NY: Chelsea House, 1983), Introduction.

[3] Richard Restak, "Assassin," *Science Digest* (December 1981): 81. Sidney J. Slomich and Robert E. Kantor, "Social Psychopathology of Political Assassination," *Bulletin of the Atomic Scientists* (March 1969): 9.

[4] "Assessing Whether Batterers Will Kill," Danvers, Massachusetts, Police Department http://sww.danverspolice.com/domvio14.htm. "Domestic Violence in the Courtroom: Understanding the Problem . . . Knowing the Victim," American Judges Foundation, no date, http://aja.ncsc.dni.us/domviol/booklet.html. "Combating Workplace Violence," Illinois State Police, Safety Messages and Programs – Combating Workplace Violence http://www.state.il.us/isp/viowkplc/vwovrw.htm

[5] James Gilligan, *Violence: Reflections on a National Epidemic*, (New York: Random House, 1997), 11-12. Emphases in original.

[6] Crane Brinton, *The Anatomy of Revolution*, (New York: Vintage Books, 1965).

[7] Calhoun, *Hunters and Howlers*, 107. See also Frederick S. Calhoun and Stephen W. Weston, *Defusing the Risk to Judicial Officials: The Contemporary Threat Management Process* (Alexandria, VA: National Sheriff's Association, 2001), 27-49.

[8] Bryan Vossekuil, Robert Fein, et al., *The Final Report and Findings of the Safe School Initiative: Implications for the Prevention of School Attacks in the United States* (Washington, D.C.: United States Secret Service and United States Department of Education, 2002), 21.

[9] William H. Erickson, Chairman, "The Report of Governor Bill Owens' Columbine Review Commission," Governors Office, Denver Colorado, May 2001, 21-22. James P. McGee and Caren R. DeBernardo, "The Classroom Avenger," *The Forensic Examiner*, May-June, 1999.

[10] T. Stanley Duncan, "Death in the Office: Workplace Homicides," FBI *Law Enforcement Bulletin*, undated, http://nsi.org/Tips/workdeth.txt. Steve Kaufer and Jurge W. Mattman, "Workplace Violence: An Employer's Guide," Workplace Violence Research Institute, 1998, http://www.wrkvio.com/articles/employers_guide.html. Chris E., McGoey, "Workplace Violence At the Office?" January 7, 2001, http://www.crimedoctor.com/workplace1.htm.

[11] "Assessing Whether Batterers Will Kill," Danvers, Massachusetts, Police Department http://sww.danverspolice.com/domvio14.htm.

[12] Patricia Tjaden, Patricia and Nancy Thoenes, *Extent, Nature, and Consequences of Intimate Partner Violence: Findings From the National Violence Against Women Survey*, Washington, D.C.: U.S. Department of Justice, National Institute o f Justice, July 2000, iv.

[13] Park Dietz, et al., "Threatening and Otherwise Inappropriate Letters to Hollywood Celebrities," *Journal of Forensic Sciences* (January 1991): 187.

[14] Park Dietz, et al., "Threatening and Otherwise Inappropriate Letters to Members of the United States Congress," *Journal of Forensic Sciences* (September 1991): 1466, 1463.

[15] Bryan Vossekuil and Robert Fein, "Protective Intelligence and Threat Assessment Investigations: A Guide for State and Local Law Enforcement Officials," (Washington, D.C.: National Institute of Justice, 1998), pp. 14-15

[16] Calhoun, *Hunters and Howlers*, xix-xxi.

[17] Gavin de Becker, *The Gift of Fear: Survival Signals that Protect Us from Violence*, (New York: Little, Brown, 1997), 117. Debra M. Jenkins, "The U.S. Marshals Service's Threat Analysis Program for the Protection of the Federal Judiciary," The Annals of the American Academy of Political and Social Science, July 2001, pp. 69-77.

[18] "Assessing whether Batterers Will Kill," Danvers, MA, Police Department. "Domestic Abuse: Symptoms of Abuse — Threats, Power Misuse, and Control," Metro Nashville Police Department, http://www.telalink.net/police/abuse/symptoms.htm. Kerry Healey, Christine Smith, with Chris O'Sullivan, "Batterer Intervention: Program Approaches and Criminal Justice Strategies," *Issues and Practices in Criminal Justice* (Washington, D.C.: National Institute of Justice), February 1998. Patricia Tjaden and Nancy Thoenes, *Extent, Nature, and Consequences of Intimate Partner Violence: Findings from the National Violence Against Women Survey* (Washington, D.C.: U.S. Department of Justice, National Institute of Justice, July 2000), 43.

[19] *Dealing with Workplace Violence: A Guide for Agency Planners*, United States Office of Personnel Management, Office of Workforce Relations, OWR-09, (Washington, D.C.: Government Printing Office, February 1998), 17. Steve Kaufer and Jurg W. Mattman, "Workplace Violence: An Employer's Guide," Workplace Violence Research Institute, 1998, http://www.workviolence.com/articles/employers_guide.htm. Jurg W. Mattman, "Preventing Violence in the Workplace," Workplace Violence Research

Institute, 1998, http://www.workviolence.com/articles/preventing_violence.htm.
[20] Mary Ellen O'Toole, "The School Shooter" A Threat Assessment Perspective," Critical Incident Response Group, National Center for the Analysis of Violent Crime, FBI Academy, September 2000, pp. 5-9. Vossekuil, et al., Safe School Initiative. K. Dwyer, D. Osher, and C. Warger, *Early Warning, Timely Response: A Guide to Safe Schools* (Washington, D.C.: U.S. Department of Education, 1998), pp. 8, 11.
[21] De Becker, *The Gift of Fear*, 103-118. Meloy, *Violence Risk and Threat Assessment*, 161-66.
[22] Washington *Post*, October 25, 2002.
[23] Leon Friedman, ed., *Assassination and Political Violence*, vol. 8 in Violence in America, (NY: Chelsea House, 1983), pp. 65-66.
[24] Linda Lalucella, *Assassination: The Politics of Murder*, (LA: Lowell House, 1998).
[25] Fein and Vossekuil, *Protective Intelligence and Threat Assessment Investigations*, pp. 12-13.
[26] McGee and DeBernardino, "Classroom Avenger."
[27] Kris Mohandie, *School Violence Threat Assessment: A Practical Guide for Educators, Law Enforcement, and Mental Health Professionals*, (San Diego, CA: Specialized Training Services, 2000), pp. 26-7.

CHAPTER FOUR

Following the Path to Intended Violence

If we were to choose the single most important finding from all the research on intended violence, we would pick the realization that intended violence is a process composed of discreet, sequential, recognizable behaviors. In order to commit an act of intended violence, individuals of violent intent must engage in each of those behaviors. The process can best be envisioned as a path leading from the initial grievance to the ultimate violence. There is but one path. Anyone who wants to get to the violent act must follow it from start to finish. In this chapter, we describe in detail the various behaviors encountered in between grievance and attack.

Recognizing intended violence as a process of integrated behaviors shifted the focus of contemporary threat management from the traditional emphasis on what individuals say – the threats they may make – to emphasizing what individuals do. What individuals say and the threats they make should never be ignored. These provide good insights into the subject's motive and intent. In intimate relationships, threats frequently become part of an escalating spiral leading to violence. Frequently, too, threats may be the first indication that the subject has focused on a particular potential victim. Nonetheless, assessing the potential risk needs to be firmly grounded on the subject's behaviors and actions, not merely on his or her words.

Nor should the assessment rely on checklists of unrelated behaviors. Intended violence follows an integrated process wherein all of the subject's actions become intertwined. The behaviors must be assessed as a whole, not just by the particular parts. Individuals of violent intent move from developing the idea for committing violence through various individual steps leading to the violent act. For anyone who intends to engage in violence, the intent itself compels certain behaviors. These actions are noticeable, if only we knew where to look and what to look for. Intended violence must be understood as a process of behaviors, a culmination of necessary acts taken in preparation to act violently. Seeing the requisite behaviors in their entirety and in sequence further enhances the threat manager's ability to identify potential problems, assess the actual degree of risk, and decide on the best strategy for managing that risk.

Figure 1 illustrates the path to intended violence.

Figure 1. Path to Intended Violence

Attack
Breach
Preparation
Research/Planning
Ideation
Grievance

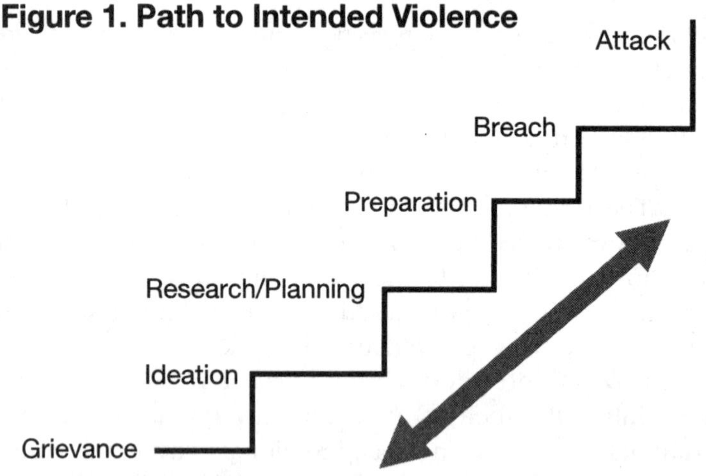

Since the process resembles a path, the perpetrator can move in either direction along it, reaching one level and then moving forward or retreating to a previous level. Time means nothing along the path. Traversing it can take months, even years, or it can be covered in hours, even minutes.

Case Study:

Royal Persistence vs. Middle School Impulse

Sal L., a Mexican citizen, knew he was the King of California. In August 1995, he went to the office of his usurper and told the governor's staff to leave. He was there to take up his royal duties. His persistent and aggressive behavior earned him a mental health commitment. From the hospital, Sal continued to threaten the governor. Law enforcement officers tried to solve the problem by repeatedly deporting him, first in October 1996, then again in April 1997 and February 1998.

Sal persisted, as any King would. At the new governor's inauguration in January 1999, the threat manager distributed copies of Sal's photograph. That morning, the threat manager found Sal sitting in the Capitol Rotunda along the route the governor would take to the inauguration. Sal carried with him a nine-inch knife and a newspaper clipping containing the governor's picture. The threat manager arranged another mental health commitment. When that expired, Sal was again deported to Mexico.

In May 2002, Sal returned to the California capitol demanding his rightful place. He wore a hand-decorated tunic and a cardboard crown handed out at Burger King. Arrested, committed, and deported again, Sal came back to the capitol in February 2003. He sneaked into the public seating overlooking the legislature. He stood up and yelled, "I am the King of California. Arrest me." When uniformed officers tried to oblige him, Sal fought back. Persistence drove him along the path to intended violence.

Conversely, Nate Brazill took the path to intended violence impulsively, not persistently. A seventh grader at Lake Worth Community Middle School, Brazill turned rambunctious on the last day of the school year in May 2000. He threw a few water balloons. The guidance counselor suspended him and ordered Brazill and another student to go home. On the walk home, Brazill told his classmate he was going to get his gun and shoot the counselor. True to his word, Brazill retrieved a .25 caliber pistol and returned to school. He went to a classroom and asked to speak to a friend, but the teacher refused. Brazill aimed the pistol and shot the teacher flush in the face, killing him instantly. For Brazill, impulse drove him along the path to intended violence.

Time is not a factor in following the path to intended violence.

SOURCE: Authors' personal knowledge; Miami Herald, June 4, 2000.

Step 1: Grievance

As we discussed in the previous chapter, individuals of violent intent are relentless seekers of justice. This does not mean that each such individual has the same reason for feeling aggrieved, only that each has a feeling of being wronged in some way. Why the individual feels unjustly treated varies from person to person. Nor need it be rational or logical. Justice may be universal, but injustice is highly personalized to each individual.

Figure 2 illustrates the place of grievance along the path to intended violence.

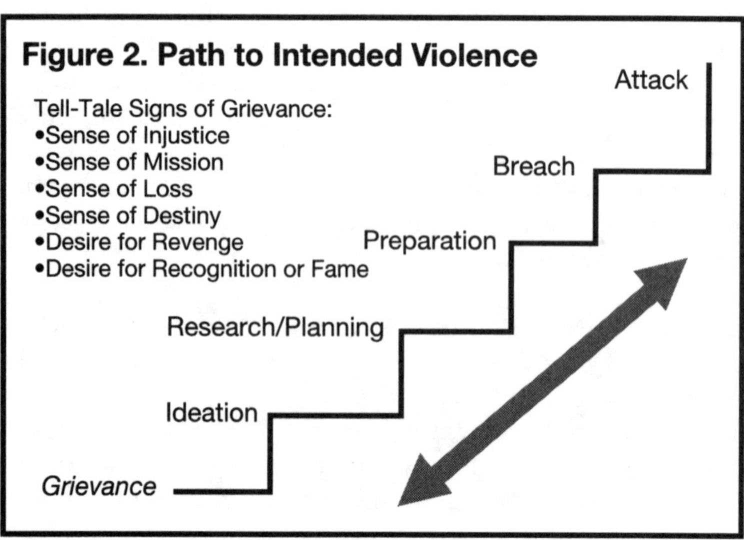

Effective threat management requires understanding that a strong, burning feeling of injustice always prompts individuals of violent intent to take the first step along the path to intended violence. Knowing that a grievance must exist helps the threat manager look for the reason. Finding out about that reason helps identify individuals of violent intent and assess their potential for risk.

Case Study:

A Father's Motive

On March 16, 1995, a package arrived at a Louisiana courthouse addressed to a specific judge. The parcel contained a bomb and a receipt from Radio Shack. Seizing on this clue, the Federal Bureau of Investigation immediately launched an investigation on the person whose name appeared on the ticket. He was an African-American teenager, who was soon cleared of sending the bomb. But the agents found out that the young man was dating a local Caucasian girl. She was carrying his child.

The investigation soon centered on the girl's father. Once confronted, he quickly confessed. He intended, he explained, to get his daughter's boyfriend out of her life and decided the best way to do that was to frame him. Sending a bomb to a federal judge seemed to guarantee the young man would go away for a long time. But why that particular judge, the investigators asked. Because, the father explained, of all the federal judges listed on the courthouse directory, this judge's name was the only one short enough to fit on the mailing label.

No single description of the reason for violence could possibly cover all the insanities of human behavior.

SOURCE: Authors' personal knowledge.

Although it is impossible to list all possible reasons prompting acts of intended violence, something always spurs the subject onto the path. However muddled, irrational, or nonsensical, every individual embarked on an act of intended violence feels that he or she has a compelling reason for stepping in that direction. Broadly described, they all carry with them a sense of injustice, of being unfairly treated or ignored. Maybe its because they feel separate from everyone else, isolated or just different. Perhaps its because they feel themselves on some mission to save the world, themselves, or some damsel in distress. They may have suffered some loss, perhaps even big enough to give themselves a sense of nothing left to lose. Some may be heartbroken, love obsessed, or enraged by jealousy. Some feel it is their destiny, an inescapable fate. Others may be propelled onto the path by good old-fashioned revenge. Many seek recognition in the form of infamy, as though they can steal someone else's hard-earned fame by the simple act of murder. Violence will make them famous, even if it costs their freedom or their lives. Still others act out some command delusion. They take their instructions from aliens or the devil or God. Regardless of the specific reason in any particular case, everyone on the path believes they have good reason for being there. More precisely, they believe they have a compelling reason.

Case Study:

Man on a Mission

Kizo ordered Kelly G. to kill as many law enforcement officers – federal and local – as he could. Kizo also wanted Kelly to attack as many federal and state government buildings as he could. Following orders, Kelly went to the local offices of the FBI in his city. At the security checkpoint, he asked to speak to an agent before going through security.

During the subsequent interview, the agent , suspecting Kelly might be armed, asked to search him. He found three loaded handguns and 220 rounds of ammunition.

Kelly also confessed about Kizo, adding that under Kizo's

orders he had made several approaches to the FBI offices, the state police headquarters, and various government buildings, always heavily armed. He dreamed of killing law enforcement officers as well as people fleeing the government buildings.

He added that he had gone to the FBI offices that particular day to report Kizo to the police. However, Kelly suspected that the FBI might be in collusion with Kizo, so he armed himself to be "prepared for a bad event."

The FBI agent arrested Kelly for firearms violations and the court ordered mental health treatment. Further investigation revealed that Kizo was the name of a fictional Yahuza character in the movie "Black Rain" starring Michael Douglas.

SOURCE: Authors' personal knowledge.

Placing the case under investigation into a specific venue or context will help the threat manager uncover the specific reason or grievance in the instant case. The danger here, of course, is forcing the facts to fit into the wrong venue. The threat manager should carefully weigh all the known facts, focusing specifically on the potential victim, the victim's situation, and the victim's previous history. Is the target a public figure or a student, a jurist trying a court case or an enraged husband caught up in a nasty divorce? By examining the target's situation, circumstances, and past, the threat manager can begin to see events and involvements prompting the individual of violent intent to feel wronged.

That examination needs to be exhaustive and comprehensive, for public figures are also spouses and co-workers. What at first blush appears to be a public-figure pursuit of the mayor may turn into a domestic dispute because he or she is getting divorced. Or it could turn into a problem with a co-worker if the mayor recently fired someone. The trick for the threat manager is not to categorize the potential victim, but to examine his or her entire situation, circumstances, and previous history.

Case Study:

Public Figure with a Private Past

A male caller repeatedly and regularly called the office of a female state senator. Each time, he asked to speak with her; each time he expressed his profound admiration for her personally and for her work. After several months of calls, the receptionist convinced the caller to leave his name. When the senator saw the name, she immediately called the threat manager.

Eight years earlier, long before she first ran for any public office, the senator taught at a local college. One of her students developed more than a crush on her. For a full year, he enrolled in every course she taught. After classes, he followed her to the parking lot. One day, he cornered her on campus and confessed his love for her. Campus police investigated the encounter and obtained a restraining order.

Now he was back, calling her office to express his deeply held admiration. Worse, the threat manager determined that the love-sick pupil lived within a mile of the senator's office. Although a public figure, her problem originated in the days before she took the public stage.

Any assessment of the victim's situation must be comprehensive, including current and previous experiences.

SOURCE: Author's personal knowledge.

Step 2: Ideation

Most people have grievances, things that happened that still rancor. Consequently, to say that individuals of violent intent have a grievance does little to separate them from the crowd. But most people put those sad events behind them and move on. They let the little injustices – and the people who caused them – go. Conversely, individuals of violent intent are incapable of putting the injustices behind them. At some point, it occurs to them that violence will correct the wrong, avenge the injustice. That is what distinguishes them: not the feeling of injustice, but the decision to use violence to avenge it. Getting that idea means taking the second step along the path to intended violence.

Once motivated by some grievance, individuals of violent intent must next strike upon the idea of resorting to violence. In other words, the intent to cause harm must be accepted and decided upon before any other actions can be taken. Intended violence results from a willful decision, a conscious choice. That choice derives from first recognizing that violence is an alternative.

Figure 3 illustrates the place of ideation along the path to intended violence.

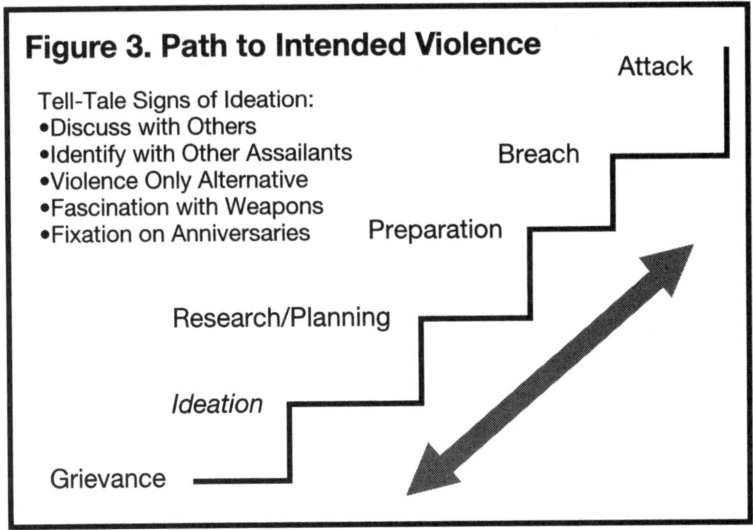

A number of tell-tale signs help identify possible ideation:

- making inappropriate communications or contacts;
- discussing the idea with others, even if only elliptically;
- identifying with other assassins;
- fixating on violence in general or specific acts of violence;
- expressing a fascination with weapons; or
- showing an interest in anniversaries or significant dates related to the grievance.

These signs are mere signals. Although ideation must occur in every case of intended violence, these signs do not necessarily appear in each case. They should be treated as potential clues, but neither inclusive nor exclusive of other clues and warning signs that an individual has decided violence will resolve his or her problems. The threat manager needs to watch for any evidence of reaching that resolution.

Case Study:

Trouble in Paradise

Bryan K. Uyesugi worked for Xerox Corporation in Honolulu, Hawaii, for nearly a decade. During that time he frequently fought with his co-workers. In 1994, police arrested him for criminal property damage resulting from an argument he had with a colleague. That arrest meant he could not obtain the firearms permit he wanted.

Although Uyesugi did not have a firearm permit, his supervisors knew he owned a large firearms collection. They knew, too, that he could not control his temper, particularly with co-workers. Worse, Uyesugi told his superiors he was afraid to bring any weapons to work for fear he might be tempted to use them.

Despite this evidence of ideation, Uyesugi contined to work for Xerox. On November 2, 1999, he finally worked up the courage to bring a gun to work. His fears were realized as he gave way to temptation. Firing a nine-millimeter pistol, Uyesugi killed seven colleagues before fleeing the scene. He surrendered to police seven hours later after a five-hour standoff. Newscasters immediately began describing the incident as trouble marring "paradise."

Ignoring signs of ideation is done at one's peril.

SOURCE: Associated Press, November 1, 2001; Washington Post, November 3, 1999.

Of course, individuals of violent intent do not normally make inappropriate communications or contacts to threat managers or other law enforcement officers. They do not usually discuss their ideas with cops or brag to the police how similar they are to some past assassin. They don't, as a matter of course, express their obsession with weapons to cops or alert them to important personal dates coming up. That would make contemporary threat management far too easy and rather boring.

But such individuals frequently engage in these behaviors with their targets, their targets' associates and friends, and with their own associates and friends. This means the threat manager needs to do one of two things, depending on the venue. For those situations involving public officials already under law enforcement protection, the threat manager should train the target and the target's family, staff, and associates on what suspicious, inappropriate, or untoward communications or contacts need to be reported to the threat manager. For those situations involving private citizens who are not already under law enforcement protection but who come to the police out of concern for their safety, the same lesson needs to be taught, but the threat manager also needs to key the initial investigation on discovering if any inappropriate contacts or communications have already been made. For public officials, training about inappropriate communications or contacts is preventive in nature. For private citizens, finding out about such communications or contacts is investigative in nature.

Exhibit 1 provides a definition of Inappropriate Communications or Contacts (IC&Cs) used by the Special Investigations Unit of the California Highway Patrol to educate its targets on what they should report. It was derived from a similar definition developed by Gavin de Becker, Incorporated. We strongly recommend that the threat manager use this definition – or something like it – as the first lesson in training those officials under the threat manager's protection and as a guide for investigating private citizen's complaints. The threat manager is wholly dependent on his or her targets reporting strange, unusual, disturbing, or disconcerting communications or contacts they receive or have received. Without such good reporting, the threat manager is blind to what may be going on in the case.

Exhibit 1. Definition of Inappropriate Communications or Contacts

Correspondence that contains the following references or information should be immediately reported to ____________________.

Threats Report all threats of harm to the principal or any other person received by written correspondence or telephone conversations. Threats may not alkways be direct or specific, but could be veiled ("You'll get yours") or conditional ("You better do…or I will…").

Inappropriate Correspondence Any correspondence that makes reference to:

- *A special history shared with the principal.*
- *A special destiny shared with the principal.*
- *A direct communication (belief that there is direct communication between the principal and writer).*
- *Religious and historical themes involving the principal (including when the writer admonishes the principal to change his/her lifestyle).*
- *Death, suicide, weapons, etc.*
- *Extreme or obsessive admiration or affection.*
- *Obsessive desire to contact the principal (including plans for meetings, interest in home address, etc.).*
- *A debt that is owed the writer by the principal (not just money but any type of debt).*
- *The principal is someone other than himself/herself (an imposter, a historical figure, the writer's relative, etc.)*
- *Persons who have been attacked in public (Lincoln, Lennon, Sadat, Kennedy, et al.).*
- *Persons who have carried out attacks against public figures (Oswald, Hinckley, Sirhan, et al.).*
- *Mental illness (psychiatric care, anti-psychotic medication, etc.).*
- *Bodyguards, security, safety, danger, etc.*

Beyond these general categories, please include anything that is disjointed in content, sinister or otherwise questionable. This should include bizarre or unreasonable solicitations. We will return anything that is not of interest.

Writers will often start with a letter, receive a response, and then send questionable material later. If you recall the writer has had a response in the past, please make note of that and attach it to the letter. When placing notes and notations on materials you are sending us, it is best to use Post-It notes, as they do not damage evidence as do staples and tape. Always include envelopes, even if they are torn.

We will require the original piece of correspondence. The letter will not be returned, therefore, you may wish to make a copy for your records.

The above criteria should also be applied to cards which arrive with flowers, telephone messages, or any other type of communication.

Threats included, what is especially important here is to be particularly sensitive to any evidence or clues suggesting that an individual has begun to think of violence as a viable course of action. Some of those clues take the form of IC&Cs, including threats. For example, we define references to security measures as inappropriate. If the subject is thinking about security, he or she may be contemplating ways to get around that security. Claims that the subject and target share some special destiny may mean that destiny is death. John Hinckley wanted to link his name forever with the actress Jodie Foster. He achieved that destiny by shooting President Ronald Reagan. What people say, it would seem, sometimes gives insight into what they are planning.

Sometimes, individuals contemplating violence provide others with brief, even elliptical, insights into the focus of their contemplations. A week or so before Francisco Duran traveled from Colorado to Washington, D.C., where he fired his semi-automatic rifle at the White House, he signed one of his business cards and gave it to a friend. He advised the friend to save the card because someday soon it would be quite valuable. Jack Gary McKnight, who shot his way into the Topeka federal courthouse, opined to a friend that he ought to kill all those whom he believed had gone after him. Russell Weston, who shot his way into the U.S. Capitol in the summer of 1998, complained repeatedly and widely that the government had him under constant surveillance. He told anyone who would listen, including staffs at several government agencies, that he intended to put a stop to it.

School shooters seem particularly prone to confiding their plans to others. Eric Harris and Dylan Kliebold posted their ideas about violence and slaughter on the Internet. They also made a videotape acting out their fantasies. As they walked toward the cafeteria, they warned another student to stay away from the school. Luke Woodham received considerable encouragement from Grant Boyette, his closest friend, who promised to join him in a shooting rampage through their high school in Pearl, Mississippi. Boyette backed out at the last minute, but urged Woodham to go through with it anyway. Frequently, it would seem, those who think about committing a violent act have trouble keeping those thoughts to themselves.[1]

Sometimes ideation appears as a fascination with another assassin. In March 1992, Michael Griffen assassinated Dr. David Gunn, the first time an anti-abortionist killed an abortion doctor. For the next year and a half, anti-abortionist Paul Hill championed Griffen's action under the pseudo-doctrine of justifiable homicide. He circulated petitions, appeared on talk shows, and began focusing on Dr. Gunn's replacement. In August 1993, Hill culminated his own trek along the path to violence by shotgunning Dr. John Britton and his escort, David Barrett. "Michael Griffen had been dismissed as being mentally unbalanced," Hill later explained, "but I was a former Presbyterian minister." Hence, he reasoned, his act of violence would have more credibility than Griffen's because he had better credentials. Hill wanted to inspire others to follow his footsteps along the path to intended violence.[2]

The Secret Service's Exceptional Cases Study cited the case of "FD," who became fascinated with the idea of assassination through her study of the Civil War. From John Wilkes Booth, she began reading obsessively about other assassins. For hours on end she played the soundtrack from Steven Sondheim's musical Assassins. Finally, and hoping to salvage something from the seeming hopelessness of her life, FD decided to become an assassin herself. She targeted President George Bush, but her intentions were discovered before she could act them out. Even those intent on violence, it would seem, have role models they follow.[3]

Sometimes the fascination is with violence in general. Frequently, acts of intended violence seem to come in spates as though the first inspired the second and the second the third. In August 1999, Atlanta newspapers gave extensive coverage to a particularly brutal case of domestic violence. Shortly afterward, Mark Barton killed his own family, then shot up two day-trading brokerage firms. A week after that, Alan Eugene Miler went on a shooting spree in Pelham, Alabama. He attacked two places where he had previously worked. Not to be outshone by the Oklahoma City bombing, the Unabomber apparently moved up the timetable of his bombing of a forestry association official in Sacramento, California. On April 18, 2000, Kenneth Ray Miller, who lived in a senior-citizen apartment house in Lincoln Park, Michigan, opened fire with a rifle on a meeting of the other residents. He killed two women. The next day, a former resident walked into a meeting at a retirement community in Peoria, Arizona, and opened fire, killing one woman and injuring four other people. Violence, it would seem, inspires violence.[4]

Some who intend violence give a glimpse of their intentions through an obsession with weapons. Workplace violence cases are populated with individuals who spent their working hours intimidating fellow employees with talk of guns, photos of guns, speculations about what they would do if they had a gun at that moment, and wishes for guns. They post photographs of guns in their work area, reveling both in the topic itself and in the discomfort it causes their colleagues. School shootings offer similar lessons, with many of the shooters obsessed with guns, knives, and bombs. Acts of violence, it would seem, sometimes start from a romance with the tools of violence.

Interest in anniversaries or key dates provide other signals that an individual may be thinking about committing a violent act. McKnight timed his assault on the Topeka federal courthouse for the day of his sentencing. "Crazy Eddie" Vaughn attacked his prosecutor on the morning his case was scheduled to go to trial. Charles Koster assassinated Judge Richard Daronco two days after the judge dismissed Koster's daughter's lawsuit.

Workplace violence often takes place on the anniversary of the employee's termination from the company. Domestic violence often takes place on the anniversary of the divorce or around the time of some contentious court hearing. Attacks on abortion clinics and providers increase around Christmas; the January 22 anniversary of the *Roe v. Wade* Supreme Court ruling; Easter; Mother's Day; and – along the Canadian border – around November 11, known in Canada as "Remembrance Day" and adopted by anti-abortionists as remember the unborn. Timothy McVeigh quite intentionally picked the anniversary of the Waco conflagration as the day he blew up the Murrah building in Oklahoma City, Oklahoma. Anniversaries and key dates provide a neat symbolic wrap-up to the plan for violence. It forges a link between the assassin's act and some larger cause, thus making the mundane act of murder a memorial to something bigger. Anniversaries become, it would seem, both deadlines and symbolic statements.

Case Study:

In the Nick of Time

Steve W. wrote the governor to complain bitterly about the state's judicial system and his insurance company. He had been in an automobile accident that left him disabled, but he could get no justice from the courts or the insurance. In return, he informed the governor that he had planted 37 bombs with timers at various locations in his city. "If violence is what they want, that's what they get."

Moving quickly, the threat manager got an arrest warrant for the threats and a search warrant on Steve W.'s trailer. The search uncovered two loaded handguns and a new hunting vest. The pouch of the vest held an improvised explosive device designed to explode when thrown to the ground. On the counter lay components for dozens of additional devices.

The threat manager found a city map with detailed drawings of the courthouse, with additional markings showing the judge's chambers. The map showed the location of the insurance company and Steve W.'s attorney's office. Steve W. also marked on the map where he intended to throw the bombs and how many he would explode at each location. On the margins of the map, Steve W. had written, "Kill, Kill, Kill" and "Kill lawyers." Steve W.'s calendar showed a doctor's appointment the next day. Notes he wrote indicated that he never intended to return. He planned to visit his parents' grave to explain his plans to them, then proceed with his bombings. This evidence led to Steve W.'s conviction.

For individuals of violent intent, it is but a small step from idea to action.

SOURCE: Authors' personal knowledge.

Step 3: Research and Planning

Once an individual decides on violence, he or she needs next to plan the event. Planning requires some degree of research, if only to determine where the target will be on the day of the attack and the best way to affect the assault. Consequently, both the research and the planning can be skeletal, such as choosing to use a pistol after fifth period in the schoolyard where little Tommy has recess. Or both can be fully fleshed out, detailed and determined, with contingencies, fall-backs, and escape routes.

Figure 4 illustrates the place of research and planning along the path to intended violence.

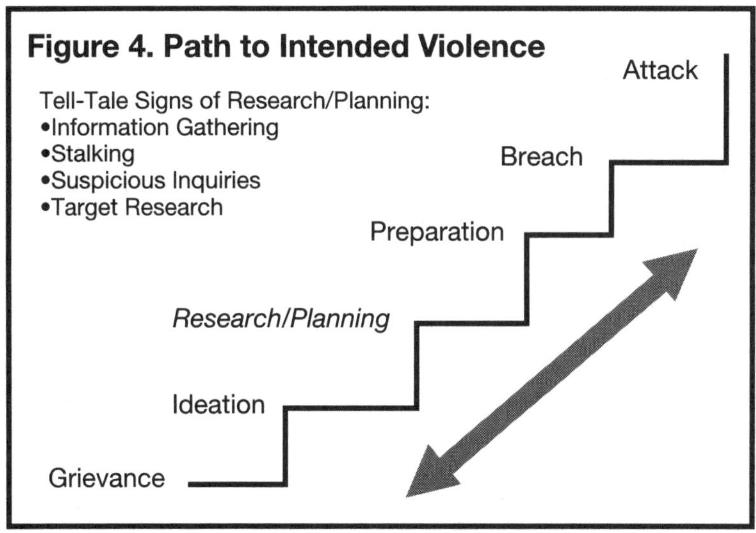

Not every case involves extensive research. On the morning John Hinckley attempted to assassinate President Ronald Reagan, he went to McDonald's for breakfast. While he ate, he debated with himself whether to go to New Haven, Connecticut, (where his obsession, Jodie Foster, attended Yale) and kill himself or remain in Washington and try to kill Senator Edward Kennedy or the president. On his way back to his hotel two blocks from the White House, he bought a Washington *Post*. From it he learned Reagan was scheduled to make a luncheon speech at the Washington Hilton, which was not far from his hotel. Convenience won the day. Hinkley decided to "take my little pistol" and see how close he could get to the president. Clearly, little research went into that.[5]

Not every case involves extensive planning. Michael Griffen killed Dr. Gunn simply by researching the kind of car Dr. Gunn drove, his routes, and where he parked at the reproductive health care clinic. When he saw Dr. Gunn's car enter the parking lot, Griffen knew the doctor would pull into the alley behind the clinic and park near the back door. Griffen walked down the alley and shot the doctor as he got out of his car. Griffen used what he knew about Dr. Gunn to devise a simple plan.[6]

The research and planning can be extensive and elaborate. Walter LeRoy Moody researched Judge Robert Vance's personal life, learning both Vance's home address and the home address of a fellow judge and friend of Vance's. Then Moody constructed an elaborate mail bomb designed to detonate by opening the package. He mailed it to Vance's home, using the information from the other judge for the return address. Unsuspecting, Vance opened the package believing his friend had sent him some law journals. Moody also mailed out three other bombs, two to the offices of civil rights advocates in Jacksonville, Florida, and Savannah, Georgia, and one to the Eleventh Circuit Court of Appeals in Atlanta. The first two were to disguise Moody's anger at Vance for rejecting Moody's appeal. He hoped to make the attacks appear ideologically (racially) motivated. With the fourth bomb, Moody intended to disguise the assassination of Judge Vance as an attack on all judges. Vance and one of the civil rights advocates were killed. The other two bombs were intercepted.[7]

Moody's research was extensive, Hinkley's almost accidental. Moody's plan was elaborate, Griffen's quite simple. Nonetheless, all three plans were informed by research on the respective targets. All three were thought out beforehand, however briefly or extensively, and all three were carried out with deadly effect.

The tell-tale signs of an individual who has reached the research and planning stage along the path to intended violence deal primarily with efforts to gain information about the target. Some of the signs are:

- target surveillance;
- target research;
- suspicious inquiries; or
- information gathering.

Of all the steps along the path, these behaviors are the most noticeable. They force the potential perpetrator out into the open to collect the necessary information. In order to research the target, the attacker has to ask questions, has to engage in behaviors associated with collecting information. The information itself has to come from direct observation, querying associates of the target, or combing through public records stored by public custodians. The target may notice being followed home, neighbors may report a stranger asking intrusive questions, fellow workers may notice an unknown car parked nearby.

Research on the target cannot be done in a vacuum. One of the earliest clues pointing toward James C. Kopp as the alleged killer of

Dr. Bernard Slepian in the fall of 1998 was testimony from one of the staff members at the abortion clinic that she had seen a suspicious car parked near the clinic a week or so before the shooting. Suspecting the car's driver of putting the clinic under surveillance, she jotted down a description of the car and its license plate number. The FBI later matched that information with a car witnesses saw near the scene of the killing.

Dr. Slepian was killed at home late on a Friday evening just after he returned from services at his synagogue. He stepped into his kitchen, turning on the light. Kopp, hiding in the wooded backyard, fired a single shot from a high-powered rifle. Kopp admitted stalking Slepian on six different occasions. He also researched other abortionists in the Buffalo, New York, area. He chose Slepian because his house offered the best place to shoot. Undoubtedly, Kopp also knew Slepian's routines, particularly that he would return from synagogue at around ten p.m., Friday night.[8]

Case Study:

The Internet Killer

It was in tenth grade, twenty-one year old Liam Youens explained on his website, that he fell in love with Amy Boyer. They were on the bus together and Boyer turned around to yell at a friend. Seeing her, Youens fell in love. Shortly thereafter, he decided to kill her and himself. "That was the basic plan for the next half decade," he noted.

Youens never risked expressing his feelings for Boyer to her. They graduated high school and he left Nashua, New Hampshire, to attend the Rochester Institute of Technology. A year later, he dropped out and returned home, determined now to track Boyer down. Although he knew where she lived, every time he attempted to approach her at home he found her surrounded by family. He decided to find out where she worked.

He posted his diary on the Internet and in it described how he thought of killing her or one of his classmates from high school. The Columbine shootings inspired him and he thought of returning to his high school to carry out his own "rampage."

But always he came back to Amy. He contacted an on-line research company for help finding her place of employment. For a few hundred dollars, the company provided Youens with Boyer's birthdate, Social Security number, address, and employer. She worked as a dental assistant on Main Street. "It's actually obscene what you can find out about people on the Internet," Youens editorialized on his web site.

Youens found Boyer at the dentist's in the fall of 1999, but he had trouble working up the "courage" to shoot an unarmed woman. By October 7, he was chastising himself on his web site for "making excuses." Five days later, he again chickened out because he had no place from which to shoot her. Three days later, on October 15, he drove his car beside her's and began firing, hitting her in the face and arms, and killing her.

Researching the target is an essential step along the path to violence, but it can take many different forms, from surveillance to surfing the Internet.

SOURCE: Boston Globe, November 29, 1999.

Obviously, the more intimate the relationship, the less need to research the target because the attacker knows enough already. Former employees know well the layout of their former places of employment. School shooters know their way around the school and the schedule of classes and recesses. Enraged spouses can easily find their former mates, at work, at home, or hiding with friends. Steve Lancaster knew his wife would be at their home helping get their kids off to school before leaving for work herself. He timed his attack on her based on that knowledge. Mitchell Johnson and Andrew Golden had been through enough fire drills at their middle school to know the procedure. They took that into account when they planned their attack. They pulled the fire alarm, then hastened to their snipers' nests. From there, they had a full view of the area where the students and teachers would evacuate. In these types of cases, research may not be as necessarily elaborate as in other cases. Nonetheless, the planning still has to take place and that incurs some risk of being noticed.

Case Study:

Knowing Where the Target Will Be

Edward Lansdale did not have to research his target's whereabouts. She had filed criminal charges against him, accusing him of sexually molesting her when she was a young teenager ten years earlier. As a result, Lansdale knew she would be at the Yreka, California, county courthouse on October 20, 2000. He also knew the jury would begin its deliberations over his guilt or innocence. Although he adamantly denied the charges, he had offered no defense and had no doubt what the verdict would be.

He began his preparations. He put his affairs in order, adding his daughter's name to the title of his house and giving his car to his ex-wife. He made out a will and recorded lengthy tape recordings addressed to various family members. He obtained a bottle of strychnine and hid a dose in his eyeglass case. He also took two pistols with him to Yreka.

On the morning of October 20, Lansdale slipped a five-shot, .22 caliber revolver into his pocket. He knew the courthouse did not screen for weapons, so he secreted the pistol in the men's room just down the hall from the courtroom. As he explained in the tape to his sister, he hoped to catch up with his accuser, then:

I'm gonna shoot her in the hand. I want to tell her that, "I'm gonna give you something that you, every time you look at your hand, you're gonna remember what you've done and how many lies you told here." I'm gonna shoot her in the hand. I'm gonna shoot her in the foot. I'm gonna tell her, "Every time that you take a step, you're gonna remember this." And I'm gonna shoot her right in her crotch.

When court recessed so the jury could deliberate, Lansdale retrieved his pistol. He caught up with his accuser at the stairs. His first shot hit her wrist. Chasing her down the steps, his second shot hit her in the lower back, the third in her buttocks, and the fourth shot passed cleanly through her husband's right leg. Lansdale stopped at the stair landing halfway between the second and first floor. He fired the last of his bullets into his right temple.

Based on what individuals of violent intent learn about their target's circumstances and environs, they plan and prepare themselves for the violent attack.

SOURCE: Detective Rick Berwick, Yreka, California, Police Department Crime Report (01020010) 00-1680, October 20, 2000.

Step 4: Preparations

Once the potential perpetrator completes the research and planning, he or she next has to make the requisite preparations called for in the plan. Preparing for the attack spawns a number of tell-tale signs, among them:

- acquiring a weapon;
- assembling equipment;
- arranging transporation;
- observing significant dates;
- conducting final-act behaviors; or
- costuming.

Figure 5 illustrates the place of preparations along the path to intended violence.

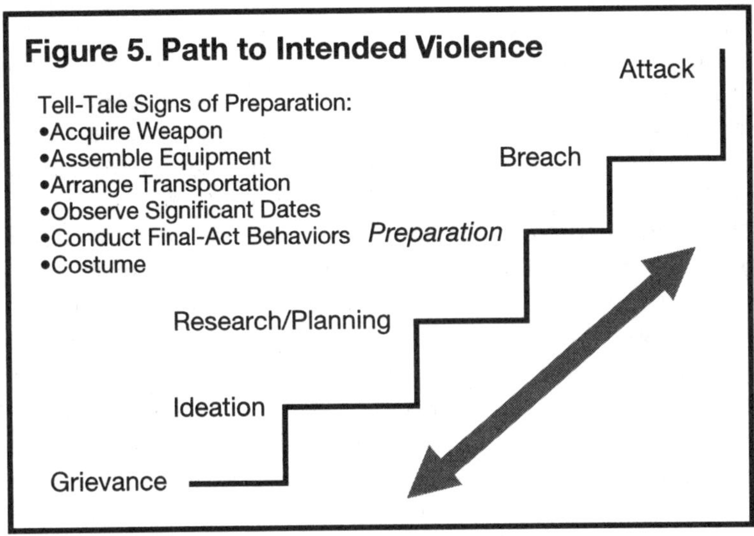

Harris and Klebold planned their attack for a year, during which they assembled their gas and pipe bombs and purchased their weapons. Steve Lancaster dressed himself in dark clothes so he would not be so easily seen as he approached his wife's home. Paul Hill practiced firing his shotgun at a local firing range. On the day of the shooting, he hid the weapon along the fence surrounding the abortion clinic. He retrieved it as soon as the truck carrying the doctor pulled into the clinic lot. Richard Farley armed himself with a substantial arsenal before he launched his attack on Laura Black and his former co-workers. Sungnam Lisowski first obtained a gun permit, then a gun, then practiced shooting before she killed her cheating husband and wounded their two daughters. After killing his mother and his wife, Charles Whitman went shopping. He purchased rifles, a shotgun, ammunition, food, and drinks. He loaded them in a footlocker, then hauled the footlocker to the top of the University of Texas clocktower. In all these cases – and in all the other cases of intended violence – the assailants prepared for their attacks.[9]

Preparations are activities and activities are noticeable. They can be disguised and hidden or carried out in secret, but they cannot be avoided. Like research and planning, they do not occur in a vacuum.

Often, they require interactions with others, the gathering of materials from diverse sources, and the assemblage of that material. The police finally tracked down Michael Bray and his two accomplices after they burned down several empty abortion clinics between Washington, D.C., and Delaware. The investigation centered on identifying the type of fuel they used, then tracing that to its source. Once they located where the arsonists shopped, it was an easy matter to determine who they were and arrest them as they prepared for their next outing.[10]

Preparations extend beyond obtaining a weapon or assembling the lethal equipment. Some attackers also have to raise the resources necessary to fund the attack. When anti-abortionist Rachelle Shannon decided to retire from arsons and become an assassin, she chose Dr. George Tiller of Wichita, Kansas, as her target. Shannon was an Oregon housewife who had no income beyond her husband's. She had always financed her fires by holding bake sales to earn the cash to buy gasoline and containers. It simply took her a few more sales than usual to raise the cash to buy a pistol and a plane ticket. Baking helped her solve that logistic.[11]

If the potential attacker has in mind some significant date, then obviously he or she has to wait for the proper day to arrive. Although many dates are personal, some dates are known to be associated with violence. Anniversaries of divorces, child-custody hearings, family-oriented holidays, and job terminations all attract individuals of violent intent. Sungnam Lisowski waited until Christmas day to kill her husband and shoot their daughters. Steve Lancaster killed his wife a week after she obtained a temporary restraining order barring him from their home. Charles Kopp shot Dr. Slepian in late October, around the time of Canada's November 11 "Remembrance Day."

Especially in cases where the assailant does not intend to escape after the assault, potential perpetrators may also engage in final-act behaviors. They put their affairs in order, arrange their funerals, set out their justifications. Hill took his wife and children to the beach for one last family outing. "All my paternal instincts were stirred as I played with my children. . . . I took them one by one, each in turn, into water over their heads as they clung to my neck." Hill recounted, "As I carried and supported each child in the water, it was as though I was offering them to God as Abraham offered his son." His family did not suspect the plan brewing in his head, but Hill well knew this was their last time together. "I enjoyed watching them through eyes unknown to them – like a man savoring his last supper," he remembered. Edward Lansdale gave his ex-wife his car and put his daughter's name on the title to his house. He made a lengthy tape recording addressed to his sister in which he explained and justified why he intended to attack the woman who accused him of abusing her as a child. He hoped his sister could sell his story to 60 Minutes.[12]

Final act behaviors can also be destructive. School shooters Luke Woodham of Mississippi and Kip Kinkel of Oregon each killed their parents before heading to school. Through a videotape of himself, McKnight asked his father-in-law to poison some trees they had planted together. Before setting off to attack the Topeka federal courthouse, he killed his dogs. In September 1999, Larry Ashbrook of Forest Hill, Texas, began destroying his house. He overturned the furniture, punched holes in the walls, poured concrete down the toilets, and tore up his family photos. On September 15, he drove himself a few blocks to the Wedgewood Baptist Church. Inside, 150 teenagers were attending a weekly prayer service. Ashbrook entered shooting. He killed six, wounded seven, then killed himself.[13]

Case Study:

The Last Will and Testament

On Tuesday, July 27, 1999, Mark Barton bludgeoned his wife to death. The next day he killed his son and daughter. Having bankrupted the family through his day-trading, he clearly did not want to leave them behind.

On Thursday morning, July 29, Barton drove into Atlanta. He did not, however, go directly to the two brokerages. First, he went to his attorney's office. There he made out his last will and testament. His lawyer later remarked that the only thing out of the ordinary about Barton's will was the stipulation that his wife and children be buried together. Most testators do not plan the funerals of their family, but Barton knew what he was doing. It was his final act before he headed to the brokers.

Because the assassin knows that the path to violence has an end point, he or she can prepare for reaching that end.

SOURCE: Authors' personal knowledge.

In addition to final-act behaviors, attackers also frequently self-consciously dress for the occasion. These costumes can be utilitarian, a disguise, or a symbolic statement. Evan Ramsay, who went on a shooting spree at his Bethel, Alaska, high school, purposefully wore loose clothing to hide the shotgun as he rode the bus to school. McKnight dressed in his Sunday best, though later the police remarked on how ugly his tie was. The Secret Service study found that many presidential assassins chose their wardrobes so they blended with the surroundings and did not appear suspicious. Going on the attack seems to require a fine sense of fashion.[14]

The point, of course, is for the threat manager to keep constantly in mind that intended violence requires logistical preparations. Knowing that preparations need be made, the practitioner can focus his or her investigation on identifying those activities. There is no standard rule for what the preparations may be. They can range from baking cakes to making bombs. The only rule is that the assailant has to prepare for the assault.

Step 5: Breach

The penultimate step to achieving intended violence is for the attacker to breach the target's security, however elaborate or minimal that might be. In other words, the assailant has to position himself or herself in some proximity to the target. For Moody, the Unabomber, and other mail bombers, that proximity was as close as the nearest mailbox. For Hinckley, it meant taking a taxi to the Washington Hilton. McKnight drove himself thirty miles to Topeka, parked in the parking lot, and set his car on fire before entering the courthouse. Evan Ramsay rode the bus to school, his shotgun stuffed down his oversized pants. In sum, the potential perpetrator has to get to the place from which the attack will be initiated.

Figure 6 illustrates the place of breach along the path to intended violence.

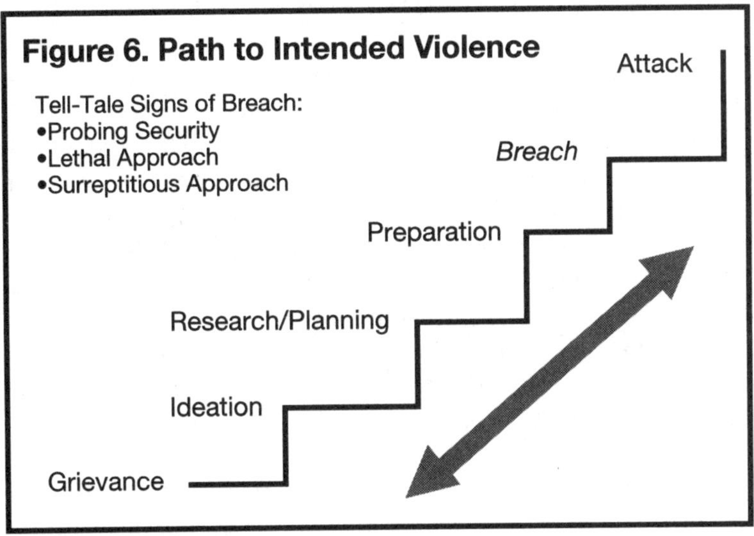

Getting there may also be heavily influenced by the personal quirks of the attacker. In the taxi on the way to the Hilton, Hinckley realized he needed to go to the bathroom, so he detoured to the restrooms at a nearby Holiday Inn. Outside it was raining. Not wishing to get too soaked while waiting, Hinkley gave the president "five or ten minutes" to come out of the hotel, after which Hinckley would go back to his room. Tragically, Reagan beat the deadline.[15]

Getting there is a logistical exercise, both noticeable and potentially preventable. The Unabomber, for example, went to great lengths to make sure the postmark on his mail bombs would not lead back to him. Rather than mail them from his Montana cabin, he sometimes traveled as far away as California before posting them. Although mailing a bomb sounds easy, it actually requires considerable effort in order to avoid detection. Eventually, such efforts are detectable.

Case Study:

Getting Close

Sometime in the mid-1990s, Larry W. realized that the president and his state governor were radiating him in order to force him to commit a crime. He went to the governor's office to complain. The receptionist listened to him patiently, then explained she could not help. Larry left and went to the nearby federal building to bring the issue to the CIA. The metal detectors alarmed as he passed through. Guards discovered a .45 semi-automatic pistol with three extra magazines, as well as a Gerber fighting knife. Larry admitted that he had the weapons on him during his visit to the governor's office.

Five years later, Larry began leaving letters addressed to the governor at stores in a small town 45 minutes from the capital. The letters accused the governor of attacking Larry with rays that burned his body. The threat manager assigned to the governor's protective detail learned of the letters and unsuccessfully tried to find Larry. He also alerted the uniformed patrols to be on the lookout.

Four days later, a uniformed patrol intercepted Larry as he approached the capitol building. Larry wore camouflage clothing and carried a large caliber revolver. As he made his way toward the capitol, he passed out flyers describing his troubles to anyone who would take them. The uniformed patrol took him into custody. The threat manager arranged to have Larry committed to the state mental hospital for observation and treatment.

Getting close can be as simple as strolling across the capitol grounds handing out flyers – and carrying a gun.

SOURCE: Authors' personal knowledge.

Step 6: Attack

As obvious as it seems, potential perpetrators only become attackers by actually attacking. In some cases, that proved not so easy. Liam Youens, the Internet killer, repeatedly approached his target, Amy Boyer, but he kept finding excuses not to shoot her. She was surrounded by family or he could not find just the right spot from which to shoot. Only after chiding himself for cowardice was Youens able to reach the final stop along the path. The Secret Service study found a number of attempted assassins who did not become actual assassins because it proved just too hard to do. Security appeared too tight or something else got in the way. In the case of FD, she intended to shoot President George Bush as his motorcade drove past her. Just as the car came into view, the man standing next to her asked for the time. As she dug out her pocket watch, Bush sped by.[16]

Case Study:

The Cowardly Anti-Semite

Buford Furrow hated Jews, minorities, federal employees and just about anyone else in anyway different from him and his ideal of an Aryan. He had affiliations with various hate-groups and white supremacists and once posed for a photograph dressed in a Nazi uniform.

Furrow also had something to prove. He wanted to make a statement to show the world his hatred and to prove to his fellow white supremacists that he was a true believer. He decided that violence would give him that proof. He could kill some Jews. The easiest way to do that was to shoot up some facility associated with Jews, like a synagogue or museum. He began researching to find just the right target.

But Furrow was also a coward. The first two places he scouted scared him away because they employed open security measures. The museum he checked out had guards and a magnetometer. It worried him that he might have to go up against somebody else armed with a gun. He kept looking.

Furrow found his target quite by accident. While gassing up his van, he noticed a sign for the North Valley Jewish Community Center. Checking it out, he discovered that it doubled as a summer day care center for kids. Kids seemed to be the perfect target for him.

Tuesday morning, August 9, 1999, just as a group of children set out on a field trip, Furrow entered the lobby of the community center and sprayed more than seventy bullets at anything that moved. Five people – three of them children – were wounded. None were killed. Perhaps Furrow was too nervous to fire straight.

Furrow fled. As he made his get-away, he chanced upon Joseph Ileto, a postman of Filipino descent. Furrow shot him nine times, explaining in his confession that Ileto was not white and was a federal employee.

Taking the last step along the path to violence requires considerable commitment and nerve.

SOURCE: www.wired.com/news/story/21210.html, August 10, 30, 1999

Using the Path to Intended Violence

We know of no other assessment tool as useful as conceptualizing the path to intended violence. Understanding the process of intended violence helps the threat manager identify, assess, investigate, and manage individuals of violent intent.

Threat managers who use the path to intended violence will find themselves better able to identify problem individuals, assess their level of risk moment to moment, settle on the appropriate protective responses, explore new areas for the protective investigation, and devise the best threat management strategies. The path to intended violence supports every element of contemporary threat management. By visualizing the subject's place along the path, the threat manager gains great insight into the potential risk. That insight then informs choosing the best protective response and threat management strategy.

Summary

In this chapter we reviewed the procedural steps composing the path to intended violence. In order to commit an act of premeditated violence, those of violent intent must have some grievance prompting them to consider violence. They must then come up with the idea that violence is the only reasonable alternative open to them, with reasonable defined as what they consider reasonable, not what any common standard of reasonableness would determine. Once determined on a course of violence, the subject next must research and plan how he or she will actually make the attack. The plan necessarily leads to preparing for the assault, usually by obtaining the appropriate weapon, but also by obtaining essential information, engaging in final act behaviors, and taking whatever other measures called for in the plan. Those preparations then allow the actual breach of the target's security perimeter, however elaborate or primitive that might be. Finally, the path to intended violence culminates in the actual use of violence.

These steps are integral to any act of intended violence. Knowing about them and being able to recognize their various clues provides the threat manager the best assessment tool, the best way of thinking about potential acts of violence. Although we discuss other assessment tools in a subsequent chapter, none works as effectively as understanding the path to intended violence.

Reference Notes for Chapter 4

[1] "Teen Guilty in Mississippi School-Shooting Rampage," CNN.com, June 12, 1998, http://cnn.com/US/9806/12/school .shooting.verdict/index.html.

[2] Paul Hill, "Why I Shot an Abortionist," June 1999, at http://www.armyofgod.com/WRBltr.html.

[3] Fein and Vossekuil, "Assassination in the United States," 327.

[4] *Atlanta Journal-Constitution*, July 30, 1999; Lycos News, http://www.lycos.com/news/flash/alabamashooting.html; Washington Post, April 19 and 20, 2000.

[5] James W. Clarke, *On Being Mad or Merely Angry: John W. Hinckley, Jr., and Other Dangerous People* (Princeton, NJ: Princeton University Press, 1990), 3-5.

[6] United States Marshals Service, National Sheriffs Association training seminar, Newark, NJ, January 20, 2000.

[7] Calhoun, *Hunters and Howlers*, 2-3.

[8] Buffalo *News*, November 20, 2002.

[9] Chicago *Tribune*, February 19, 1997; Erickson, et al., The Report of Governor Bill Owens' Columbine Review Commission, 25; Hill, "Why I Shot an Abortionist."

[10] New York *Times*, January 21, 1985.
[11] ATF Interview with Rachelle Shannon.
[12] Hill, "Why I Shot an Abortionist," 4-5. Detective Rick Berwick, Yreka, California, Police Department Crime Report (01020010) 00-1680, October 20, 2000.
[13] "Gunman Kills Seven, Then Himself, in Texas Church Shooting," Steve Pegram Ministries News, September 16, 1999, http://stevepegramministries.com/News-ChurchShooting_9-16-99.htm.
[14] Mohandie, *School Violence Threat Management* 87; Secret Service presentation, National Sheriffs Association training seminar, Newark, NJ, January 20, 2000.
[15] Clarke, *On Being Mad*, 6.
[16] Secret Service presentation, National Sheriffs Association training seminar, Newark, NJ, January 20, 2000.

PART II. THE CONTEMPORARY THREAT MANAGEMENT PROCESS

CHAPTER FIVE

Identifying Individuals of Violent Intent

Identifying individuals of violent intent first requires the threat manager to establish a good, dependable reporting process. Individuals who plan violence do not normally alert the police of their intentions, but they do behave in ways that frequently bring them to the attention of those they want to harm or their associates. It behooves the threat manager, then, to train the staffs of protected officials and the officials themselves in what to report. Private citizens who seek protective assistance should also be well schooled. Businesses and schools should also be offered training sessions on dealing with violence against those institutions. The groundwork for identifying individuals of violent intent lies in training and community outreach. This ensures that the threat manager will hear of untoward incidents as soon as possible.

Getting reports is but the first step in identifying individuals of violent intent. The threat manager must next evaluate or assess the initial reports, and do so quickly. The initial assessment will drive subsequent decisions regarding levels of protection, courses of investigation, and management strategies. It will also allow the threat manager to prioritize this particular case compared to other active cases or to other professional responsibilities. A good threat management program does not require a full-scale protective investigation for every case anymore than it requires 24-hour protection every time a target receives an inappropriate telephone call. Quite the contrary, good threat management depends on intelligent, consistent assessments upon which decisions about investigating and protecting can be made and priorities established.

Threat management cases rarely open sedately. The initial report carries with it an implicit urgency prompted both by the actual circumstances and the target's degree of panic. At the same time, initial reports just as rarely contain enough facts to allow the threat manager to confidently assess the actual risk level. Frequently, the initial information is flat wrong or grossly exaggerated. The target, possibly through fear or desire for attention, often embellishes what he or she saw, heard, or suspected. The mayor's secretary reports receiving a letter filled with obscenities, but is too shy to read the letter over the telephone. A female battering victim informs her local police station that she saw her estranged husband outside her house at 2:00 a.m. peering into the den window. The supervisor of the governor's protective detail passes on the make, model, and license plate number of a car that appeared to follow the governor's motorcade from last night's fundraiser. These kinds of reports cannot be ignored or set aside to await more details. The threat manager must respond to them – and quickly. The challenge, then, is settling on that first response knowing that each case is different, that initial reports are flawed, and that each case requires its own unique management strategy.

Ironically, the most dangerous situations are the most recognizable. Everyone easily recognizes a high-risk situation. Danger is apparent at the moment of dangerousness. Someone shoots at the county supervisor. A man becomes violently belligerent in the district attorney's reception area. The uniformed patrol finds a box outside the state capitol building with wires protruding from it. Threat managers recognize these incidents as clearly in the breach phase of the violence process. At this stage along the path to intended violence, both the danger and the protective response are crystal clear. Get the target out of the danger area, find and confine the subject, and defuse any suspicious or dangerous objects.

Case Study:

Vehicular Homicide

Clara Harris suspected her husband was having an affair. On July 24, 2002, she hired private investigators to confirm her fears. That afternoon, Harris decided not to wait on the results of the investigation. Instead, she drove to a

Galveston, Texas, hotel and found her husband in the arms of one of his employees. Outside, a Blue Moon detective stood ready to videotape her husband and his mistress when they left their rented room.

Harris first fought with the girlfriend, ripping her shirt off in the scuffle. She then ran to her silver Mercedes Benz. Speeding through the parking lot, Harris jumped the median and slammed the car into her husband. She then circled the drive and ran over his body two more times. Beside her, her 16-year-old stepdaughter frantically tried to stop the car.

Violence as it occurs is easy to assess.

SOURCE: Associated Press, August 2, 2002.

Because at its most dangerous, danger is blatant, the threat manager's first questions should be: "Where is the danger coming from?" and "How imminent is it?" In other words, the threat manager first assesses the *immediacy* of the risk. The quickest way to do that is to focus on how the Inappropriate Communication or Contact (IC&C) was delivered or noticed by the person reporting it. A telephone threat requires one level of protective response; a suspicious package requires an entirely different, more urgent, response. Similarly, the threat manager reacts to a nasty letter sent to a council member completely differently than to a report that a disgruntled homeowner is at the zoning board office demanding entry into the chairman's office. The difference in responses derives from the urgency created by the presence of the package and the angry homeowner at places where each can cause damage or injury. Telephones and angry letters do not kill; bombs and people can. Their danger is clear and present.

Case Study:

Assessing on the Fly

On March 8, 1988, Deputy City Prosecutor Jessica Silvers of Van Nuys, California, obtained a conviction against Jeremy Sigmond on four misdemeanor counts of reckless driving and weapons violations.

The next day, Sigmond returned to court, this time armed with a gun. He aimed it at Slivers. Since he did not shoot right away, he probably intended to kidnap her. Regardless, the court bailiff made an immediate assessment that the situation was obviously high risk and required the appropriate protective response. He pulled his pistol and fired. In the ensuing exchange of gunfire, the bailiff was wounded, shot in the stomach, but he killed Sigmond. The prosecutor was unhurt.

In emergency situations, the assessment of danger must be immediate and the response appropriate to the level of danger.

SOURCE: Washington Post: March 10, 1988

The overwhelming majority of threat management cases do not present such clear and present dangers. Since the level of risk is not immediately clear, assessing these cases is difficult. With no lethal indicator, such as Harris driving her Mercedes toward her husband or Sigmond aiming his pistol, the protective response must be squarely based on an accurate assessment of the current situation. The initial assessment essentially asks, "How close is the danger to the target right this minute?" Ticking boxes or angry individuals stomping toward the target are immediate high risks. Telephone calls and nasty letters do not approach that level – at least not at that moment.

But the lack of immediate danger does not mean the call or letter can be safely ignored. It simply means the response to those kinds of situations requires a more deliberative, thoughtful, and systematic approach. That kind of approach must permeate the entire contemporary threat management process. Most cases initially seem ambiguous, with the subject's actions and intentions obscured. This uncertainty requires the threat manager to start the case by thinking through the known and the unknown. That is, the case must begin by assessing the known facts and identifying the unknown facts. Assessments require systematically thinking through facts and circumstances to form a realistic appraisal of the subject's intentions at this time, always recognizing that assessments – like intentions – have short shelf lives.

Acting without assessing compounds the problem. It also means rushing into a response without considering all the known facts, recognizing what is not known, and weighing alternatives and options. In addition to distorting the assessment, any actions taken by the threat manager inevitably influences the target, who may gauge his or her response to how the threat manager reacts. Overreacting can unnecessarily panic the target; under-reacting may tell the target that he or she has nothing to worry about. At the same time, a person poised at any point on the path to intended violence can be driven forward by the wrong response. Threat management thus requires considerable finesse, both with the subject and the target. By assessing the situation, the threat manager takes the time to think through the problem in order to design the best protective response, identify areas of further inquiry, and begin developing appropriate management strategies.

Case Study:

Underestimating the Danger

Ms. B. announced her intention to give up her seat in the state legislature in order to run for governor. About half-way through the campaign, her staff opened a letter postmarked from a city 500 miles away. In the letter, Dan proclaimed that he and Ms. B loved each other and, living together, they would govern the state. He also announced his intention to join Ms. B.

The staff found the letter greatly amusing, but because of the postmark they sensed no great urgency. Instead, they routed the letter to the threat manager through the state's inter-office mail.

The next morning, Dan called Ms. B's campaign headquarters. He told the receptionist that he had arrived at the airport and needed someone to pick him up and take him to Ms. B's house. With this contact, the staff members changed their assessment of the situation and immediately contacted the threat manager. He picked Dan up at the airport.

During the subject interview, Dan calmly described how on several occasions, he had contacted Ms. B telepathically. She had agreed that they should live together and govern the state. Dan sold his possessions, packed his few belongings, wrote the letter to Ms. B, and bought a one-way ticket to the state capital. Dan's personal diary confirmed these details, including the telepathic conversations.

Based on the diary and his attempted approach, state psychiatrists admitted Dan to a mental health facility. Ms. B's staff members vowed never to rely on inter-office mail to contact the threat manager.

Good and timely communications are essential ingredients to sound threat management.

SOURCE: Authors' personal knowledge.

The threat management process can best be conceptualized by the flow chart illustrated in Figure 1.

Figure 1. The Contemporary Threat Management Process

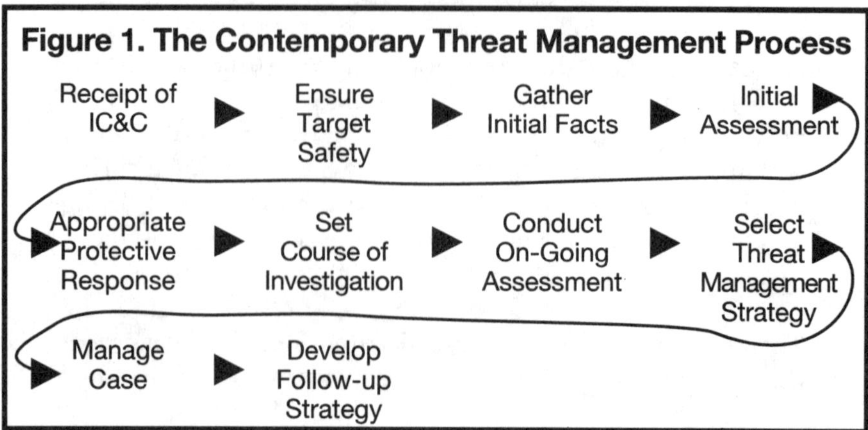

As the flow chart illustrates, contemporary threat management proceeds methodically. If individuals of violent intent have a path they follow, so, in turn, do threat managers. The process requires continually thinking through the problem, weighing all the known and unknown aspects of the case, and carefully and prudently selecting strategies best designed to decrease any potential risk.. The threat manager must establish lines of communication to ensure that any IC&C will be promptly reported. Once the threat manager identifies an individual of concern, the threat manager should ensure the target's immediate security, begin to collect all relevant facts, and then use those facts to think through the problem and devise the best management strategies. Proceeding hastily or, worse, unthinkingly, is to gamble against the odds. The threat manager must move deliberately, with each step carefully thought out and the reasons for taking it justifiable and documented. To do less risks more.

Getting the Facts

Facts alone fuel assessments. An attack already launched is easy to assess, but the potential for an assault gets murkier and murkier the less one knows about the case. Identifying individuals of violent intent requires the threat manager to focus on four separate areas. The first is setting up a reporting process whereby potential targets or victims, their staffs, and family report IC&Cs to the threat manager. The remaining three areas cover the threat manager's initial response to any such reports.

Area 1: Establishing a Reporting Process

Some of the potential targets of intended violence occupy positions that offer them some degree of security. Public officials, corporate managers, and celebrities usually have a buffer zone giving them some protection. People working in that buffer zone can be used as a unique early warning system to alert the threat manager to any IC&Cs directed at the potential target. These individuals include receptionists, mail handlers, security guards, telephone operators, and anyone else with access to the target. Setting up that warning system requires training the individuals who comprise it. The training must include such topics as recognizing IC&Cs, what to report, and where to send the report.

Other potential targets do not enjoy a buffer zone protecting them from individuals of violent intent. Indeed, they may be living with the very person who poses the most risk to them. They may be working with that person or going to school with him or her. Consequently, the threat manager has to find ways to educate these potential targets. Public outreach efforts, school presentations, and workplace workshops help spread the word. Of course, when someone expresses a concern about their living partner or a colleague at work or school, the threat manager can tutor that person on recognizing IC&Cs, what to report, and where to make the report. The training can also include security briefings on measures to take to improve individual security.

The key for the threat manager is to open a communication avenue that facilitates getting information from the potential targets to the threat manager. The training should stress accurate, factual reporting of anything of concern. Since the path to intended violence is easy to understand and easy to illustrate, it makes a wonderful training tool. Potential targets, their staffs, and families can easily conceptualize the process and its stages. Knowing the kinds of things to look for helps keep them alert. Getting the facts straight can be greatly facilitated by advance training for those individuals most likely to receive an IC&C. The threat manager should use it to train anyone who might receive or notice any IC&C. And not just once. Refresher classes and reminders need to be conducted routinely. New employees should be briefed as soon as possible.

Case Study:

The Importance of Training

The chairman of the board of an international corporation contacted law enforcement to express his concerns about the public's reaction to some controversial measures the corporation had taken. The publicity focused on the chairman as the personification of the corporation. The threat manager privately briefed the chairman on recognizing IC&Cs and taking personal security measures.

In addition, the threat manager conducted a training class for the chairman's staff. He included the receptionists, mail handlers, corporate ombudsman, and personal assistants.

When the threat manager began describing the various elements of an IC&C, he noticed the staff members whispering to each other and exchanging knowing glances. The threat manager immediately recognized the reaction and paused his presentation to ask the staffers if they recognized any IC&Cs they had received.

Several of the staff described several particular cases they remembered when someone wrote the chairman's office with an angry complaint. They explained that whenever they received strange communications, they put them in the bottom file drawer because they did not know what else to do with them.

After the training, the threat manager took possession of the communications and reviewed their contents. The file contained a number of veiled threats as well as communications from individuals who had come to the threat manager's attention before. The communications allowed the threat manager to alert corporate security about several individuals to watch out for.

Training is essential to sound threat management.

SOURCE: Authors' personal knowledge.

Properly trained, these individuals will know how to write down exact quotes, note observable clues, and describe other relevant information. Properly trained, they will preserve evidence, use caller I.D., and employ other tactics to help the threat manager's protective investigation. Properly trained, they will not panic unnecessarily nor let their emotions carry them away.

Area 2: Locating the Target

Second, once an IC&C has been reported, the threat manager must ensure the immediate security of the potential target. By this, we do not mean setting up a protective detail or taking any elaborate steps. Rather, it simply means asking for the target's current location. If the target cannot be located, the threat manager may have to take the time to find him or her. In most cases, however, the target's location will be known. Indeed, the target will probably be the person reporting the IC&C.

This step should not be confused with the more deliberative assessment the threat manager makes after getting as many facts about the case as possible. That deliberative assessment will determine the protective response. The step of initially locating the target involves making an on-the-run determination of the immediacy of any risk and the current exposure of the target. The deliberative assessment and choice of protective response comes later, maybe later that hour or later that day.

This step, obvious though it sounds, is frequently overlooked. Moving quickly to locate the potential target also merges with taking the next step of getting the facts because the threat manager can learn if the target knows anything about the IC&C or the circumstances surrounding its delivery. The threat manager can determine if the potential target has recently noticed anything suspicious, out of the ordinary, or troubling. In certain venues, the potential target may know the subject, may in fact know him or her intimately or very well. The target's assessment in those situations can prove very beneficial.

Information from the potential target can then be factored into the initial assessment. It also provides the manager a chance to brief the potential target on what is known up to now, what security measures to observe, and how to report future IC&Cs.

Case Illustration:

Changes in the Weather

The personal assistant to a popular local television weatherman contacted law enforcement about a woman named Linda who had sent amorous e-mails to the weatherman's home and office computer. The weatherman wanted the e-mails stopped. The assistant provided the threat manager with copies of three of the e-mails from Linda, but had no additional information. In the e-mails, Linda stated her intention of visiting the weatherman at home. She asked for his address, then complained at his failure to give it to her. The assistant assured the threat manager that the weatherman was safely in the studio, but the weatherman refused to meet with the threat manager.

The weatherman's refusal to meet the threat manager aroused her suspicions. She insisted on an interview. Reluctantly, and with considerable embarrassment, the weatherman admitted that he knew Linda. She had been his babysitter when she was 14 and he was 10. Without explaining why, the weatherman confessed that he had looked her up through an Internet service and had initiated the e-mail exchanges with her. When her e-mails became too familiar and affectionate, he backed off. He became more disturbed when she began calling his cell phone, even though he gave her the number.

The weatherman claimed that he had deleted all the previous e-mails exchanged between him and Linda except for the three previously provided and the latest he had received. He gave the threat manager the last e-mail. It contained moderate pleas for him to contact Linda. She also complained that his continued silence hurt her feelings.

Although the weatherman insisted on an aggressive law enforcement response to scare Linda away, the threat manager adopted a "Watch & Wait" strategy to see if Linda would stop contacting the weatherman on her own. Three days later, Linda sent another e-mail telling the weatherman how much he had hurt her and that she wanted nothing further to do with him. Linda kept her promise.

Prominent public figures have private lives that can lead to IC&Cs.

SOURCE: Hypothetical example based on authors' professional experiences.

Area 3: Getting the Facts

Next, the threat manager should gather as many facts as fast as possible, always taking extreme care to filter out the facts from speculations and panic-driven exaggerations. This process falls short of a full protective investigation. At this point, the threat manager should focus on analyzing the IC&C and interviewing the individual reporting it – and the potential target, if different – as thoroughly as possible. The initial facts can only come from the IC&C itself and from the individual reporting the concern. On many occasions, the report comes from someone other than the target. Indeed, there is no consistency at all in who reports the incident, which means there is no consistency in the quality of initial reports.

The reporter's own fears and embarrassment compound the inconsistencies. Individuals who receive IC&Cs, especially if they are the potential target, tend to exaggerate or distort, to misquote and misperceive, the IC&C. Informants in particular frequently fabricate in the hope for some personal benefit to themselves from squealing. These distortions, whether intentional or not, further complicate the threat manager's need to get to the facts. Training potential targets and their associates helps to stick to the facts. The training should teach them how to respond to an IC&C and should alert them as to what clues they should be looking for. Even with training, distortions will remain. The threat manager needs to filter out all the distortions before making the assessment.

Case Study:

The Imaginative Informant

A prisoner in the county jailed charged with drug offenses informed a deputy sheriff that he knew about two men who were stealing explosives to use in an attack on the governor. The deputy contacted the threat manager. During the threat manager's initial interview with the prisoner, the prisoner provided specific details about the two men, the types of explosives and where they stole them, and when and where they planned to use them against the governor. In exchange for this information, the informant asked for an early release. Once out of jail, he wanted to be a paid informant working the case.

The threat manager, following standard – and highly recommended – procedure, arranged for a polygraph test on the informant. The prisoner failed on all the particulars of the explosives' theft and the assassination plot.

Back in his cell, the prisoner confessed that he lied to get back at two colleagues who had burned him in a drug deal. He also wanted to get out of jail early. The threat manager asked why he made up the story of the assassination plot. The prisoner explained that he knew he would get everyone's attention and be taken seriously if he claimed to have information effecting the safety of somebody as important as the governor.

It should come as no surprise to experience police officers that informants do not always tell the truth.

SOURCE: Authors' personal knowledge.

The threat manager should carefully scrutinize the IC&C, paying particular attention to how it was delivered. The following questions will help focus the initial analysis:

- If it is a communication, what does it say and how is it phrased?
- Is there anything about the IC&C and how it was delivered that indicates that the subject researched the private or personal affairs of the target?
- Does the subject refer to anything that might relate him or her to the potential target?
- Does the subject mention other individuals? If so, the threat manager should contact them.

Once the threat manager is confident that he or she has a clear view of the facts of the case based on information from the potential target, any staff members who actually saw or heard the subject's IC&C, and the IC&C itself, the threat manager should take a moment to ask broader questions. These should cover such issues as any other events or activities going on that might have gone unreported before. Has the potential target received strange calls or visitors recently, has his or her property been vandalized, has he or she been in situations that made them feel uncomfortable or suspicious? Have their families or neighbors reported anything out of the ordinary? Often, staff members will not mention these unless specifically asked by the threat manager. They forget about them or do not see their relevance to the events at hand.

Case Illustration:

Putting Two and Two Together

The director of a city agency calls 911 to report a disgruntled individual had just threatened to go to the agency building and bomb it. The police respond and the bomb squad activates. The threat manager also responds because of the threat.

The threat manager interviews the director, who insists that the disgruntled citizen is on his way to the agency office. He explains that two of his staff members had each fielded an angry phone call from the same individual. The office manager concurs with the director. The manager acts very frightened and pleads with the threat manager for protection.

The threat manager quickly determines that neither the director nor the office manager actually took the phone calls. He tracks down the two staffers who spoke to the angry caller. In separate interviews with each, the threat manager determines that a man had called to complain angrily that he had not received a payment due him from the city agency. In the last call, the man asked for the agency's address and said he would come to the office to straighten the problem out in person. Neither staff member knew anything about a bomb threat, just that the caller was clearly agitated and upset over the missing payment.

During the re-interview with the director and office manager, both looked sheepishly at the other. The office manager said, "Don't you people know? We had a bomb threat last week and had to evacuate the building. The director and I were afraid this morning's caller was the same person as last week." In effect, the director and office manager put two separate, unrelated incidents together to make an emergency situation.

Frequently, getting the facts solves the problem.

SOURCE: Hypothetical example based on authors' professional experience.

The threat manager should also remember to ask questions about the past. Staff members may have called only because now they are concerned. They could have ignored other approaches or not seen their significance. In addition, questioning all the staff members in an affected area may also disclose previously unreported contacts.

Case Study:

The Relentless Suitor

A staff member of a female city council member contacted the threat manager to express great concern over a male subject. The subject had visited the councilwoman's office the day before and dropped off a written marriage proposal for her. At first, the staff was amused at the letter, thinking nothing more about it than that it was some harmless nut who had fallen for their boss. For that reason, they did not report the incident to the threat manager.

The next day, the man returned and demanded an answer to his proposal. At that point, the staff members became nervous about the visitor. One of them called the threat manager to report the two incidents.

The threat manager carefully read the written communication and thoroughly interviewed the staff member who dealt with the subject on the second visit. After satisfying herself that she had gotten an accurate picture of what transpired during the two visits, the threat manager began questioning other members of the councilwoman's staff. From these interviews, she learned that within the last ten days the subject had made at least 18 contacts, including letters, telephone calls, and visits to the office. Such relentless pursuit convinced the threat manager to increase her initial assessment from moderate to high risk.

The initial gathering of facts must be thorough, reaching beyond what happened in the instant report to delve for information on recent events.

SOURCE: Authors' personal knowledge.

Area 4: Analyzing the Facts

Finally, the manager needs to analyze the known facts to determine the appropriate level of protection, set a course for investigation, and begin identifying relevant management strategies. In the next chapter, we describe a number of assessment methods the threat manager can use to focus his or her thinking. For now, we want to emphasize that the assessment should be systematic, standardized, and well documented. Each case and each report should be consistently treated the same. A systematic approach ensures that the threat manager does not overlook any relevant facts in the rush of urgency. Standardization provides the threat manager with a larger context to gauge how this case compares to previous cases. Documentation provides a written record of each case for future reference and to establish a database of inappropriate communicators. Since these individuals frequently become repeat offenders, both toward the current potential target and to new ones, such a database can add more context to a new IC&C committed by a previous communicator. Documentation also allows the threat manager to track trends and share information with other law enforcement entities. Combined, a systematic, standard, documented approach allows for the most accurate assessments.

Case Study:

The Repeater

A couple of years after Timothy McVeigh blew up the Murrah Federal Building in Oklahoma City, Oklahoma, a person signing the name Johnny King began mailing postcards to federal courthouses and federal judges across the country. Each postcard conveyed identical messages: the receiving courthouse or judge should be destroyed as utterly as the Murrah building.

Deputy U.S. Marshal Protective Investigators dutifully reported receipt of the postcards to the headquarters Analytical Support Unit (ASU), which entered each one into its threat database. Although the field deputies thought they were receiving unique postcards, the analysts at headquarters soon recognized that Johnny King was a habitual threatener who could not possibly attack as many courthouses and judges as the dozens of postcards threatened. Recognizing that pattern helped the field investigators focus their resources on more pressing cases.

Maintaining a database of inappropriate communicators facilitates identifying repeaters.

SOURCE: Authors' personal knowledge.

Maintaining a database also allows the threat manager the ability to identify anonymous inappropriate communicators by comparing the style and substance of previously received IC&Cs or making connections between communicators using different names or aliases. Sharing databases with other law enforcement agencies greatly expands the threat manager's ability to investigate these type of anonymous IC&Cs. Although the threat manager cannot share law enforcement information with private security companies, no such restriction applies to the company sharing its information with the threat manager. Many private security firms willingly help by opening their files to threat managers. In sum, keeping files in a retrievable format like a data base and sharing that information with other law enforcement agencies should become an integral part of the threat management process.

Case Illustration:

The Hate Monger

The rabbi of the city's largest synagogue received a detailed threat letter. The letter contained precise descriptions of how the author intended to torture and kill the rabbi. It also contained lengthy anti-Semitic accusations and complaints. The threat manager also noticed that the writer consistently misspelled a popular vulgarity.

During the threat manager's initial interview with the rabbi, no additional information beyond the contents of the letter could be ascertained. The threat manager checked the database of IC&Cs she had been maintaining for the past five years. She searched for similar misspellings and anti-Semitic expressions. Since her database resided within a computer program, she was able to use the program's search capabilities to find exact phrase matches. Her database also had a field for unique attributes such as unusual misspellings. After running the misspelling, the threat manager identified four matches, the earliest one dated three years earlier, the latest dated three months prior. Each of the letters contained very similar anti-Semitic expressions. One of the previous letters had a name and return address.

The threat manager retrieved all four letters from the evidence room and turned them and the latest letter over to the police lab. The lab linked the letters to the same writer. Based on the database matches and the physical evidence, the threat manager obtained an arrest warrant on the writer. The evidence also sustained a successful prosecution.

Previous IC&Cs can help solve current IC&Cs.

SOURCE: Hypothetical case based on authors' professional experiences.

Assessing Just the Facts

Before detailing the initial assessment process in the next chapter, the threat manager needs to internalize three rules of thumb.

Rule 1. Avoid the *What If?* Game

First, especial attention should be paid to ensuring that the assessment is solidly based on the known facts and only the known facts. Assessments are seriously distorted by assumptions, speculations, and guesses. Intelligent guessing, sometimes even speculating and assuming, are occasionally useful tactics in guiding a protective investigation. They have a profoundly negative impact on threat assessments. Thinking through the case requires sticking to the known facts. Once the manager starts assessing assumptions, the assessment becomes a house of cards in a strong wind.

Practitioners who start factoring assumptions into their assessments are playing the "*What If?*" game. The game involves guessing about *what might be* rather than assessing *what is.* This game exercises the imagination, often to the point of letting it run riot. But the game is in no way an intelligent assessment of what is truly known. Potential targets love to play the *What If?* game. They can play it endlessly. Assessors should avoid it at all costs. Asking *What If?* questions are not assessments. They are unfounded speculations that contain an underlying assumption that the *if* condition is true. These questions – *What if* the subject has a weapon? *What if* the subject has a criminal record? *What if* the subject is waiting right now in ambush? – throw no light on the case. On the contrary, they very much cloud the view. Knowing that a subject delivered an inappropriate communication over the telephone tells us one thing, but it does great harm to assume that the caller might just be on the way to visit the victim. Facts and facts alone are the only counter to the *What If?* game.

By assessing only the known, the threat manager defers finding out about the unknown until the investigation. The assessment simply locates the subject's current position along the path to intended violence. Without further inquiry – without a protective investigation – the subject's *direction* along the path cannot be determined just by the initial assessment. Evidence that a subject has reached the ideation milestone does not mean he or she is inevitably headed toward the research and planning point, anymore than that milestone means the subject is getting ready to make preparations. Hence, any initial assumptions about which way the subject is headed are mere speculations. Speculating is entirely different from assessing.

Once the protective investigation begins, the *What If?* questions can be translated into investigative inquiries – Does the subject have a gun? Does the subject have a criminal record? Is the subject preparing for an assault? By assessing only the known, the threat manager bases the assessment on solid facts, not flimsy assumptions.

Case Study:

Assuming Too Much

On March 10, 1993, the attorney prosecuting an important foreign terrorist trial in the northeast received a telephone call on his home answering machine. The message was left "by a female with an accent." Although garbled in part, what could be understood was reported as:

> *Hello, you sluts. I know you're there and you will die. You can do as much as you want, you're staked out. I know you're frightened now it won't help. . . Police we'll catch . . . we will catch . . . You are sluts, bye.*

The initial gathering of facts determined that the prosecutor's telephone listing was in his wife's maiden name. The family lived outside the jurisdiction where the prosecutor worked.

The threat assessors began playing the "*What If?*" game. They assessed the risk to the prosecutor as high, basing their assessment on several assumptions. First, they assumed the message was directed at the prosecutor, even though the language suggested that the target might be female. Second, and based on the first assumption, they further assumed that the caller had to go to considerable effort to get the telephone number since the listing was in the wife's name and the family lived outside the prosecutor's district. Third, the assessors assumed that the message had something to do with the trial of the foreign terrorists, even though the caller made no reference to it. Fourth, they assumed that the caller's accent matched the nationality of the defendants.

Based on this assessment, the prosecutor received a protective detail throughout the course of the trial. No other IC&Cs were reported.

After a month's analysis, language experts concluded that the caller did not have a discernible accent. After exhausting all investigative leads, the lead investigator further concluded that the call may have been a "fluke."

Playing the *What If?* game ruins any threat assessment.

SOURCE: Authors' personal knowledge.

Rule 2. Look for Positives And Negatives

The second rule of thumb is that good news is allowed. Indeed, it should be welcomed. Often, those making assessments focus only on information that might escalate the risk. They ignore positive information suggesting a decrease in risk. Knowing that an ex-husband has a new girlfriend may be good news in assessing the potential for violence against the former wife. Similarly, finding out that an individual who had been expressing obsessive affection toward a public figure had recently been prescribed medication for a bipolar condition suggests the individual is aware of his mental problem and is doing something about it. Finding out that an individual who had been fired from one job got another job at a higher salary should also be taken as good news. These examples are positives. They need to be recognized as such.

This does not mean that a single piece of good news sways the assessment any more than a single piece of bad news may. Assessments have to account for all the known facts – good and bad. In contemporary threat management, good news needs to be factored into the assessment every bit as much as bad news. But the assessment itself has to weigh all the facts, bad and good.

Case Study:

Face Values

The supervisor of the mayor's protective detail contacted the threat manager. He explained that several times over the past month, an individual named Thomas W. attempted to contact the mayor at public events. Each time, Thomas told law enforcement officers providing security at the event that he was the mayor's cousin, in town for an extended visit. The officers had been put off by Thomas's aggressive efforts to get inside the protected area near the mayor. They complained that with each refusal, Thomas became more frustrated and angry at the next attempt.

The threat manager obtained Thomas's photograph from his state Department of Motor Vehicles. On a hunch, he asked the supervisor of the protective detail to show the image to the mayor. The mayor confirmed that Thomas was his cousin. Through a communication breakdown, the evening shift of the protective detail had not been informed about Thomas's access privileges.

Threat managers should keep in mind that sometimes individuals are who they say they are.

SOURCE: Authors' personal knowledge.

Rule 3. Assessments Have Short Shelf Lives

The third rule is to remember that assessments are only current at the time they are conducted. They do not project very far into the future, nor do they enjoy a very long shelf life. The assessor considers everything known up to this point, but as the investigation continues and new information is uncovered, new assessments must be made. As a result, assessments should be treated as an on-going facet of contemporary threat management. They should be conducted frequently or whenever new facts crop up. This includes not only new information about the subject, but also any change in the potential target's circumstances.

Case Study:

Changing Circumstances, Changing Assessments

Over the course of a three-year period, Arthur G., a prison inmate, regularly wrote government officials. He complained in profane and colorful language about his treatment at the hands of prison officials. The letters frequently contained allusions to violence and other inappropriate expressions. As a result, the threat manager was given each letter from the various government officials who received them.

Based on Arthur G.'s incarceration, the threat manager assessed each IC&C as low risk. After entering each new letter in the threat data base, the threat manager assigned the case to inactive status.

Next came a letter from the inmate addressed to the Chief Justice of the state Supreme Court. The threat manager noticed that this letter contained more aggressive and profane comments than previous letters. It also contained a promise from the inmate of his intent to visit the Chief Justice soon "for payback."

This change in tone, combined with the unusual promised visit, prompted the threat manager to check on Arthur's current status. He discovered that Arthur had recently been released from prison on parole. The threat manager immediately contacted Arthur's assigned parole officer, who stated that Arthur had never reported in and was now designated "at large." A quick search of police reports further revealed that Arthur was wanted for armed robbery and auto theft.

The threat manager alerted security personnel at the state Supreme Court and issued a bulletin on the case to law enforcement. Two days later, police officers arrested Arthur during an attempted robbery half a mile from the state Supreme Court building.

Threat assessments must change with the changing circumstances of each case.

SOURCE: Authors' personal knowledge.

Summary

In this chapter, we discussed the process by which threat managers identify individuals of violent intent. Most of the identification relies on getting reports from the people most likely to notice someone embarked along the path to intended violence. But reports of IC&Cs do not suffice. Once received, the threat manager should take the time to ensure the target's immediate safety, then begin gathering as many facts about the case and the subject as are then available. That initial investigation will support the protective response and the threat assessment.

In the next chapter, we describe a number of assessment tools the threat manager can use to assess the degree of risk. Here we offer several cautions about the nature of fact gathering in support of those assessments. First, at all costs, threat managers need to avoid playing the *What If?* game. It has no place in the preliminary fact gathering and it can prove quite costly in making assessments. Second, threat managers should look for positive as well as negative clues and information. Law enforcement officers sometimes become too jaded for they are taught all crimes have a criminal behind them. Threat management is not yet about crime because none may have occurred. Consequently, threat managers frequently find that the initial suspicion or report about an individual greatly exaggerated the problem. Finally, because situations change moment to moment, gathering the facts must change with them. That means that any assessment by nature has a very short shelf life that ends once new facts emerge.

CHAPTER SIX

Assessing Individuals of Violent Intent

Threat assessments combine deductive reasoning and intuition. They rely on understanding the facts in any situation, but also interpreting what that particular combination of facts means and how it affects any potential risk. In making assessments, threat managers need to proceed deliberately and intelligently, but they must also listen to their previous experiences and their gut feelings. If a situation feels funny or disconcerting or unnerving or in any way risky, the threat manager needs to act on those intuitive signals, even if he or she cannot fully articulate why the situation causes the discomfort. Threat assessments use a scientific, fact-based approach, but they are no less an art as well.

In this chapter, we provide a number of assessment tools and concepts threat managers can use in combination or singularly. Each tries to discipline the approach to ensure the threat manager assesses the facts methodically and deliberately, considering all the possible facets of the case and asking the right questions. Several experts in the field have developed assessment tools. We include a number of these in describing four assessment approaches. Used together, they allow the threat manager to conduct comprehensive assessments, thus increasing the confidence level in the process. Each assessment tool can be phrased as a simple question. The threat manager will find that though the assessment questions appear simple, the answers can be vastly complicated.

The assessment tools address four broad, but related questions. In each case, the threat manager should always ask:

1. What are the circumstances and context of the Inappropriate Communication or Contact (IC&C)?
2. What are the stakes involved from the subject's point of view?
3. Is the subject acting like a Hunter?
4. Is the subject acting like a Howler?

The questions work best in combination because each focuses on different aspects of the subject's behaviors, motive, and intentions. The first question asks the threat manager simply to describe the IC&C, how it was delivered, to whom it was delivered and directed, what message it says or conveys, and what might have prompted it. The second question addresses how the subject views the situation in terms of what may or may not be at stake for him or her. The threat manager needs to ask this question quite broadly for the stakes from the subject's point of view may be personal, monetary, emotional, ideological, delusional, or even fraudulent. The question addresses how desperate or driven toward violence the subject feels. The third question seeks to determine if the subject has engaged in attack-related behaviors or behaviors common to assassins as we described in Chapter 4-3. The fourth question takes the opposite tack. It asks if the subject's behaviors compare similarly to the way non-attackers – the Howlers – behave.

Threat managers should consistently use each assessment tool on every IC&C in every threat management case. Consistency contributes to enhancing the threat manager's experience and expertise. It establishes comparative outcomes and standardized risk levels. By using these assessments each time, the threat manager will know that high risk means the same thing in each case, the same way low risk means the same thing for every case. Consistency also buttresses the record of the case in the event anyone questions how the threat manager handled the IC&C.

Combined, answering the four questions gives the threat manager a *fairly* complete picture of the situation *at the time the threat manager asked the questions.* We emphasize *fairly* because the completeness of the picture obviously depends on the answers the threat manager finds. We emphasize *at the time* because the accuracy of any assessment depends entirely on how current the information used remains. Situations change and new circumstances arise that alter the situation and compel new assessments. The mere involvement of the threat manager, especially once the subject becomes aware of that involvement, can dramatically change things, further requiring new assessments.

For each question, we provide simple gauges to help the threat manager assess the facts.

I. What Are the Circumstances and Context of the IC&C?

Purpose: To assess the circumstances pertaining to this particular IC&C and the context in which it occurred.

In beginning any assessment, threat managers would be best advised to look first at the circumstances and context of each particular IC&C. We abbreviate this as the Cir-Con factors. Cir-Con focuses the threat manager's attention on the details of the IC&C, but also fits those details within the overall situation, especially any known connection between the subject and target. Even identifying that no link can be established adds to the assessment. Essentially, Cir-Con assists the threat manager in gathering what he or she knows about the IC&C and the general situation into an understandable format, which lends itself to the threat assessment.
Table 6- 1 summarizes the Cir-Con factors.

Table 6- 1. The Cir-Con Factors

What can be inferred from the IC&C's method of delivery?

Assessment: Telephone and written IC&Cs are generally potential low risk; verbal and suspicious activity IC&Cs are potential high risk. Informants must first be assessed for credibility and reliability.
Sources of Evidence: Evidence for method of delivery comes from the person who received or noticed the IC&C. That is, from the individual who answered the phone, opened the mail, spoke to the subject, noticed the suspicious activity, or heard from the informant.

What is the IC&C's message, intent, request, or demand?

Assessment: Is the overall message of this particular IC&C to warn or to cause an emotional response from the target or is the intent to gather information or harm the target?
Sources of Evidence: Evidence for message or intent comes from the content of the communication or the circumstances of the suspicious activity and the observations of the person who received or noticed it.

How much target knowledge can be deduced from the IC&C?

Assessment: The more the subject knows about the target – or attempts to find out -the the higher the potential risk.
Sources of Evidence: Evidence of target knowledge comes from the

content of the communication or the circumstances of the suspicious activity and reports from the target.

Why did the subject choose this target?

Assessment: The greater the involvement or concern of the subject with the target, the higher the potential risk.
Sources of Evidence: Evidence for determining why the subject picked this target comes from the content of the communication or the circumstances of the suspicious activity, from the target, and from the current situation of the target.

Has the subject's life, circumstances, or situation changed significantly?

Assessment: The more changes that have occurred or the greater the significance of the change, the higher the potential risk.
Sources of Evidence: Evidence of significant changes in the subject's life, circumstances, or personal situation comes from the content of the communication, the observations of the target, or the issues involved in the situation prompting the IC&C.

Does this IC&C suggest a significant change in the subject's previous behavior or demeanor toward the target?

Assessment: Comparing the previous relationship between subject and target with the current IC&C allows the threat manager to determine if the IC&C signifies a move toward potential violence, no move beyond the status quo, or a move away from violence. Changes can go either way, toward risk or away from it.
Sources of Evidence: Evidence of changes in the subject's behavior comes from the content of the communication or the circumstances of the suspicious activity, the target, the threat manager's files, law enforcement records, mental health status (such as ceasing to take medication), and observations from subject's family or acquaintances.

Has the subject made other IC&Cs in the past?

Assessment: Subjects who chronically harass public officials, but take no action to cause harm, are potential low risk. Subjects who have committed assaults or escalated their threatening behaviors in the past are potentially high risk.
Sources of Evidence: Evidence of previous IC&Cs comes from the

threat manager's files, other law enforcement agencies, and the target.

What is the target's current situation?

Assessment: The greater the target's involvement in controversial or confrontational issues, especially those pertaining to the subject, the greater the risk.
Sources of Evidence: Evidence of the target's current situation comes from the target, the news media, and the issues generated in any issue involving the target.

Has the target received other IC&Cs in the past?

Assessment: Changes in the pattern of IC&Cs received by the target, whether as escalations from the same subject or increases in the number of subjects, would indicate increasing potential risk.
Sources of Evidence: Evidence of the target previously receiving IC&Cs comes from the threat manager's files and from the target.

In answering each of the questions described in Table 6-1, the threat manager can choose one of three possible answers. The answer may indicate high risk or it may indicate low risk. But the answer can very well be "Unknown." Threat managers should never force an answer if they do not know it. Not only does it throw off the assessment, but recognizing that the question cannot now be answered helps set the course for the protective investigation.

Cir-Con Questions – Circumstances

1. What can be inferred from how the IC&C was delivered?

IC&Cs are delivered by telephone, in writing (usually through the mail), verbally to the target or some known associate of the target, a third party, through a suspicious activity, or through an informant.

With the exception of informants, how the IC&C was delivered is the willful choice of the subject. Even with informants, the subject chooses to reveal his plans or feelings to the informant (unless, of course, the informant is lying). By choosing the method of delivery, the subject unavoidably reveals his or her intentions at the moment of choosing. Neither telephones nor letters (always excepting mail bombs) can cause physical harm, but approaching close enough to make a verbal IC&C or skulking about acting suspiciously puts the subject close enough to the target that some physical harm can result.

Approaches also put the subject at risk of getting caught. His or her willingness to take that risk suggests a desire to gather target information or an intent to carry through with an attack. Thus, with a phone call or letter, the threat manager can generally determine that the immediate potential risk is low. Verbal IC&Cs or suspicious activities suggest the immediate potential risk is high.

On occasion, subject's write out their complaints or hostile feelings toward the target, then hand-deliver them or leave them someplace where they will be easily found. The subject might give an envelope to the guards at the front desk, an office receptionist, or other person stationed to greet visitors. We know of cases where the subject scrawled inappropriately phrased graffiti on restroom walls in the target's building or left paper messages on statuary. Although written, the actual delivery included a physical approach to some place where the subject could reasonably assume the target might be. Such an approach obviously escalates the potential level of risk, but not necessarily to high. If the approach was made solely to leave the message, that would indicate that the subject at the *moment of delivery* did not intend an assault. However, the threat manager should also carefully assess the degree to which the approach allowed the subject to gather target information for use in planning a later attack. Did the delivery allow the subject to test security, scope out the target environ, or otherwise gain information useful to planning. Leaving a message on public grounds suggests something very different from finding a message in the target's outer office. In addition, the threat manager needs to remember that the subject was brazen enough to deliver the communication in person. Having successfully done so, he or she might decide to do it again or to escalate.

Informant IC&Cs require a different tact. Rather than assess the IC&C, the threat manager first has to determine the credibility and reliability of the informant. Only after those have been assured can the threat manager assess the information. Obviously, the more credible and reliable the informant, the more seriously his or her information should be taken.

2. What did the subject mean or intend by the IC&C?

Exactly what is the subject accomplishing with this IC&C? If a communication, what precisely is being said? Did the content request anything, such as help, money, reuniting, re-employment, a second chance, or some delusional desire? Or did the content make demands, especially with an implication of negative consequences if the target fails to meet the demands? If a suspicious activity, what is the action and why is it suspicious? Stated another way, is the overall message or intent of this particular IC&C to warn or to cause an emotional response from the target or to harm the target? Or did the subject intend to gather information on the target?

3. How much target knowledge can be deduced from the IC&C?

Is there anything about the IC&C, its delivery, or its message that indicates the subject knows any personal details about the target. Telephoning a publicly listed number suggests nothing, but telephoning an unpublished or unlisted number suggests target research. Going to a government or corporate office, school, business, or former home where the estranged spouse still lives suggests nothing, but appearing at a place not publicly or previously known suggests target research. Similarly, showing up at places that require bypassing security also arouses concern. A general reference about the target's family or personal affairs suggests nothing, but a detailed description of the spouse or children, their activities, or some difficult-to-find personal information about the target again suggests target research. Estranged spouses obviously have considerable personal knowledge about the other spouse, but they should not know things about the spouse since the separation. Evidence of such knowledge suggests target research. The more the subject knows about the target – or attempts to find out – the higher the potential risk.

4. Why did the subject choose this target?

What is the link between this subject and this target? Is there evidence that the subject is involved with – or concerned about – some issue involving the target, the target's business interests, official position, or status? The involvement can be personal, but the concerns can be ideological, political, emotional, financial, even delusional. The greater the subject appears to view the involvement or concern, the higher the potential risk.

5. Is the Intimacy Effect *at play?*

The *Intimacy Effect* postulates a clear ratio between intimate relationships – current or former – and the value of threatening words when current or former intimates become engaged in a dispute. The greater the intimacy, the higher the risk of threats actually portending potential violence in a dispute. The degree of intimacy – both physical and emotional – in the relationship between the subject and others can have a profound effect on the subject's feelings. The intimacy can be both physical and emotional, as between current or former spouses or lovers, or it can be simply emotional, as between current or former friends, neighbors, business colleagues, or associates. The *Intimacy Effect* is what makes Family Court so contentious and volatile. Similarly, situations involving workplace complaints, terminations, business dissolutions, teasing at school, or feuding neighbors also become more acrimonious simply because the disputants know each other, share a history, and now disagree with each other.

If the circumstances of the IC&C include some physical or emotional intimacy involving the subject and someone else (not just the target) involved in the situation, then the threat manager has to factor into the assessment a heightened, emotionally driven intensity pressing upon the subject. Have schoolmates tormented the subject, shaming him or her in front of friends, thus prompting from the subject an expression of a desire for vengeance? Has a supervisor recently passed a subordinate over for promotion, given a negative evaluation, or moved to terminate the subordinate, with the result that the subordinate threatens some dire consequences? Has an estranged spouse spoken ominously about the future for either spouse? Threats exchanged between individuals who know each other carry far greater weight as indicators of risk than threats directed at strangers. The greater the intensity of the relationship between subject and target, the higher the potential risk.

Cir-Con Questions – Context

6. Has there been a significant change in the subject's life, circumstances, or personal situation that might have prompted this IC&C?

Change can cause a rippling effect, frequently stressing the subject and generating the IC&C. By identifying from the subject's point of view any recent or on-going changes in the subject's life, circumstances, or current personal situation, the threat manager can better grasp what stressors might be pressing upon the subject. Knowing, for example, that the subject is going through a divorce and that the judge recently imposed new restrictions on child visitation can help the threat manager gauge the overall context in which the IC&C occurred. Change should be assessed from the subject's perspective. It should be measured in two ways: how much seemed to change and how important the change seemed to be to the subject. The threat manager should factor into the assessment how many changes occurred or how great their significance to the subject. Critical changes include such events as death of a loved one, divorce, school expulsion, school or business transfer, bankruptcy or financial problems, embarrassment, change in social status, or loss of friends.

7. Does this IC&C suggest a significant change in the subject's previous behavior or demeanor toward the target?

Comparing previous IC&Cs with the current IC&C allows the threat manager to determine if the current IC&C signifies a move toward potential violence, no move from the status quo, or a move away from violence. Changes can go either way, toward potential risk or away from it.

8. Has the subject made other IC&Cs in the past?

Past behaviors are the best indicator of future behaviors. Determining that a subject has a history of IC&Cs – and further determining what the outcomes of those were – can give the threat manager enormous insight into the potential outcome of the current IC&C. Individuals tend to follow patterns in their behaviors. If they act inappropriately toward the target, they probably acted inappropriately in disputes with neighbors, over public controversies, or in other ways. Subjects who chronically harass numerous targets, but take no action to cause harm, are low risk. Subjects who have committed assaults or escalated their threatening behaviors in the past are obviously high risk.

9. What is the target's current situation?

Often, little can be known about the subject until the threat manager has time to conduct a protective investigation. This is not true for the target of the IC&C. All the threat manager has to do is briefly interview the target. The questions should cover the target's current or recent involvement with the subject or with any issues mentioned by the subject. The threat manager should also determine if the target has noticed anything suspicious or untoward, what he or she may know about the subject, and anything else of significance to the case. In cases where the subject remained anonymous, ascertaining what the target knows, suspects, or has been doing lately may provide the only leads to identifying the subject. Is the target controversial? Is the situation in which the target may be involved receiving a lot of publicity? Has the target been involved in recent controversy or highly publicized event?

Any evidence of suspicious or disturbing activities around the target indicates potential high risk. The greater the target's involvement in controversial or confrontational issues, especially those pertaining to the subject, the greater the potential risk.

10. Has the target received other IC&Cs in the past?

Determining the target's history with previous IC&Cs will help the threat manager gauge several different aspects of the current case. Some targets, for whatever reason, seem to attract more IC&Cs than others. The current IC&C could be similar to that. Targets who have received IC&Cs in the past will probably tend to handle new ones with greater aplomb. Previous IC&Cs from other subjects related to the same situation may suggest widespread or intense feelings about the target or the target's involvement in whatever the situation.

If previous IC&Cs came from the same subject involved in the current case, then the threat manager can look for escalations or de-escalations – changes, in effect – in the current IC&C. Changes in the pattern of IC&Cs received by the target, whether as escalations from the same subject or increases in the number of subjects, would indicate increasing risk.

Case Illustration:

Using the Cir-Con Factors

The public telephone line to the mayor's office rang twice before the secretary answered. A male voice, speaking with icy calm, said, "Tell the Mayor that neither bodyguards nor fences will keep me away. I know my rights even if she doesn't. She is mine." The caller hung up.

Because of the reference to security, the secretary reported the IC&C to the threat manager. After quickly interviewing the secretary and the supervisor of the mayor's protective detail, the threat manager determined that neither knew of anything or any event that might have prompted the call. Nor had the mayor received any other IC&Cs. A check of the threat files and neighboring law enforcement agencies also proved negative. The threat manager determined that:

1. The method of delivery was telephone, *a low-risk indicator.*
2. The point of the message was to frighten or disturb, *a low-risk indicator.*
3. The IC&C gave no evidence of target knowledge, *a low-risk indicator.*
4. The subject targeted the mayor because of some action taken by the mayor affecting the subject's perceived rights. This suggested some personal involvement for the subject, *a potential high-risk indicator.*
5. The *Intimacy Effect* was *unknown at this point.*
6. Changes in the subject's life were *unknown at this point.*
7. The subject's previous behavior was *unknown at this point.*
8. No record of previous IC&Cs was found.
9. Target's current situation indicated no problems, *a low-risk indicator.*
10. The target had never received an IC&C before.

Based on the initial assessment, the threat manager determined that the immediate level of risk was low in terms of the protective response, but that measures needed to be instituted to ensure than any future IC&C directed toward the target were reported immediately to the threat manager. The threat manager also began a protective investigation by reviewing recent announcements made by the mayor's office and recent issues coming before the city council to determine if anyone had expressed undue concern or interest to other city officials.

SOURCE: Hypothetical illustration drawn from authors' personal experiences.

II. What Are the Stakes Involved from the Subject's Point of View?

Purpose: To determine – from the subject's point of view – the strength of the subject's motivation to commit an act of intended violence.

Threat managers can apply two different tests to determine how the subject views the stakes involved in the situation prompting the IC&C. The first requires looking at the issues in the subject's grievance for any evidence to measure how strongly the subject feels about the issues. The second test consists of applying Gavin de Becker's JACA scale, an acronym he developed meaning Justification, Alternatives, Consequences, and Ability.

Both tests require the threat manager to view the issues as the subject sees them. The assessment does not necessarily measure reality. Rather, it measures how the subject understands the situation. Many individuals get fired from their jobs. A rare few of them retaliate violently. Over half of all marriages in the United States end in divorce. Only a small proportion end in violence. No doubt, a majority of school kids get teased. Only a few feel tormented and only a handful of them return to school armed with guns, bombs, or knives. One of the many things that distinguishes individuals of violent intent from others grows out of their belief that the stakes justify violence. In determining the stakes, threat managers actually look for evidence concerning or revealing the subject's reaction to the situation, to things happening to him or her, to the subject's vision of the future, to the subject's faith or hope or belief that all will be well – or will not be.

The Stakes

A subject's stake in a situation can be personal, ideological, political, financial, related to deeply held religious or moral beliefs, emotional or delusional. Assessing the stakes is not about taking some objective measure of the actual stakes involved in the situation. Rather, the threat manager should look for any evidence in the IC&C or the circumstances of the case that the subject perceives or believes that the stakes are high. This may involve intangible issues, such as honor, justice, family support, emotional ties, perceived rights, or ideological beliefs, that make the grievance far more important to the subject than what an objective observer would see.

Case Study:

Ideological Stakes

In the summer of 1991, a federal judge in Wichita, Kansas, ordered the federal government to take measures to keep a local abortion clinic open. Thousands of anti-abortion protestors had traveled to Wichita to demonstrate against the clinic and block patients from entering it.

The court order outraged the protestors. On August 5, one particular protestor felt so strongly about the judge's ruling that he went to the judge's home. When the judge and his wife returned from a neighborhood stroll, the protestor accosted them on their front lawn. A brief scuffle ensued when the judge tried to push the protestor off his property.

A subject's stake in a case may involve deeply held beliefs.

SOURCE: Authors' personal knowledge.

Evidence of the subject's investment in the situation – emotional, financial, personal, or ideological – can come from the IC&C itself, from the subject's demeanor, from credible associates of the subject, or from the stakes of the situation itself.

Table 6-2 provides a way to measure what may be at stake from the subject's point of view.

Table 6-2. Measuring What Is At Stake for the Subject

No Stakes

Assessment: Neither the IC&C nor the subject's demeanor suggest that he or she made the IC&C because of any attachment to certain beliefs or personal involvement in the situation prompting the IC&C.

Normal Acceptance

Assessment: The subject claims a grievance, but appears to be accepting the stakes in a normal way. For example, an employee feels wrongly fired, but begins looking for a new job. A career criminal facing the possibility of a lengthy prison sentence may do so without objection or complaint. Spouses may accept an adverse divorce decree – even a costly one – simply as the price of getting divorced.

Mild Loss

Assessment: The subject feels perturbed enough about some loss or other grievance to communicate inappropriately, but the communication does not go to extremes nor claim a great or total loss. Having made the complaint, the subject appears to focus on future issues beyond the grievance.

Much to Lose

Assessment: The subject complains that the stakes involved in the situation are high and that he or she has much (though not all) to lose – or already lost – by the outcome. The subject appears excessively nervous or concerned about the outcome and his or her focus on the circumstances of the situation appears unusually intense. The IC&C may discuss at length or in strong terms all that the subject perceives to be at risk.

Everything to Lose

Assessment: Whether or not it is true, the subject clearly believes that the stakes involved in the situation risk the subject losing everything dear to him or her. The loss is described in exaggerated, grandiose ways, the subject acts or describes himself or herself as desperate, at wit's end, with no future or future prospects. The subject appears obsessively nervous or worried about the case. Does the subject show any interest in life beyond the outcome of the case? Have there been outbursts by the subject? Is the subject preparing for death by such actions as writing a will, giving away belongings, or putting affairs in order? Are the stakes indeed high and the subject repeatedly and earnestly stresses how high they are?

The presence or absence of inhibitors in the subject's life offers a good insight into how the subject may perceive the stakes. Inhibitors are tangible and intangible things that have enough value to the subject that they discourage actions that might put the inhibitor at risk. They can be listed as:

- Home
- Family
- Career
- Resources
- Reputation
- Health
- Alternatives
- Belief System
- Self-Esteem
- Dignity

Inhibitors work much like dominoes standing in a row. As long as each remains standing, each exerts an inhibiting effect on the subject acting out violently. But as each domino topples, the inhibiting effect dissipates. Indeed, as a domino falls, the momentum toward violence can increase.

When one inhibitor falls, it frequently knocks others down. Individuals caught in a downward spiral often begin losing everything dear to them. They lose their jobs, they lose their home, their spouse, their money. One by one, frequently seemingly all at once, everything of importance to the subject slips beyond his or her grasp. As each domino falls, the stakes for keeping the remaining ones standing get higher.

Often, the target can appear to the subject as the cause of the inhibitors toppling. Getting fired from a job imperils maintaining a house, car, kid's education, health care, future career options, and one's dignity. Subjects easily blame all these problems on the supervisor or company that dismissed them. Subjects caught up in some dispute with the government or the courts can fare worse. The legal process can literally disinhibit the subject. The government can take an individual's freedom, seize his or her assets, brand the individual a social outcast. The government can separate families, keep parents from their children, embarrass, and punish. These actions, all lawful and legitimate, act to drive the subject to greater desperation. Desperate people do desperate things.

Case Study:

"Die on My Feet"

Jack Gary McKnight knew he would be sentenced the next day to ten years in prison. He had been growing marijuana on his Kansas farm, almost all for personal use, and could not believe the government had now turned him into a criminal. The state of Kansas also instituted proceedings to seize the farm for failure to pay drug taxes. In order to avoid her own ten-year sentence, his wife agreed to testify against him.

McKnight set up a videotape recorder to film himself. As he spoke, he began listing all the inhibitors being taken from him. "They're going to take my wife," he cried, "They're going to take my house. They're going to take my farm, my job, my dogs, my guns, then make me live like a dog for the rest of my life."

McKnight saw all his stakes on the table – and he kept losing them. Worse, the game seemed to him to be rigged. He believed the government cheated and thus treated him unjustly. It was bad enough to lose, but what dramatically increased the value of his stakes was his profound sense that the losses were all so unfair. Ultimately, the only domino McKnight thought he had left was his dignity. He vowed to "die on my feet before I live on my knees."

The next morning, McKnight shot his way into the Topeka federal building, killing a court security officer, wounding two civilians, and terrorizing 11 court clerks before killing himself.

Threat managers should always measure the subject's stakes from the subject's point of view.

SOURCE: Calhoun, Hunters and Howlers.

By far, the dignity domino constitutes the most important inhibitor. Fortunately, it usually falls last. Unfortunately, subjects will use violence – as McKnight did – to keep it propped up. A case from Kentucky in 2000 also violently illustrates the point. "Crazy Eddie" Vaughn never minded his nickname. Nor did he object too much getting busted for marijuana possession or the occasional drunk and disorderly. But he apparently drew the line when the state indicted him for sexually abusing a minor. That attacked his character and reputation, thus raising the stakes too high. Despite repeated protestations of his innocence, Vaughn's lawyer convinced him the state would win a conviction. Rather than face that, on the morning set for the trial Vaughn went gunning for the prosecutor. Both men shot each other to death in the hallway outside the prosecutor's bedroom. The prosecutor was protecting his family; Vaughn his reputation.[1]

The stakes need not make sense to any rational person or reasonable assessment. They only need to be important to the subject. Some subjects act out delusions or have other mental illnesses that effect how they understand or view the stakes. Even when not mentally ill, individuals have their own highly personalized way of viewing events. The lesson for the threat manager, then, is not to assess the stakes involved, but to investigate and assess how the subject weighs the stakes.

Case Study:

The Dignity Domino

In 1988, an assistant U.S. attorney (AUSA) in the Southern District of New York was threatened by one of the highest-ranking dons of the Colombo organized crime family. The don tried to let a contract to have the AUSA killed. The AUSA had prosecuted the don and obtained a conviction, but the threat had nothing to do with that. Rather, the don wanted the AUSA murdered because the AUSA had openly speculated on whether or not the fur coat worn by the don's wife could be seized as an illicit asset. From the don's twisted point of view, such speculation insulted his wife. He could not allow such an offense to his family's dignity to go unpunished.

> The dignity domino is often the last to fall, but always the most important to keep upright.
>
> *SOURCE: Calhoun, Hunters and Howlers, 3.*

The *Intimacy Effect* frequently influences the importance of an individual's stakes. It introduces a kind of competition into the situation – "If I can't have it, she won't have it, either" or "He can't fire me, I'm too important." Such subjects frequently choose to sacrifice all their inhibitors just to spite the target. In addition, if a loss to the subject translates into a gain to the target, the subject can get even further incensed at the situation. Gang-related shootings readily illustrate the point. A loss to one gang means victory to the opposing gang. In defending itself, the first gang can either take action to preempt the attack or avenge its loss after the attack. Either way results in violence.

JACA

Threat managers have another simple tool to help assess how the subject views whether or not he or she has anything at stake in the situation prompting the IC&C. Gavin de Becker, a leading international expert on threat assessment, crafted four simple questions the threat manager should ask about every IC&C and, as the protective investigation uncovers more details, should also ask about the subject. De Becker titled the set JACA, an acronym for Justification, Alternatives, Consequences, and Ability. Essentially, the threat manager asks if any evidence, either in the IC&C or collected by the protective investigation, indicates whether the:

- subject feels *justified* in acting violently;
- subject sees no *alternatives* to violence;
- subject accepts the *consequences* of committing a violent act;
- subject believes he has the *ability* to commit violence.

JACA works only if the threat manager can put him or herself inside the head of the subject to answer the questions. This means viewing the events and circumstances strictly from the subject's point of view. It requires the threat manager to empathize with the subject, which can sometimes be a rather distasteful experience for anyone, especially a law enforcement officer.[2]

Yet, it is not really that difficult – or that bad. Again, take the case of Jack Gary McKnight. Police arrested him for possession of marijuana with intent to sell, compounded by the presence of semi-automatic weapons in his possession. Once his case transferred to the federal courts, those conditions meant a mandatory sentence of 10 years with no possibility of parole. Because of a family history of heart problems, McKnight did not expect to live another 10 years, especially not if he spent them in prison. He had no criminal history and thus little familiarity with the criminal justice system – nor with criminal life. At the same time, the state of Kansas moved to seize his property. His girlfriend agreed to testify against him in order to receive a lighter sentence for herself. (Since they lived together, she, too, was arrested and charged.) McKnight, a former Marine, also hunted as a hobby. The weapons the police found were shotguns, rifles, and several pistols, none of which McKnight used to grow marijuana.

Having thus been stripped by the government of most of his inhibitors, is it hard to imagine that McKnight felt *justified* in striking back violently by attacking the federal court? Faced with a mandatory 10-year sentence, could McKnight have seen many *alternatives* to resolving his problem with the criminal justice system? Were the *consequences* of violence any worse than going to jail? And as a hunter familiar with weapons, McKnight certainly knew he had the *ability* to fight back. Yet, in recognizing how McKnight no doubt rationalized his violence, we need not condone it. Instead, we need only recognize how he felt, thought, and rationalized his situation because by doing so the threat manager can set a course of action to manage McKnight and the threat he ultimately posed to the court.

Table 6-3 defines JACA.

Table 6-3. The JACA Scale

Justification

Assessment: Does the subject believe that he or she is justified in resorting to violence? Does the subject feel that he or she has suffered some grievous injury or loss, some insult or violation?

Alternatives

Assessment: Does the subject believe that he or she has no other alternative but violence? Is the subject at the end of his or her rope, frustrated and unable to identify other ways to solve his or her problems?

Consequences

Assessment: Most people understand the consequences of violence – prison , injury, or death – yet sometimes those results seem more acceptable than the subject's current problems. Is the subject willing to suffer the consequences of acting violently toward the target?

Ability

Assessment: Does the subject perceive himself or herself as able to act out violently? Does the subject believe that he or she is capable of attacking the target? Has the subject resorted to violence in the past? Those who have used violence before are usually more confident in using it in the future.

In addition to its utility as an assessment tool, JACA also can assist the threat manager in identifying strategies for defusing the risk. For example, the threat manager might offer different alternatives to resolving the subject's grievance or issues. Since strongly felt emotions frequently prompt IC&Cs, the subjects may not be able to recognize all the alternatives open to them. Perhaps the subject does not fully comprehend the full range of consequences, especially to his or her family, loved ones, or future. If the threat manager points these out, it may help convince the subject to back off. At the worst, the threat manager can set up a protective detail around the target, thus forcing the subject to question his or her ability to attack successfully. Since all elements of JACA must be present, taking away one of them means managing the subject away from violence.

Case Study:

What Else Can You Do?

To this day, years after Jeffrey Wade Wallace shot his way into the Key West, Florida, bar where he used to work, he believes himself the victim of an intricate, national conspiracy. The bar, he maintains, was the center of an organized-crime drug and prostitution ring with strong ties to Satanism, President Bill Clinton, and Garrison Keillor, the novelist and host of the "Prairie Home Companion" radio program. To end the conspiracy and its resultant crimes, Wallace attacked the bar. He killed one person and injured three others.

"The best example I can give," Wallace explained, "is you're in your house and somebody breaks in and you have to defend yourself and you end up killing somebody. It's terrible, but what else can you do."

The imagined crimes gave Wallace the Justification; he saw no other Alternatives; he felt he had no choice but to accept the Consequences, no matter how terrible; and his weapon gave him the Ability. A complete JACA.

SOURCE: "The Well-Marked Roads to Homicidal Rage," New York Times, April 9, 2000.

III. Is the Subject Acting Like a Hunter?

Purpose: To determine if the subject has engaged in specific behaviors associated with committing an act of intended violence or common to assassins in general.

Asking if the subject acts like a *Hunter* or a *Howler* helps the threat manager focus on the behaviors that distinguish those who intend to commit an act of violence from those who – however aggrieved – have no such intention. Hunters travel all the way down the path to intended violence. Howlers may go part of the way, but never all the way. Each may have a grievance, real or imagined, but only the Hunter allows that complaint to propel him or her to violent action. Howlers may complain, often inappropriately, loudly, and frequently, but they do not go from complaint to action.

Profound differences separate Hunters and Howlers. Hunters behave in a threatening manner. They stalk, research, prepare themselves, make approaches, and finally attack. Howlers frequently threaten, but virtually never behave in a threatening manner. They write or call, often repeatedly. But they do little else. Often, their communications are voluminous and addressed to multiple targets, frequently to individuals or officials with whom they have never had any contact. By recognizing these differences, the alert threat manager can distinguish between the Hunter and the Howler, using that distinction to assess the value of the threat.

The concept of Hunters and Howlers directly addresses the subject's intent to pose or not to pose a threat. Hunters intend to cause harm, Howlers intend to cause fear or discomfort. Those different intentions result in different behaviors and modes of expression. The Howler who makes a threatening telephone call, no matter how graphic the description of violence, can only scare the target, nothing more. Only the Hunter consummating the hunt can injure or kill.

Consequently, when the threat manager asks if the subject is acting like a Hunter (or a Howler), the underlying question is whether or not the subject is acting like he or she truly intends to cause harm. Both can be motivated, both can be capable of violence, but only the Hunter cradles the intention for committing an act of violence. Obviously, the threat management strategies for managing Hunters and Howlers are entirely different.

Two tests determine if the subject acts like a Hunter. Applying the concept of the path to intended violence is the first test. It works across all venues of intended violence. Identifying characteristics common to assassins in the United States (and known as the Dietz-10 after the psychiatrist who first described them) is the second test. It works best for public-figure attackers or threats to government facilities.

The Path to Intended Violence

The path was described in detail in Chapter 3 and will not be repeated here. In terms of conducting the assessment, using the path helps focus the threat manager on specific, attack-related behaviors.

Table 6-4 lists each step along the path and summarizes some of the tell-tale signs that the step has been reached.

Table 6- 4. Summary of the Path to Intended Violence

Grievance

Tell-Tale Behaviors: Expressed feelings of injury, injustice, anger, fear, revenge, outrage, or ideology.

Ideation

Tell-Tale Behaviors: Delivered an IC&C, discussed plans for violence with others, identified with other assassins, fixated on violence, fascinated with weapons, interested in specific anniversaries or key dates.

Research and Planning

Tell-Tale Behaviors: Stalked, researched target, made suspicious inquiries, gathered information about the target or the target's personal life.

Preparations

Tell-Tale Behaviors: Acquired weapon, assembled equipment, arranged transportation, respected significant dates, conducted final acts, costumed.

Breach

Tell-Tale Behaviors: Approached target with weapon.

Attack

Tell-Tale Behaviors: Assaulted the target with weapon.

Evidence of these behaviors can come from the content of the IC&C, how or even where it was delivered, or from things the target may have noticed, such as suspicious cars in the neighborhood or unusual inquiries. For example, references to personal information about the target, such as family arrangements or size, type of car, personal habits, spouse's employment, or favorite haunts, all indicate some degree of target research or stalking. If the subject states in the

IC&C that he or she recently bought a gun, then the threat manager must respond as though the subject has reached the preparation stage. Telephoning an official's publicly listed office number would not suggest target research, but calling an unpublished home number might. Similarly, ascertaining from the target that nothing uncommon has occurred recently would not suggest research or planning, but finding out that the target's neighbors have received a number of unusually inquisitive phone calls about the target would indicate research. When the threat manager asks if the subject acts like a Hunter, the answer would include any evidence of such attack-related behaviors as target research, attack planning, or preparing for an attack. For purposes of the assessment, any claims by the subject in the IC&C should be accepted at face value. Later, the threat manager corroborates these claims as part of the protective investigation. The rule for accepting the subject's assertions extends even to ones clearly wrong. Say, for instance, the subject states that the target lives in a particular neighborhood or drives a particular model car. The threat manager may know that the information is inaccurate. However, the claim itself gives evidence that the subject researched the target. Bad research is still research behavior. Hunters and howlers distinguish themselves by their behaviors, however productive or unproductive those behaviors may turn out to be.

Pinpointing the subject's location along the path to intended violence also indicates the level of risk. Subject's who have begun making preparations for an attack clearly represent a high risk. Subjects whose IC&C indicates they have reached the ideation stage, but have gone no farther are at this point low risk, though obviously they bear further watching. The path to intended violence narrows the focus of the assessment to subject behaviors directly related to committing acts of intended violence. Since those who pose a threat may never make a threat, identifying threatening behaviors becomes all the more important.

Case Study:

The Elevator Stalker

In 1987, a local television station in Tampa, Florida, received two calls. Each time, the caller identified himself as "Scorpio." He claimed that "there is a contract out on [an

> Assistant U.S. Attorney (AUSA)]. He will be eliminated. I rode alone with [AUSA] in the elevator at the courthouse in Tampa yesterday at 10:00 a.m." The AUSA confirmed to investigators that a lone man had been on the elevator with him at about that time.
>
> The content of the telephone calls, once corroborated, gave evidence that "Scorpio" had stalked the target at the courthouse. In other words, Scorpio had at least reached the research and planning stage along the path to violence.
>
> Consequently, the threat manager assessed the case as high risk based on the subject's behaviors and apparent direction along the path to intended violence.
>
> *SOURCE: Authors' personal knowledge.*

The Dietz-10

The second test for identifying Hunters uses a comparative method to look for specific factors common to cases of violence toward public figures. Knowing these factors helps the threat manager to compare the characteristics of the current subject with the characteristics of known assassins. The method is known as the Dietz-10. Psychiatrist Park Dietz identified 10 characteristics common to assassins in the United States.[3]

Table 6-5 lists the Dietz-10.

Table 6-5. Dietz-10 Characteristics Common to American Assassins

Mental Illness

Assessment: Does the subject display evidence of some mental disorder? Evidence of this need not come from a mental health expert. Is the subject acting strangely? Does he or she claim some mental disorder?

Exaggerated Idea of Self

Assessment: Does the subject appear to have an exaggerated idea of himself or herself? For example, does the subject project himself or herself as equal or higher in stature to the public official? Is the subject making unreasonable or unjustified demands?

Previous Inappropriate Contacts

Assessment: Has the subject had a previous inappropriate contact with some public figure, including the current target? Have their been previous incidents? Have other targets had problems with the subject?

Random/Targeted Travel

Assessment: Has the subject engaged in either random travel or targeted travel? For example, has the subject shown up at the courthouse or some location where the target was?

Interest in Assassinations

Assessment: Does the subject show any interest in another stalker or assassin? Many assassins study previous assassins and assassinations, frequently mimicking them.

Circumvent Security

Assessment: Does the subject have the ability to circumvent ordinary security? According to Dietz, it should be assumed that most individuals can circumvent security.

Diary or Journal

Assessment: Has the subject created a diary or unusually extensive files documenting a grievance or dispute?

Previous Approaches

Assessment: Has the subject made previous approaches to any public figure? Other law enforcement agencies and other targets should be contacted to see if anyone else has had encounters with the subject.

Recent Weapons Acquisition

Assessment: Has the subject obtained a weapon recently or does the subject show any fascination with weapons? Assassins frequently obtain weapons just for this particular assassination.

Target Research

Assessment: Has the subject researched the target or victim? Is there any evidence of stalking?

Evidence for making the Dietz-10 comparison comes from the content of the communication or the circumstances of the contact, from the target, from other law enforcement agencies, or from the issues involved in the grievance.

The more of the Dietz-10 characteristics a subject has, the greater the risk. In addition, threat managers should evaluate the characteristics by their combinations with other characteristics. Subjects who exhibit an exaggerated idea of themselves, keep a diary, and have the ability to circumvent security cannot be automatically assessed as high risk. However, subjects who conducted target research, recently bought a pistol, and who suffer from a mental illness clearly pose a high risk. Yet, in each example, only three characteristics obtained.

Threat managers can also use the Dietz-10 as a guide for their protective investigation. For example, the threat manager may initially have no information about whether or not the subject keeps a diary. When the threat manager eventually interviews the subject, it might be wise to ask about a diary or get permission to look for one. Similarly, interest in other assassins may not be readily apparent during the initial assessment, but may become so during the course of the investigation. The subject may have a library on assassination or keep pictures of assassinations on his or her wall. Although the assessments themselves tend to be short-lived, the elements composing them are constants. They should be kept constantly in mind throughout the course of the case.

Case Study:

Eight Out of the Dietz Ten

Rachelle Shannon began her anti-abortion career innocently enough. She attended a few demonstrations and began reading the newsletters. In her reading, she chanced upon a list of names and addresses of individuals imprisoned for burning down clinics. Shannon began corresponding with some convicts. They inspired her to start burning down clinics herself. She financed her expeditions by holding bake sales. Later convicted of a handful of arsons, police suspected her of many more [1. Previous Approaches; 2. Previous Inappropriate Contacts].

Then in March 1993, Michael Griffen assassinated Dr. David Gunn. Inspired again, Shannon wrote Griffen several times [3. Interest in Assassins]. Again not satisfied cheering from the sidelines, she determined to become an assassin herself [4. Exaggerated Idea of Self]. Her research on prominent abortion providers led her to choose Dr. George Tiller of Wichita, Kansas [5. Target Research]. After a few more bake sales than usual, Shannon had enough cash to purchase a pistol and a plane ticket from her home in Oregon to Wichita [6. Recent Acquisition of a Weapon; 7. Targeted Travel].

On August 19, 1993, Shannon waited outside Tiller's clinic. As he left work for the day, she approached his car and fired her pistol [8. Circumvent Security].

It is not known if Shannon kept a diary or if she suffered from some mental illness, but what is known gives her a score of eight on the Dietz-10. In addition, the particular eight factors, combined, added up to a higher risk.

SOURCE: New York Times, August 20, 21, 22, and 28, 1993; ATF interview with Shannon.

IV. Is the Subject Acting Like a Howler?

Purpose: To look for specific behaviors – or lack of behaviors – associated with not committing an act of intended violence.

Although Hunters engage in the same kinds of attack-related behaviors regardless of venue, Howlers do not. Indeed, the mark of a Howler in one type of intended violence may well be the exact opposite mark in another type. For example, subjects who repeatedly communicate direct threats to public figures almost always turn out to be Howlers. They are upset and angry and want the public figure to hear their complaints, but they seek nothing further than that. The act of complaining, even threatening, satisfies them. Conversely, subjects who know their targets and who issue threats, both direct and veiled, often end up carrying out those threats. As every street cop knows, many spouses who threaten their partners eventually assault them. Subjects who talk about violence or describe their plans to commit a violent act at work or school also have a high risk of eventually acting out. School shooters frequently confide their plans to their chums. Subjects who ultimately engage in violence at the workplace often begin by using the threat of that violence to intimidate their co-workers or supervisors.

Consequently, threat managers need to keep in mind what type of intended violence they might be assessing when they ask if the subject acts like a Howler. The *Intimacy Effect* very much comes into play here, especially in evaluating threats. There seems to be a very direct relationship between the chances the subject will carry out a threat and the degree of intimacy between the subject and the target. The more intimate, the more likely the chance.

So why look for Howlers? Primarily because asking if the subject acts like a Howler reminds the threat manager to look for positive as well as negative evidence. Threat managers must avoid always assuming the worse. Doing so wastes resources and energy and, even worse, results in raising suspicions about subjects who never intended to act violently. Far more subjects eventually turn out to be Howlers than Hunters. Although we do not mean by this that threat managers can afford to play the odds, we do suggest the odds are usually greater that the subject is a Howler.

But if the marks of a Howler differ depending on the type of possible intended violence under assessment, how does the threat manager identify behaviors associated with Howlers? Threats toward public figures suggest the possibility of a Howler. Yet, threats toward co-workers, schools, or domestic partners suggest the possibility of a Hunter. Does the threat manager risk blinding him or herself to potential risk by looking too hard for redeeming evidence? Here the research on intended violence leaves a vacuum. Only a few studies have tried to distinguish non-attackers from their opposites. We know of no study that does this across all venues.

Experience, bolstered by commonsense, helps fill the void. We hypothesize two markings that distinguish Howlers across all venues. First, those subjects who make an IC&C of some sort but who never escalate beyond that initial IC&C can be considered possible Howlers. For example, a worker might receive a bad performance evaluation and in direct response utter a threat to the supervisor. If he or she then calms down and returns to work without ever making another threat, that behavior typifies a Howler. Howlers are emotional beings, very prone to angry or hurt outbursts. Once the emotion passes, they lose any interest in carrying out what they might have said in the heat of the moment. Assessing the circumstances of the utterance may lead the threat manager to determine that whatever was said was said emotionally and the emotion has now dissipated.

Second, we hypothesize that Howlers maintain and build up their inhibitors. Hunters either lose or strip themselves of theirs. We have already suggested that threat managers should look for the absence or loss of inhibitors when assessing whether or not a subject acts like a Hunter. At the same time, threat managers should look for the presence or increase in inhibitors when determining whether or not a subject acts like a Howler. Those individuals with many inhibitors, and especially those individuals who add to their inhibitors with new ones, will probably turn out to be Howlers.

Case Study:

Motive and Ability Without Intent Makes a Howler, Not a Hunter

On September 13, 1999, Illinois police arrested Clayton Waagner after an intensive manhunt. A convicted felon, police had an outstanding Michigan warrant against him for weapons violations. But police also suspected Waagner – a fervent anti-abortionist – of planning violence against abortion facilities. At the time of the arrest, he had firearms, gasoline cans, a dummy hand grenade, ammunition, and a list of eight abortion clinics in Georgia and Tennessee. In a subsequent interview with the *Pittsburgh Post-Gazette*, Waagner described his plans to kill abortion doctors. "I figured for every one I killed, I'd get another one to quit," he explained. Thus motivated, Waagner used the Internet to locate abortion clinics, then monitored a police scanner to gather information on the clinic's security. Waagner also surveilled several clinics. As proof, he provided detailed descriptions of clinic staff, buildings, vehicles, and parking lots. The Feminist Majority later verified the accuracy of his research. The effort Waagner put into his research, planning, and preparing clearly showed he had plenty of motive and ability.

He just never quite mustered the intent. Waagner confessed to the newspaper that his "nerve failed him." He further explained, "I would much rather be sitting on death row right now for having succeeded than sitting in some county jail for having failed. It's not that I regret getting caught. It's that I regret getting caught as a failure." He added, "The last thing I expected was that I'd have trouble shooting" abortion doctors, but he never could bring himself to do it. Without the courage of strong intentions, neither motive nor ability can overcome that last hump along the path to intended violence.

SOURCE: "Plot to Kill Doctors and Terrorize Clinics Revealed," Anti-Abortion Violence Watch: Reporting on Domestic Terrorism Against Women's Health Clinics, a publication of the Feminist Majority Foundation's National Clinic Access Project, April 21, 2000, p.1.

Using the Assessment Tools

Any assessment, whether using the tools described in this chapter or others, measures only the current situation. They become outdated almost as soon as the threat manager completes them. Assessments help determine the appropriate protective response, set the course for any protective investigation, and inform which management strategy to adopt. As new evidence and new information develops, the threat manager has to factor that into new assessments. Consequently, threat managers should not view assessments as one-time exercises. Rather, they should be treated as on-going processes forming a continuous re-evaluation of the level of risk and the effectiveness of the protective response and the management strategy.

Summary

In this chapter, we described a number of assessment tools the threat manager can use to determine the level of risk based on the information known at the time of the risk. The assessments boil down to four general questions:

1. What are the Circumstances and Context surrounding the IC&C?
2. What is at stake for the subject making the IC&C?
3. Is the subject acting like a Hunter?

4. Is the subject acting like a Howler?

A number of tools help the threat manager organize the available information and focus in on making the best assessment. The threat manager can then use the assessment for determining the appropriate protective response, course of investigation, and selection of the best or most appropriate threat management strategy.

Reference Notes for Chapter 6

[1] Louisville *Courier-Journal*, June 13, 2000.

[2] Gavin de Becker, *The Gift of Fear*, 93-7.

[3] Thomas Taylor, *Dodging Bullets: A Strategic Guide to World-Class Protection* (Jacksonville, FL: Institute of Police Technology and Management, 1999), 123-30.

CHAPTER SEVEN

Investigating Individuals of Violent Intent

Protective investigations focus on collecting facts concerning the circumstances of the Inappropriate Communication or Contact (IC&C) and what prompted it, the subject, the target's relation to the subject, the subject's past behaviors, and the subject's current behaviors. Threat managers gather information and evidence to inform an accurate and complete assessment of the potential risks and the best way to defuse them. Like the assessments they feed, protective investigations must be grounded in facts. They require an objective, rational approach to the problem at hand: Does the subject pose a risk to the target *at this time?*

Note the emphasis on "at this time." That roots the protective investigation – and the assessment – on past and present issues, not future ones. No one conducting a protective investigation can foresee the future, especially the subject's future behaviors. The future will introduce its own volatile mix of variables in its own time. Predictions are the province of angels and fools. They have no place in protective investigations. These investigations do not entail guessing the future or gazing at Ouija boards or fondling crystal balls or reading palms. They do not rely on intuition or gut feelings or any other intangibles. All the threat manager can reasonably do is assess what has already happened and what is currently known about the subject. Neither the protective investigation nor the threat assessment look beyond the here and now. Rather, it is solely and exclusively about what happened before to get to this situation and how to handle that situation now.

Protective Investigations

Protective investigations use many of the same tactics employed in criminal investigations. However, they concentrate on different areas, ask different questions, and serve different purposes. Both criminal and protective investigations rely on analyzing forensic evidence, discerning motives, interviewing eyewitnesses, interrogating subjects, and monitoring the subject's behaviors. Criminal investigations use the information to prove what the subject has already done – who committed the crime and why. Protective investigations collect information for assessing the level of risk and how best to stave it off through appropriate threat management strategies.

Protective investigations serve two equally important purposes. Both must be addressed. First, they collect or corroborate information the threat manager uses to conduct on-going assessments. Second, protective investigations seek to identify the most effective threat management strategies for successfully defusing any potential risks. In other words, they aim to solve whatever the problem is. Successful protective investigations require achieving both goals. To fail at either exposes the target to potential harm. Because of these dual purposes, protective investigations can be as complex and difficult as any criminal investigation. They require intelligence, finesse, subtlety, diplomacy – and sometimes just plain luck.

This chapter describes a number of areas of inquiry and investigative leads for the threat manager to follow in achieving the first goal of a protective investigation, gathering information to feed the on-going assessments. The next two chapters deal with the second goal, selecting and implementing the most appropriate threat management strategies.

Threat managers stand apart. Many competent criminal investigators fumble protective investigations. Those who focus solely on criminal acts, on finding a *corpus delecti* and a hard trail of physical evidence, do not make good threat managers, however much they may excel at solving crimes. Protective investigations require looking way beyond criminal evidence. They include gathering evidence that shows the subject may not act violently. Threat managers ask such odd-ball questions as:

- What is at stake for the subject?
- Is the subject communicating an intent to act violently to friends or colleagues?
- Are there any positive influences in the subject's life to dissuade him or her from acting violently?
- Does the subject indicate any faith in the future for him or herself?

- Do the subject's behaviors suggest the subject does not intend violence?
- What, if anything, can be done to resolve the subject's issues with the target?
- Does the subject give any indication that his or her issue or grievance can be resolved peacefully and reasonably?

Only by addressing all the evidence and circumstances, positive and negative, can the threat manager accurately assess the situation and select the most appropriate threat management strategies.

Although no set formulae exist for conducting a protective investigation, certain activities should always be done to ensure thoroughness. The initial facts should be deliberately assessed first. Information should always be corroborated and documented. All leads should be exhausted. New assessments should be conducted whenever the threat manager uncovers new information. Appropriate threat management strategies should be brought into play and their effectiveness continuously evaluated. The threat manager should periodically review the status of the case until he or she can confidently inactivate it.

Criminal investigations clear with the arrest and conviction of the perpetrator. Threat management cases do not have such firm resolutions. Threat managers cannot turn from a protective investigation until he or she can articulate why the subject does not pose a risk to the target at this time. That is a challenging standard. Often, it involves essentially proving a negative, always a daunting task. For example, someone makes some sort of IC&C, but takes no other action toward the target. Can the threat manager prove that some emotion – anger or fear – sparked the IC&C, but that emotion has now dissipated? At what point does inactivity translate into no longer posing a risk to the target at this time?

The opposite also occurs. A subject might commit a crime, such as making a direct threat. The arrest and conviction closes the criminal investigation, but not the protective investigation. With the right resources, connections, and initiative, prisoners locked behind bars can still pose a significant risk to the target. In addition, many prisoners eventually get out of prison. Individuals of violent intent often have an inexhaustible supply of patience, frequently because the penal system imposes that patience upon them. In other situations, the subject continues to pose a potential risk, but the threat manager cannot develop sufficient grounds to support an arrest or mental health commitment. In those cases, the threat manager has to establish procedures to monitor the subject over the long term. Threat managers rarely enjoy open and shut cases. Indeed, as we discuss in the last chapter, we avoid the terms "open" and "cleared" when describing the status of threat management cases. Rather, we classify them as active, long-term, chronic or habitual, and inactive. We define these categories in greater detail in the last chapter.

To further complicate the issue, the threat manager will find no two cases quite alike. The threat manager has no standard guide. He or she must assess each case on its own facts and circumstances. The threat manager needs to approach the protective response, protective investigation, and management strategies all as parts of an ever-changing process. During that process, the threat manager deals with events and incidents which he or she must factor into the risk assessment and the evaluation of the strategy's effectiveness. Because each case presents its own unique set of factors and complexities, effective threat management requires treating each case seriously until the threat manager can determine the actual risk, either by proving none exists at this time or by adopting effective management strategies. To do less leaves the target exposed.

Case Study:

Heard It Over the Radio

James G. called the county commissioner's office to complain that the commissioner kept transmitting radio signals into James' head. James wanted the transmissions stopped. He told the receptionist that he was tired of being put off. He intended to "take action" against the commissioner.

The threat manager first ensured the immediate safety of the elected commissioner, then opened a protective investigation. She learned through her contacts that James had called another county agency. He told officials at that agency that he planned to start shooting people because the commissioner, using radio satellites, told him that he, the commissioner, was coming to James' house to kill him.

The threat manager also ran some records checks. She found that a week earlier, James had purchased a handgun. She interviewed James, who readily admitted that he bought the gun to defend himself when the elected commissioner came for him. He added that he would also use the gun to show the commissioner he "meant business." Based on his threats and delusions, the threat manager convinced the state psychiatrists to accept James for observation. She then used the mental health statutes to seize the handgun.

Protective investigations do not solve crimes, they prevent them.

SOURCE: Authors' personal knowledge.

Although threat management cases can erupt suddenly and require an emergency response, threat managers should never conduct protective investigations hastily. Once the threat manager ensures the target's immediate safety, the protective investigation can begin. The threat manager should proceed deliberately, fully pursuing all leads. The case study about the radio transmissions amply illustrates the benefits of proceeding with due deliberation. Doing so allowed the threat manager to find out about the previous contact with the government agency and the purchase of the weapon. These facts then informed her approach to the subject, as well as helped her convince the state psychiatrists to admit James for observation and, ultimately, treatment. Her protective investigation followed a logical course that covered all possible sources of evidence. Making haste may waste the target.

Case Study:

Making Haste

During the Montana Freemen's trial in 1998, an individual approached the heavily guarded courthouse entrance, hesitated, looked around, then quickly departed. An alert security officer reported the suspicious behavior to law enforcement officers. The officers pursued the subject into a restaurant where he had joined another man.

The officers approached the individual and asked for identification and an explanation. Although embarrassed, the subject cooperated. His lunch companion watched with growing resentment. He and the subject were both medical doctors, both were prominent members of the community. Now his friend was being publicly humiliated.

Later that afternoon, the lunch companion called the clerk's office. Without identifying himself, he requested the U.S. Attorney's phone number. The doctor indicated he intended to complain about the security measures set up for the trial, including the incident at the restaurant. Because of the reference to security, the clerk reported the call as an IC&C. He used the telephone's caller ID to get the name.

Law enforcement officers chose to confront the caller before conducting an investigation. They did not fully interview the clerk and therefore did not learn about the subject's reference to the luncheon encounter. That would have led them to the officers who had interviewed the other doctor. Instead, they chose to track down the subject. Unfortunately, other duties prevented them from going to the subject's home until late that evening. Despite the late hour, the officers interrogated the subject about the phone call, accepted his story, and left.

The doctor was not so willing to close the case. Not only had law enforcement officers accosted his friend in a public place, they had now subjected him to a grilling – all because he had made an innocent phone call. The doctor wrote several letters to his senators and congressmen complaining about the "Gestapo-like" tactics of the law enforcement officers. As a result, the officers became the subjects of several congressional inquiries.

Making haste creates more problems than it resolves.

SOURCE: Authors' personal knowledge.

Once the threat manager ensures the target's immediate safety, the need to hurry diminishes considerably. In the case of the impatient Montana law enforcement officers, neither incident required such abrupt responses. After trailing the initial subject into the restaurant, the officers could have avoided embarrassing him by simply asking to speak with him privately. When the clerk reported the phone call, the officers did not get a full report. Had they done so, they would have learned about the lunch incident, which would have led them to the officers who had investigated that. Those officers would have told them that their subject was a well-known doctor in the community and the individual making the call was his associate. That information may well have been enough to assess the situation as no risk.

By rushing into the restaurant and demanding an explanation and, later, going to the second subject's home without getting a complete report from the court clerk, both sets of officers incurred several risks. First, they injected themselves into situations about which they had too little information to determine if they really had a problem and if that problem entailed a danger to any of their targets or themselves. The restaurant interview could have been handled more delicately. The response to the telephone call was worse. Without first trying to gather information about the subject, his issues, and his intentions, the officers had no way to assess the risk to themselves in visiting the second subject at his home. Nor could they develop questions and lines of inquiry to pursue beyond simply asking why he was interested in the security around the courthouse. Even worse, the investigation they failed to conduct only entailed a detailed interview of the court clerk, nothing more than that.

If during the interview the subject lied, the officers had no way to determine that he had. If he chose to withhold information, the officers had no way to notice any gaps. Perhaps more importantly, without some inkling of the subject's motives, the officers chanced escalating the risks by visiting the subject and further arousing his feelings about the security measures for the trial. They paid for their mistake by having to answer several congressional inquiries. Perhaps that taught them that boldness is no antidote to rash behavior.

Since protective investigations require extensive work, we do not recommend activating one for every IC&C. Some IC&Cs are clearly low risk. Resources should not be expended on them once the assessment shows that the threat manager is dealing with a Howler.

For example, determining that a prison inmate sent an inappropriate letter may not need any extensive investigation beyond confirming that he or she remains in prison for an extended time and he or she has no outside support or resources. This can usually be accomplished through a check with the prison authorities. At that point, the threat manager can arrange to have the inmate's outgoing mail screened and ask the prison authorities to notify the threat manager of any change in the prisoner's status. Since protective investigations require extensive work, they should only be initiated when really needed.

Case Study:

Love's Labours Lost

Kevin M. was a petty criminal doing time in a Florida county jail. One day, a group of federal prisoners overnighted in Kevin's jail. Among them, Kevin met the love of his life. The next day, the federal prisoners left.

Kevin decided the only way he could be with his new friend was to get himself transferred to federal prison. That, he decided, required committing a federal crime. Since being incarcerated in a county jail crimped his ability to break a federal law, Kevin did the only thing he could think to do. He began writing threatening letters to federal officials throughout the country. His targets included judges, U.S. Attorneys, deputy marshals, congressmen, and the president.

Rather than waste limited resources investigating each of Kevin's threats, federal law enforcement officers arranged with the sheriff's office to keep informed of Kevin's incarceration. The officers entered each letter into their database, but decided to let Kevin serve out his county sentence, then charge him with making threats. It would be a while before Kevin made it into the federal system.

Not every IC&C requires a comprehensive protective investigation, though once an investigation is opened, it should be as thorough as possible.

SOURCE: Authors' personal knowledge.

The *Intimacy Effect* and Protective Investigations

The *Intimacy Effect* offers a unique benefit for any protective investigation. In cases where target and subject know each other, the target offers a wealth of information and insight about the subject. By extensively interviewing the target, the threat manager can uncover a treasure-trove of details about the subject; what is prompting the IC&C; how the subject handles stress, rejection, bad news, and good news; and how keenly he or she feels about the issues at hand. Intimate partners, co-workers, school chums, even judicial officials have inside knowledge about their partner, troubled co-worker, angry chum, or outraged litigant. They also may have records on the subject, including personal histories, evaluations, previous encounters, and other information shedding light on the subject's motive, intent, and ability.

Cases generated by the *Intimacy Effect* also offer the advantage of measuring exactly what is at stake from the subject's point of view. Attacks on public officials may occasionally involve high-stake geopolitical issues, but most of the time the motives prompting these attacks are, as the Secret Service researchers found, surprisingly banal. Violence spawned by the *Intimacy Effect* often involves fairly high stakes, at least in the view of the subject. Understanding what is at issue for him or her will immeasurably help the threat manager assess the degree of risk. Any insight that can be gained from the potential targets, based on their knowledge and familiarity with the subject, should be exploited very early on in the protective investigation.[1]

Ironically, the *Intimacy Effect* can distort the opinions and beliefs of the target. Because the subject and target had some kind of relationship in the past and the target is now targeted by the subject, the target may entertain unkind feelings and opinions about the subject. For example, an ex-wife may exaggerate the risk posed by her ex-husband. A supervisor may feel too embarrassed to admit his or her own fears about a subordinate. Even intimates not targeted by the subject can misrepresent the situation. A mother, for example, may refuse to recognize her son's potential for violence. Consequently, though the *Intimacy Effect* offers the threat manager an abundance of information, the threat manager should carefully distinguish between the facts presented by the intimate and the opinions expressed by that individual.

Case Study:

Parental Support

While waiting at the school bus stop, William Charles Cyrus, 16, and David Hicks, 15, began arguing. The argument continued as they boarded the bus, then escalated into a fistfight. When the bus reached Little Rock Hall High School, Hicks started climbing down the bus steps. Cyrus pulled a .22 caliber pistol and shot Hicks in the back.

Panicked, Cyrus fled home. When officers arrived to arrest him, they could not convince his mother and stepfather that he had done anything wrong, much less shot another student. The parents cursed the police, then physically tried to prevent them from taking Cyrus into custody. According to a police spokesman, the parents "created quite a problem for the officers." The police ended up arresting Cyrus for the shooting and his mother and stepfather for disorderly conduct and hindering apprehension.

Threat managers cannot assume that any individuals familiar with a subject under investigation will support or assist that investigation.

SOURCE: United Press International, February 10, 1981

Conducting Protective Investigations

Threat managers must first plot out the protective investigation in a precise, orderly manner. The protective investigation must proceed systematically to ensure that it addresses all potential sources of information, with all leads pursued in depth. We prefer to conceptualize the process of the investigation much like the rippling effects of a stone tossed into still waters. The waves of the investigation ripple outward in concentric circles. The threat manager should begin the investigation by looking for evidence close in to where the IC&C was received, then expand outward looking for other sources of information. Each circle builds upon the previous ones until all areas of inquiry are thoroughly exhausted. The analogy to a circle serves, too, as a useful reminder to avoid myopic, single-focused investigations. Everything should be checked, all leads thoroughly pursued, and all directions covered.

Protective investigations are not criminal investigations culminating in an arrest once sufficient evidence to support the charges has been developed. Protective investigations end, if and only when, the risk to the target has been defused. Even then, that might be but a temporary respite. The threat manager must be prepared to re-address the case at any point in the future if the subject communicates with the target or begins showing renewed interest in acting out violently.

Since other events in the subject's life and circumstances can further enhance the risk, the threat manager has to inquire into everything going on with the subject. Individuals who find themselves in stressful situations often act violently. It relieves the pressure. Falling inhibitors can start knocking other inhibitors down, thus escalating the strains on the subject and making the need for relief more pressing. Unless the threat manager identifies all the problems, he or she cannot accurately assess the risk. Nor can the most appropriate threat management strategy be selected. Only by covering all aspects of the situation can the threat manager accurately and confidently assess and defuse the potential risk.

Case Study:

The Trigger

Ronald Taylor, 41, only wanted his apartment door fixed. Unemployed, he lived off disability checks resulting from a mental illness. His symptoms included the delusion that whites persecuted him because he was Black.

On Friday, March 1, 2000, Taylor called the building manager to complain about the door, but nobody responded to his complaint. Sometime later, he called again, leaving a "profanity-laced tirade" on her answering machine.

Unbeknownst to Taylor, the manager had already assigned

two maintenance workers – both white – to check out the door. Shortly after Taylor left his vulgar message, the two workers arrived at his apartment. But the wait and seeming lack of responsiveness had already sent Taylor over the edge. He greeted the two men by attacking one of them. When the second worker intervened, Taylor shot him in the chest.

Taylor then went on a rampage through the area in Pittsburgh, Pennsylvania, where he lived. He went first to a nearby Burger King where he killed a 71-year old. At a nearby McDonald's, he shot to death one man sitting in a car and critically wounded another man sitting in a van. When the restaurant's assistant manager came out to investigate the ruckus, Taylor shot him.

In all, Taylor killed three and wounded two, all of them white.

Even seemingly innocuous or routine events, such as a broken front door, can trigger long-smoldering and completely unrelated feelings that then erupt into violent acts.

SOURCE: Associated Press, November 1, 2001.

First Circle: Examining the Circumstances and Context

Protective investigations open with the receipt of an IC&C or some other event or situation indicating that the subject may be thinking about violence. The threat manager should first carefully analyze the circumstances and context of the IC&C. Next, the threat manager should interview the individual who received or noticed the IC&C carefully and thoroughly. The target, the target's staff, and, if warranted, the target's family should also be fully questioned. The threat manager should not restrict the questions to the circumstances of the IC&C, but should also branch out into what the individual knows and thinks about the subject and the situation. The threat manager should also determine if anything unusual, suspicious, or untoward has recently come to anyone's notice. If the IC&C was made anonymously, the threat manager should sound out the recipient and target for their suspicions as to the identity of the subject. Obviously, cases infused with the Intimacy Effect will generate more information than cases involving public figures who do not know the subject sending the IC&C. Nonetheless, important clues can be uncovered by inquiring into the circumstances and context of how the IC&C was delivered, where it was delivered, and when it was delivered.

At this point, the investigation reaches a branch. If the subject is known or identified, the investigation goes in one direction. If the subject is unknown, then the investigation has to focus on finding out who committed the IC&C. Identifying the subject relies on the same techniques as identifying a criminal and need not detain us here. It depends on fairly standard investigative procedures. Once the threat manager identifies the subject, the investigation should move to the second ripple.

Second Circle: Establishing Content and Motive

Written, telephonic, and informant IC&Cs contain language that the threat manager can analyze for such important evidence as the subject's motive, expressed intent, and understanding of his or her ability to take future actions. Often, these communications contain lots of bluff and bluster. The threat manager needs to take care not to take the subject to literally, but to analyze and understand what prompted the IC&C and what the subject hoped to accomplish by it.

Why is the subject making the IC&C?

Potential Leads:

The threat manager should carefully determine all the facts related to the IC&C, including its content, if any, its delivery, to whom it was directed, and the timing of the delivery (in other words, why now?). Did the subject ask for anything? Does the IC&C seem more designed to cause an emotional reaction, such as fear or anger? Did the subject take care with the IC&C, organizing its contents thoughtfully so that the recipient could clearly understand the content. Or did the subject rush to get some message out that comes across incoherently or jumbled? If written, how so? Did the subject use handwriting, typing, or cutting and pasting from a printed source? If telephoned, did the subject use a phone number easily obtained or did getting the number require some effort or research?

Does the subject seem to believe that any action of the potential target threatens the subject's inhibitors?

Potential Leads:

Often, the subject feels prompted to act inappropriately because he or she fears some action of the target will be detrimental to him or her. Employees who fear being fired may respond with threats or threatening actions. Domestic partners going through a separation may likewise react threateningly. Delusional subjects may believe a public figure controls them, or aliens want the public figure assassinated. Whether real or delusional, what the subject believes is happening, especially any beliefs that what is happening is detrimental to his or her interests, are powerful motivators. It is crucial to both the threat assessment and the protective investigation for the threat manager to make a conscious effort to understand the situation from the subject's point of view. It is that viewpoint that will ultimately determine if violence is the answer.

Did the subject provide any facts or information that can be corroborated?

Potential Leads:

For assessment purposes, the threat manager should accept any claim made by the subject. Protective investigations, however, require a healthy skepticism and corroboration of the claims. Verifying what the subject says can lead to other information about the subject. It also gives a measure of the subject's veracity, tendencies to exaggerate, dishonesty, or delusional thought patterns.

Case Study:

Blowing the Whistle

"My death is on your hands," Robert Pickett wrote in a letter to his hometown newspaper, the Evansville (Indiana) Courier and Press on February 2, 2001. Pickett, who worked for the Internal Revenue Service, had applied to the federal courts for whistleblower status. The court rejected the lawsuit.

Throughout the letter, Pickett dropped numerous clues of

an intention to commit a violent act, including his suicide. He referred to himself as already dead, the "victim of a corrupt government." He claimed a mental illness resulting from his situation. "To protect themselves, these bureaucrats deliberately took improper actions which aggravated my mental illness," Pickett charged, "This torture caused me great mental anguish, including two suicide attempts and several hospitalizations." He concluded the letter chillingly: "I would rather not continue with life since I will only be subjected to further persecution."

On February 7, 2001, Pickett fired two shots into the White House compound. When police and Secret Service officers approached, he turned his pistol on them. One uniformed Secret Service officer shot him in the leg. Other officers took him into custody. Police negotiators concluded that he intended to die, either by his own hand or suicide-by-cop.

Frequently, what subjects say in their IC&Cs give threat managers plenty of information about their mental state, intentions about violence, causes of their grievance, and intensity of their feelings. The subjects just may not take the next step and tell what they plan to do about it.

SOURCE: Washington Post, February 8, 2001.

Re-Assess

Once these areas of investigative focus and investigative leads have been exhausted, the threat manager should conduct another set of assessments using the same procedures described in the previous chapter. Where is the subject on the path to intended violence? What do the Circumstances and Context (Cir-Con) Factors indicate? Have the stakes changed? Has the Justification, Alternatives, Consequences, and Ability (JACA) scale changed? Is the subject acting like a Hunter? Is the subject acting like a Howler? Does the reassessment indicate a change in the potential risk? Has the protective investigation uncovered any risk-enhancing factors thus far? Has the protective investigation uncovered any risk-reducing factors thus far?

Third Circle: Getting Information on the Subject

Once the threat manager identifies the subject, the threat manager needs to compile a definitive biography on the subject. The threat manager can get information to put this together from any number of sources, including information from the target, the subject's criminal or mental health history, job record, school record, law enforcement records, public data bases, or individuals who know the subject. The investigation should not focus solely on the subject's relationship with the target or any issues referred to in the IC&C. Rather, the investigation must seek out any information about the subject that might throw light on the potential for violence.

Is there anything in the subject's background suggesting a propensity for violence or explosive behavior?

Potential Leads:

This obviously includes such events as arrests, but should also take into account any interest in, or familiarity with, weapons, domestic relations, family history, employment record, military experience, youthful experiences, previous victimizations, or previous run-ins with law enforcement.

The threat manager should check the records of the National Crime Information Center (NCIC), as well as with the local police and sheriff's office where the subject lives and works. Local police records should also be checked to see if the police have ever been called out to the subject's home or neighborhood. If the subject does have a criminal history, the threat manager should review the police files carefully to determine the circumstances, provocation, and type or extent of the violence during the incident. In particular, the threat manager should find out what happened, how it happened, and, if possible, why it happened. Arrest records should not be accepted at face value. Oftentimes, the details of the case tell a wholly different story from the recorded charges.

In addition, the threat manager should check into any alcohol or drug abuse by the subject. If the subject is on parole or probation, his status and behavior while under supervision should be checked.

In checking these sources, the threat manager should always keep in mind that the absence of a criminal record, lack of any documented mental health history, or no record of treatment for alcohol or substance abuse does not mean the risk from this subject is diminished. In many cases, the subject's first crime or first noticeable symptom of mental illness is the violent assault on the target. Consequently, finding evidence of criminal or mental health records tells the threat manager a lot, but not finding such information does little by way of informing the assessment.

Case Study:

The Provoked Fisherman

A threat manager investigating a company employee who told his supervisor, "Watch your back around me," learned from the National Crime Information Center that the subject had been arrested some years earlier for assault with a deadly weapon. On its face, such a record disturbed the threat manager since it seemed to increase the potential risk in the current case based on the principle that past behaviors are the best indicators of future behavior.

But the threat manager knew to dig deeper and look at the circumstances of the previous case, especially any provocations or extenuations. From the investigative files, the threat manager learned that at the time of the arrest, the subject was going through some stressful work problems compounded by messy divorce proceedings. That day, he decided to put his troubles aside and go fishing. As he cast along the banks of the Sacramento River, two river bums approached. One of the bums pulled a knife on the fisherman while the other began to steal the fishing gear. The fisherman wrested the knife away, then pressed it to the bum's throat and ordered the second bum to flee. Once he was gone, the fisherman released the first bum. The two men pressed assault charges, but the investigation cleared the fisherman.

The threat manager learned from the circumstances of the previous case that the subject reacted to stress appropriately by engaging in activities that relieved it. Further, although highly provoked, the fisherman also used the minimum force necessary to extricate himself from a dangerous situation. Based on the principle that past behaviors best indicate future behavior, the threat manager assessed the arrest for assault with a deadly weapon as a risk-decreasing factor in the current case.

Previous resorts to violence need always to be examined for their circumstances, provocations, and extenuations.

SOURCE: Authors' personal knowledge.

What is the subject's current situation?

Potential Leads:

Many IC&Cs to public figures and former intimates come from prisoners or patients confined to mental hospitals. Threat managers have a far easier time controlling incarcerated or committed subjects than those who can move about freely. It is a simple question, often overlooked, but the threat manager should ask, "Is the subject in prison or jail or in a mental health facility? If so, for how long?"

Case Study:

The Paranoid Attack

A criminal-history check of a subject under assessment showed an arrest for assault. However, the charges were dropped. Although this appeared to be only a minor entry on the subject's criminal history, the threat manager sought out the details of the incident.

The threat manager learned that the subject, without provocation, attacked a person on the street. The subject accused the person of following him and trying to kill him. The charges were later dropped after the subject agreed to seek psychiatric counseling.

From this information, the threat manager learned that she was dealing with a subject who suffered paranoid delusions. Further, while in this mental state, the subject acted out violently by physically attacking another person.

This information proved very relevant for evaluating the subject's potential for violence.

Threat managers should never take criminal history checks at face value.

SOURCE: Authors' personal knowledge.

What is the subject's current mental health condition?

Potential Leads:

How does the subject present him or herself in the IC&C? What is the subject saying and how is he or she acting? Is there evidence of delusional or paranoid behavior? Is there evidence of command hallucinations such as the subject acting out orders? If the subject has been prescribed medication, is he or she taking it? If the subject is under mental health treatment, is he or she attending sessions with the doctor?

Does the subject own or have an interest in weapons?

Potential Leads:

Are any weapons registered to the subject? Did the subject ever own a weapon in the past? Is there evidence of any interest or fascination with weapons, not just firearms, but knives, swords, and explosives as well? Does the IC&C refer to or mention weapons?

Has the subject recently purchased a weapon? Has he or she sought to obtain a weapon from friends or family members? Has the subject made any comments associating weapons with the target?

What inhibitors currently exist in the subject's life?

Potential Leads:

This includes finding out about the subject's living arrangements, emotional involvements, immediate and extended family ties, employment, employment history, finances, physical and mental health, religious interests, real and personal property, reputation, and self-esteem.

Does the subject perceive any of those inhibitors toppling or in danger?

Potential Leads:

In addressing the possibility of a subject's inhibitors toppling, the threat manager needs to evaluate the reality of that possibility and the subject's perception of that reality. If the subject perceives a loss of inhibitors for any reason, that perception may be enough to influence his or her behavior. The threat manager should look for any recent significant changes or disruptions in the subject's life, such as unemployment or marital breakup.

Has the subject suffered some recent loss?

Potential Leads:

Has the subject had a recent death in the family? Has there been any recent job loss or change in employment status? Has the subject been arrested or charged with any crime? Has there been a divorce, change in child custody, loss of visitation rights, or change in living arrangements? Has anything happened to cause the subject embarrassment or loss of dignity?

Has the subject engaged in any final act behaviors?

Potential Leads:

Has the subject recently made out a will? Has he or she made any final statements or begun giving possessions away? Has the subject added another individual to a bank account, house title, or other property or possession?

Has the subject engaged in any attack-related behaviors?

With the path to intended violence in mind, can the threat manager identify any behaviors taken by the subject that might indicate that the subject has stepped out along the path? Has the subject engaged in research behaviors or planning activities or made preparations for an attack?

What are the subject's issues that prompted the IC&C?

Potential Leads:

The threat manager needs to collect evidence on what is motivating the subject to make the IC&C and to focus on this particular target. Often, this determination can be simple. Subjects losing a domestic partner focus their wrath on that partner. Employees fired from a job or facing disciplinary action retaliate against their supervisors and co-workers. But not all cases have an easily identifiable motive. Paranoid schizophrenics and subjects suffering delusions may not have a readily recognizable or rational motive. The threat manager needs to approach this issue with imagination.

How does the subject interact with other people?

Potential Leads:

The threat manager should try to determine how the subject deals with his or her spouse, neighbors, fellow workers, and others. However, in taking this step, the threat manager should exercise great care and caution. Contacting neighbors, family members, or fellow workers always risks someone telling the subject of the threat manager's interest in him or her and the nature of the questions the threat manager asked. Consequently, not only may the subject find out about the protective investigation, but the subject may also get some insight into what the threat manager knows and wants to know.

Although much valuable information can be developed from these sources, contacting them can further outrage the subject if handled indelicately. As a general rule, contacting neighbors, co-workers, fellow students, associates, or friends should only be done in those cases the threat manager has already assessed as high risk or when the threat manager feels confident that the person contacted will not betray the contact to the subject.

If the threat manager contacts neighbors, fellow workers, or others who know the subject, the threat manager should use the occasion to get as much information on the subject as possible. This includes asking about the subject's current situation and what prompted the IC&C. The threat manager should also broach such questions as:

- How does the subject react to adversity?
- Has the subject ever talked about violence or made references to it?
- Does the subject own weapons or seem fixated with them?
- Is the subject mentally and physically capable of planning and carrying out an act of violence?
- Does the subject seem to be experiencing a recent loss or some feeling of desperation?
- Are the family members or neighbors concerned about the subject's propensity toward violence?
- Are there inhibitors or disinhibitors in the subject's life?
- Does the subject talk about the future positively or ominously?

Re-Assess

Once those areas of inquiry and investigative leads have been exhausted, the threat manager should conduct another set of assessments using the same procedures described in the previous chapter. Where is the subject on the path to intended violence? What do the Cir-Con Factors indicate? Have the stakes changed? Has the JACA scale changed? Is the subject acting like a Hunter? Is the subject acting like a Howler? Does the reassessment indicate a change in the potential risk? Has the protective investigation uncovered any risk-enhancing factors thus far? Has the protective investigation uncovered any risk-reducing factors thus far? Should the case be classified active, inactive, habitual, or long-term?

Fourth Circle: Interviewing the Subject

As delicate as interviewing neighbors, family members, colleagues, and associates can be, their delicacy pales in comparison with the risks entailed during a subject interview. Interviewing the subject carries the same risks as interviewing others who know the subject. The subject will learn of the threat manager's interest in him or her. And the subject will learn something about what the threat manager knows and wants to know about the subject.

But two additional factors further complicate the risk. First, the interview combines into a hybrid mix the protective investigation with threat management. The interview collects information to improve the threat assessment. It also lets the threat manager exploit opportunities for defusing the risk. During the course of the interview, the threat manager may find a chance to refocus the subject or offer him or her assistance with a problem. An opportunity may arise allowing the threat manager to confront the subject, either with an explicit warning or a more active response, such as arrest or mental health commitment.

Second, interviews by definition are fluid. They resist by-the-book directions because they are so situation dependent. The face-to-face interplay between the threat manager and the subject controls the course of the interview. How the interview progresses depends entirely on how the subject and the threat manager react to each other and to the circumstances surrounding the interview. Managing how the interview progresses requires the threat manager to take the time prior to the interview to identify his or her goals and to keep alert to those goals throughout the interview. At the same time, the threat manager needs to retain enough flexibility during the interview to change goals as opportunities arise. In sum, threat managers should view subject interviews as contradictory beasts, belonging both to the protective investigation and to the application of threat management strategies.

All of this is simply to say that subject interviews require preparation and forethought going in, but flexibility and innovation throughout. They present an opportunity to achieve any of the following goals:

- Gather information from the subject to add to the assessment;
- Explore ways to stop the subject's problematic behavior;
- Confront the subject by explaining why his or her behavior is a problem and then warn the subject of the potential consequences of continuing the problem behavior;
- Obtain evidence of criminal behavior, especially an admission of guilt.

The threat manager's approach to the interview should match both the goals set for the interview and the priority of those goals. For example, if the goal is to gain information and then find a method to stop a subject's problematic behavior, then the initial approach should be friendly, non-confrontational, and designed to establish a rapport with the subject. Once all relevant information is obtained, the threat manager can shift the tone of the interview to a confrontational approach, if the situation requires it.

Advantages of Subject Interviews

Subject interviews provide the best direct source of information about the subject, his or her concerns, and his or her intentions. They also offer the best opportunity to explore ways of stopping the problem behaviors. Simply by listening carefully and empathetically, the threat manager can encourage the subject to feel that someone in a position of authority or influence has listened to his or her problems or concerns. Such feelings can help defuse the subject's anger or emotions and thus lessen the risk. Subject interviews also lend themselves to those cases in which a direct confrontation with the subject may defuse the risk.

Disadvantages of Subject Interviews

Subject interviews entail their own risks. Since the interview brings the subject and threat manager face to face, the potential risk of physical danger is high. Interviews also always carry the potential of further angering the subject or convincing him or her to go underground or flee. They expose the threat manager and his or her agency to potential complaints or lawsuits. In certain cases, interviews help the subject initiate a mind game or war with the threat manager since he or she will have the threat manager's contact information.

When to Interview

As a general rule, an interview is usually required when the threat manager needs to find ways to stop the subject's problematic behaviors, but the subject has yet to commit a crime. We also recommend subject interviews when the content of the inappropriate communication is ambiguous or confusing. In addition, the threat manager should delay interviewing the subject until he or she has completed the other areas of investigative interest. Threat managers will find it counterproductive to interview a subject before the threat manager has collected as much information about the IC&C and the subject as possible.

When Not to Interview

The threat manager should probably not attempt an interview when the subject's behavior suggests that he or she would not respond to an approach. For example, attempting to interview extreme anti-government ideologues probably risks worsening the situation more than improving it. Threat managers should discourage subject interviews when the subject's behavior is not clearly inappropriate and law enforcement attention on the subject cannot be justified. Subject interviews should also be avoided or postponed if the threat manager determines that letting the subject know about law enforcement's interest in him or her would escalate the risk. This is especially counterproductive when the protective investigation has uncovered evidence of a crime and the threat manager is putting together a prosecution package.

We discuss here first the pros and cons of using the subject interview as part of the protective investigation. In the next two chapters, we explore the pros and cons of the subject interview as a venue for deploying two different management strategies: *Refocus or Assist* and *Warning or Confront.* Each aspect of subject interviews has its own advantages and disadvantages, its own determinants of when or when not to use each.

Subject Interview for Information Gathering

Threat managers have only one clear rule about interviewing the subject of a protective investigation: Never conduct the interview without a partner. Other than that, the decisions about whether, when, and where derive from the circumstances of the case. Sometimes, the subject's behaviors give the threat manager little or no choice but to talk to him or her. If, for example, the subject appears at some location near the target, the threat manager will need to conduct an interview. Any time law enforcement officers detain or arrest a subject, then an interview becomes necessary. In those situations when the threat manager has little time to prepare prior to the interview, the threat manager should – at a bare minimum – try to find out five fundamental pieces of information about the subject:

- past criminal history, especially any previous violence;
- past mental health commitments, again especially if violence was involved;
- any firearms registered to the subject;
- accurate and complete details of the subject's behavior that brought him or her to the threat manager's attention;
- any previous IC&Cs.

This information will allow the threat manager to develop an effective interview strategy and devise appropriate tactics for officer safety.

However, threat managers will rarely find themselves in situations requiring an immediate interview. Usually, the threat manager can proceed deliberately and methodically in preparing to talk to the subject of a protective investigation. In most cases, the threat manager enjoys the great advantage of choosing whether, when, and where to sit down with the subject to discuss his or her inappropriate behaviors, grievances, and issues. We strongly recommend that the threat manager exploit that advantage by fully preparing.

All subject interviews for information gathering share one central goal. The threat manager seeks to gain as much information as possible from the subject. And not just what the subject may reveal about his or her involvement in the IC&C under investigation. The threat manager should also probe the subject about his or her current situation, life experiences, outlook on the future, recent experiences, living arrangements, finances, employment, mental competency, issues, grievances, and feelings about the target. Any information gleaned from the interview should then be factored into a new threat assessment to produce a fresh understanding of how much of a risk the subject poses at the time of the new assessment. The threat manager can then use the new assessment and the information gained from the interview to intelligently choose the most appropriate threat management strategy.

Because the threat manager wants to get the subject talking fully and frankly, subject interviews for information gathering differ considerably from interviews conducted during a criminal investigation. During the latter, police officers usually take on a tough, accusatory demeanor in an effort to pressure and discomfit the suspect. Subject interviews for information gathering seek to draw the subject out, to get him or her talking about him or herself, situation, circumstances, emotions, desires, and intentions. Taking a tough approach or starting with accusations will produce a defensive response from the subject. The threat manager will get little or no useful or relevant information.

Consequently, the threat manager should do everything possible to make the subject feel comfortable and at ease. The threat manager should act sympathetically and appear eager to listen to anything the subject wants to say. Often, threat managers will find that these subjects have been waiting for someone to whom they can complain and unburden themselves of all their troubles. Because they have a grievance, they need someone with whom to grieve. By appearing to sympathize, the threat manager invites the subject to tell his or her side, to unload all and every gripe. This approach frequently results in the subject gushing out all his or her self-justifications, complaints, injustices, slights, and wrongs. Since they now finally have someone to talk to, oftentimes talk they will.

We recommend the following five rules of etiquette when interviewing subjects for information gathering.

1. Dress and Act Non-Threatening

As part of the confidence building, both threat managers should dress in plainclothes and approach the subject without any overt display of power or force. If the situation requires backup, other officers should remain close but out of the subject's sight. Informing the subject of the purpose of the interview is neither necessary nor in many cases a wise strategy. Simply explaining that the threat manager merely wants to talk about any problems the subject may have often suffices. In that way, the subject may see the threat manager as someone who can help with a problem rather than as a law enforcement officer enforcing the law.

2. Mind Your Manners

The threat managers should treat the subject with deference, courtesy, and respect. Since most IC&Cs do not violate any law, the threat managers should avoid treating the subject like a criminal or even someone under suspicion of a criminal violation. After all, in most protective investigations, the threat manager merely suspects the subject of some potential risk. He or she will have little definite information and the suspicions could turn out to be unfounded or misdirected. The threat managers should listen not only carefully, but also patiently. The threat manager shuld let the subject talk freely as long as he or she wants. To avoid rambling discussions, the interviewer should use questions to guide the subject back to the topic at hand. But let the subject carry the burden of the conversation. Only from what he or she says will the threat manager obtain the information necessary to assess the potential risks.

3. Do not Overreact

The threat managers should not be surprised or put off by outbursts of anger or frustration, provided they do not escalate toward violence. Letting a subject blow off steam – and feel that he or she has expressed pent-up anger and frustration to someone in authority – can often help resolve the issues prompting the IC&C. Simply having someone listen can dissipate the anger. Frequently, too, such eruptions provide the threat manager the opportunity to suggest appropriate ways for the subject to deal with or address the problems or grievances.

4. Keep on Track

Keeping to a reasonably strict chronology of the case will structure the interview. It provides the threat manager a better opportunity to compare the facts uncovered during the protective investigation with the facts as described by the subject. One of the best ways to get the interview going is simply to ask the subject to start at the point when his or her problems or issues began. One of the best ways to keep the interview going is to ask, "Then what happened?"

5. Save the Emotions for Last

The interviewer should avoid asking about the subject's feelings until some rapport or comfort level has been established. Feelings are volatile – asking about them is equally volatile and intrusive. But at some later point, asking about them is crucial to understanding the subject's perspective. Begin the interview with questions about the facts and events. As the subject responds and grows more comfortable answering questions, the threat manager can shift to questions probing how the facts and events made the subject feel and how the subject reacted to them. Finally, the threat manager can guide the interview toward future-oriented questions such as asking the subject how he or she expects the issues to be resolved. What would the subject like to see happen? How does the subject expect that to happen? What does the subject intend to do next?

At all events, the threat manager should avoid any confrontational-style demeanor when using the interview to gather information. Confrontation, as we will discuss in Chapter 9, can in certain circumstances be an effective management strategy, but it is counterproductive when the interview is being used during the information-gathering phase as part of the protective investigation.

Case Study:

The Chatty Bankruptee – 1

Although C.F. filed for bankruptcy in New England, she never accepted the fact that she had lost her wealth and position in high society. She blamed the judge for closing her business and taking away her two houses, her boats, and her cars. Over several years, she wrote her congressional representatives and the president complaining about the judge. However, the U.S. Marshals Service did not open a threat management case on C.F. until she wrote the judge accusing him of murdering her family and causing her mental health problems. C.F. also indicated that she had researched the judge's personal life.

After thoroughly reviewing the case files and interviewing the judge, court clerk, and C.F.'s two former attorneys, the threat managers set an appointment with her, explaining only that they wanted to discuss her case with her. Prior to the appointment, the threat managers consulted with a forensic psychologist on the best way to approach her. The psychologist explained that C.F. would see their visit as an opportunity to enlist official help. He predicted that she would be up all night writing out a chronology of her case and all her troubles. She would have voluminous records to show them. She would, he predicted, barely let the threat managers introduce themselves before embarking on a monologue. But don't worry, the psychologist assured them, most people run out of steam after about 20 minutes. Then the threat managers could ask their questions.

After the interview, the threat managers congratulated the psychologist on his prescience. C.F. had stayed up all night preparing a handwritten, 15-page chronology of her case. She brought out a large box containing her case files. From the interview, the threat managers determined that C.F. did not pose a physical threat to the judge, but would no doubt continue her campaign to expose what she perceived as the injustices done to her.

But, the threat managers chided the psychologist, he was wrong about one thing. C.F. went way beyond 20 minutes. "Oh, I figured that," he replied, "I just didn't want to discourage you."

Often, those who feel they have a grievance toward a target simply need someone in authority to listen to their troubles. The threat manager learns by listening.

SOURCE: United States Marshals Service, National Sheriffs Association training seminar, Newark, NJ, January 20, 2000.

Advantages of Subject Interviews for Information Gathering

Subject interviews for information gathering offer the best opportunity available to the threat manager to find out the facts and circumstances of the case from the subject's point of view. Beyond getting the subject's perception of the events of the case, subject interviews also give an opportunity for the threat manager to learn other information about the subject. Exhibit 7-1, developed by the Special Investigations Unit of the California Highway Patrol, provides a list of questions and topics the threat manager should keep in mind. Notice that these questions do not focus on the specifics of the case, but on the physical, emotional, and mental state of the subject.

Exhibit 7-1

ASSESSMENT WORKSHEET

NAME (Last, First, Middle)

AKA, MAIDEN, FORMER MARRIED

CASE NUMBER

TELEPHONE NUMBER

SSN _________ DATE __/__/____ TIME __:__ INTERVIEW CONDUCTED

AGE _ DOB __/__/____ HEIGHT _'__" WEIGHT ___ EYES

___HAIR ___ FACIAL HAIR __

STREET ADDRESS ____________ CITY _______ STATE __ ZIP CODE _______

HOW LONG? LAST ADDRESS

1. MARITAL STATUS: MARRIED DIVORCED SEPARATED SINGLE SPOUSE'S NAME NAMES AGES OF CHILDREN
2. PRESENT CONDITION: LAST SLEPT (when, how long) EAT/ DRINK
3. HEALTH ISSUES: UNDER DOCTOR'S CARE YES NO DOCTOR'S NAME PHONE DISEASES MEDICATIONS TAKEN (what, when, why)
4. WHO TO CONTACT FRIENDS/FAMILY (address, phone)
5. EMPLOYMENT: COMPANY TITLE / DUTIES TELEPHONE ADDRESS SALARY HOW LONG?
6. FINANCES: WELFARE SSI SDI CASE WORKER/ PHONE NUMBER
7. EDUCATION: DEGREES OBTAINED: GED TRADE AA BA MA PHD HIGHEST GRADE LAST SCHOOL ATTENDED
8. TRAVEL: VACATION EMPLOYMENT TARGETED
9. VEHICLES: COLOR YEAR MAKE BODY LICENSE
10. NEIGHBORS: GOOD REPORTS; QUIET FEW VISITORS; NORMAL CONTACT; DISRUPTVE; UNCOOPERATIVE; ASSAULTIVE/INTIMIDATING
11. MILITARY: BRANCH RANK DATE IN DATE OUT SPECIALTY
12. SKILLS/ HOBBIES:
13. PERSONAL GOALS: SHORT TERM LONG TERM
14. WEAPONS POSSESSION: DIRECT ACCESS/ INTEREST LEGITIMATE USE FASCINATION RECENT ACQUISITION

15. ALCOHOL/ DRUGS: WHAT? HOW MUCH? WHEN? ANY TREATMENT PROGRAMS (Where, How often)
16. PURPOSE: PURPOSE FOR LATEST CONTACT WITH TARGET
17. PRIOR/OTHER CONTACTS: PRIOR CONTACTS, ATTEMPTED CONTACTS, MULTI-MEDIA, STALKING, CONTACT WITH OTHER PUBLIC FIGURES, ETC.
18. TARGET KNOWLEDGE RESEARCH?
19. DIARY / JOURNAL: YES/ NO
20. THREAT: WOULD YOU CONSIDER YOURSELF A THREAT
21. CRIMINAL RECORD: (When, agency, crime, disposition, jail, prison, etc.) DECEPTIVE RESPONSE
22. PAROLE: PAROLE OR PROBATIONS: YES? NO? CONTACT PERSON:
23. PSYCHIATRIC TREATMENT: DISTANT PAST FREQUENT/ RECENT INVOLUNTARY / COURT ORDERED DOCTOR'S NAME PHONE MEDICATION
24. KEY DATES: BIRTHDAY / ANNIVERSARY TRAGEDIES / ETC.
25. SUICIDAL THOUGHTS: SUICIDAL THOUGHTS OR ATTEMPTS?
26. HOMICIDAL THOUGHTS OR ATTEMPTS?
27. ASSASSINS/ VIOLENCE IDENTIFICATION WITH ASSASSINS OR NOTORIOUS VIOLENT ACTS?
28. ACTUAL PROBLEM SUBJECT WANTS HANDLED BY TARGET

Case Study:

The Naked Nazi

After reviewing several bizarre letters containing violent references from a subject to a government official, the threat manager opened a protective investigation. After exhausting all investigative leads, the threat manager decided to interview the subject at the subject's residence.

The threat manager and his partner found the subject in a one-room apartment in a downtown flea-bag hotel. The subject had decorated the walls with enough pictures of Nazis to cover the wallpaper. On closer inspection, the threat manager saw that the subject had interspersed pictures of himself naked among the photographs.

Conducting subject interviews at the subject's residence will give the threat manager clues as to the subject's mental state; personal interests; tastes in books, magazines, and movie videos; newspaper clippings; financial resources; and personal hygene.

SOURCE: Authors' personal knowledge.

Disadvantages of Subject Interviews for Information Gathering

Although much valuable information can be gleaned from a subject interview, it can also be dangerous for several reasons. It can pose a physical risk to the threat manager and the subject. Further, it risks escalating the problem by offending or provoking the suspect. Since protective investigations frequently entail no crimes, the subject may feel the threat investigator has no call to even investigate, much less conduct an interview. Consequently, and excepting those cases in which the subject's behavior compels an interview, the decision to contact the subject should not be made automatically or as a matter of course. The threat manager should base the decision on a careful deliberation weighing the specifics of the case, what might be gained by the interview, and what might be lost.

When to Conduct Subject Interviews for Information Gathering

When the threat manager controls the decision to interview, it should only be made after the threat manager has all the information he or she can possibly get about the case and the subject. This allows the threat manager to then weigh the pros and cons of approaching the subject. If the threat manager decides to talk to the subject, having all the available information can help determine the style, tone, and course of the interview. Being cognizant of all the issues troubling the subject will also help the threat manager establish a rapport with the subject, thus opening the way to gaining more information from the interview. It also provides the necessary facts against which to measure the subject's veracity.

Too often, threat managers rush into the interviews without being properly prepared. The threat manager must ensure that he or she knows everything available about the subject, the subject's issues, and the circumstances and context of the IC&C. Only then can the threat manager confidently guide the interview and assess the subject's responses.

Yet, even given all the caveats and potential risks, unless the threat manager has a persuasive reason for not conducting an interview, then in most cases the threat manager should go ahead with it. Simply too much can be learned and observed to pass over the opportunity lightly. The answer to the *whether* question, then, depends on the threat manager's confidence that what will be gained from the interview outweighs any risk of exacerbating the situation. In the majority of cases, the scales tip toward gaining the information.

Case Study:

Getting Some Papers

A subject began a letter-writing campaign to several government officials detailing his paranoid delusional belief that they intended to kill him. Prior to approaching him for an interview, the threat manager made a number of checks into the subject's background. Firearms records showed the subject had recently purchased a semi-automatic handgun.

The threat manager and his partner decided to contact the subject at his residence. They also arranged for uniformed backup nearby, but hidden from the subject's view. After introductions were made at the front entranceway, the subject became visibly agitated. He turned from the door, mumbling something about getting some papers to show the threat managers. Conscious of the recent purchase, the threat managers stopped the subject before he reached the master bedroom. A quick look revealed a fully loaded handgun on a table just inside the bedroom door.

Based on the subject's delusions and the apparent attempt to get the weapon, the threat managers took him to a mental health facility for evaluation. They took the weapon for safekeeping. Once the subject was committed, the threat managers initiated procedures to confiscate the handgun.

SOURCE: Authors' personal knowledge.

Where the interview should occur is also easily answered. The most advantageous site is at the subject's residence. The subject is more likely to be comfortable there and hence more likely to be expansive in his or her answers. Visiting the residence provides the opportunity to check out the subject's living conditions and to look for any signs of weapons, undue interest in the target, any final act behaviors, or indications of preparing for an act of violence. But going to the residence can be dangerous as well. One officer should be the designated interviewer while the partner attends to officer safety.

Case Study:

The Bloody Interview

A subject dropped a letter off at the governor's office in a large western state. The letter contained delusional references and a demand for $22 million in lottery winnings that the subject believed were due him. The letter also contained a prediction that dire consequences would befall the governor if the subject was not paid.

The threat managers ran a criminal history of the subject and found charges for assaults as well as several drug violations. The state firearms registration showed no listing for the subject. When the threat managers contacted the local law enforcement dispatcher, he described the subject as a local "nut" well known to the police. The dispatcher also stated the subject was HIV positive. At this point, the threat managers decided to interview the subject. They did not pursue any further leads with the local police. Doing so might have alerted them to the fact that the subject was currently under investigation for assault with a deadly weapon, namely a knife. He had also been committed several times for mental health problems.

Two threat managers visited the subject at his residence. He appeared delusional and under the influence of drugs. The subject was bleeding from self-inflicted razor cuts on his arms and hands. The threat managers also noted a number of razor blades and knives on the floor and table.

Based on the wounds, the threat managers told the subject they intended to take him for a mental health evaluation. The subject leapt over a couch and grabbed a plaster statue, which he brandished at the threat managers. When they tried to take him into custody, he violently resisted. During the fight, both threat managers were exposed to his HIV tainted blood. One was gouged in the face by the subject's sharply pointed fingernails.

Interviewing the subject at the subject's residence provides many opportunities to learn about the subject, but it also entails considerable risks. The best antidote to that risk is for the threat manager to fully research the subject prior to the interview.

SOURCE: Authors' personal knowledge.

When Not to Conduct Subject Interviews for Information Gathering

Threat managers should never treat subject interviews lightly. Approaching the subject can make matters worse. Particularly with IC&Cs toward public officials, the subject uses the IC&C to express their anger, even outrage, at something the official did or represents. Having expressed their opinion, these subjects now feel better. They start getting on with the rest of their lives. Interviewing them simply reminds them of what they were mad about to begin with. It risks stirring things up all over again. As Gavin de Becker likes to point out, threat managers often have to choose between two opposing strategies: *watch and wait* or *engage and enrage.*

The *Intimacy Effect* also comes into play with subjects who have committed an IC&C toward someone with whom they have or had a personal relationship. Interviewing these subjects may fuel their anger toward the target. The subject may interpret the threat manager's approach as a betrayal by the target or as a challenge to the subject. The approach may threaten the subject's perception of his or her relationship with the target. It may prompt an escalation in his or her behavior toward the target.

Summary

This chapter defined protective investigations, especially as they differ from criminal investigations. Protective investigations seek to uncover information on subjects who commit an IC&C in order to assess whether or not the subject poses a risk to the target at this time. They differ from criminal investigations both in their style and their approach. Criminal investigations focus on determining if a crime occurred and, if so, who committed it. Protective investigations look into the possibility of a crime occurring and how best to prevent it.

The chapter pointed out ways a protective investigation can or should be conducted. We proposed treating the investigation in stages, with each stage reaching farther out than the previous one. By this we mean the threat manager should initially focus on the circumstances and context within which the IC&C took place. That entails analyzing the content or circumstances of the IC&C for any insights into why it was done. Next, the investigation should reach out to the target and the target's staff, family, or associates to determine if any of those individuals have any evidence or information that sheds light on the subject's intent, motive, or ability. Next, the threat manager should consider the benefits and detriments of contacting the subject's family, neighbors, associates, legal overseers, or others. Finally, the threat manager, having now gathered information on the subject and the IC&C from all possible sources, needs to decide about interviewing the subject.

Obviously, no prescription for a protective investigation can cover all the leads, possibilities, twists and turns, and avenues that investigations take. We have tried here to stake out the general areas these investigations should cover. But our list is not exhaustive. Since each protective investigation has its own peculiar and unique sources of information, the threat manager should take care to identify and exploit all of them.

What we have also tried to do here is not only give general directions toward productive areas of inquiry, but also to frame the kinds of questions threat managers can ask. Many of these questions are unique to protective investigations. They are not the kind of thing criminal investigations usually ask. If the threat manager gets nothing more from this chapter than a broadened imagination to use in approaching protective investigations, then the chapter has well served its purpose.

Notes to Chapter 7

[1] Robert Fein and Bryan Vossekuil, "Assassination in the United States: An Operational Study of Recent Assassins, Attackers, and Near Lethal Approaches," Journal of Forensic Sciences, March 1999, 333.

CHAPTER EIGHT

Managing Individuals of Violent Intent: Non-Confrontational Strategies

Threat management strategies conveniently divide into two distinct and even categories. Four of the strategies rely on measures that purposefully avoid confronting the subject – indeed two of these strategies depend on the subject not knowing he or she has come to law enforcement's attention. The other four strategies involve a confrontation with the subject using government power and authority to restrict the subject's behaviors or physically confine the subject. In this chapter, we discuss the pros and cons of the non-confrontational strategies. The next chapter evaluates the confrontational strategies.

Although for purposes of discussion we divide the strategies into two chapters, we envision the strategies arrayed across a continuum from least to most intrusive. Figure 8-1 shows how the strategies align. The concept of a continuum emphasizes an important process threat managers should always keep in mind. Threat management strategies should always be applied in direct proportion to the behavior of the subject. It makes no sense, and risks great harm and embarrassment, for the threat manager to arrest someone who simply wrote a public official, spouse, co-worker, or anyone else and included a casual reference to violence. Although clearly inappropriate, such references may not be illegal. Similarly, a mental commitment would not hold up for a schoolboy who mentions to a friend that he knows where Daddy keeps his gun. Clearly, school and law enforcement officials need to know about such comments, but their reaction to them should be kept always in perspective. Conversely, it would be appropriate to arrest an estranged husband for violating a temporary restraining order instructing him to stay away from his spouse. As punishments must fit their crimes, threat management strategies must be in balance with the behaviors to which they respond.

Figure 8-1. Range of Threat Management Strategies In Ascending Order of Confrontation

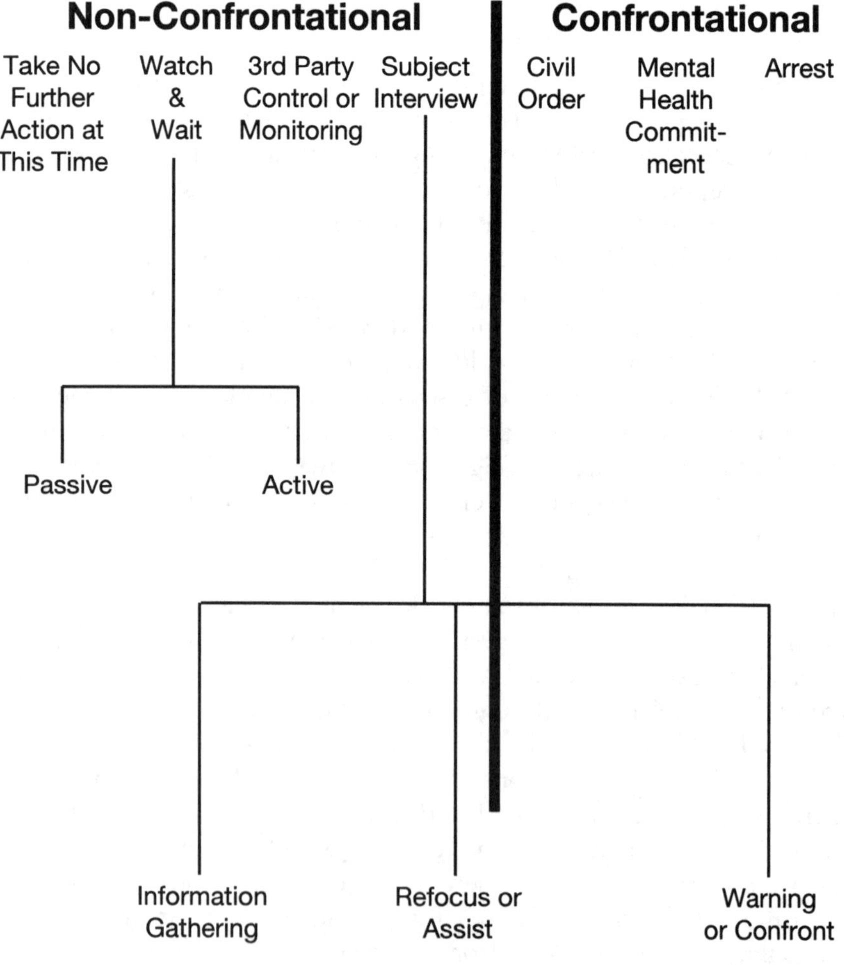

Although we graphically present these strategies as though arrayed along a continuum, threat managers should avoid treating or selecting them as though each was exclusive of the other or their employment must be sequential. Depending on the circumstances, several strategies may work well in combination with others. One strategy may provide a temporary break until another strategy comes into play. Watch and wait regularly gives the threat manager time to assess the effectiveness of another strategy. Threat managers frequently use temporary restraining orders in conjunction with criminal prosecutions. Arrests lead to third-party controls or monitoring. Refocus or assist often dovetails into taking no further action. Successful threat management requires innovation and flexibility, not by-the-book approaches.

Case Study:

Multiple Strategies, Quick Responses

Although the couple had broken up some months before, James C. kept calling Jenny at work. Each time, he left lengthy, angry, and threatening messages on her voice mail. After a almost a week of such calls, Jenny's co-workers and supervisor convinced her to go to court for a restraining order.

Since the threat manager had previously arranged to be notified of all such orders, he learned of Jenny's predicament once the court issued the order. The threat manager reviewed the facts of the case and decided on an initial Watch & Wait strategy to see how James reacted to the restraining order.

James did not react well. Whenever he got drunk or high, he called Jenny's work number and left vaguely threatening messages. At first, Jenny decided not to report the calls for fear of getting James in more trouble. One night, James crossed the line. Slurring his words, he left a long, explicitly threatening, vulgar message. The next morning, Jenny burst into tears when she heard the message. Her supervisor and the office manager noticed her reaction and contacted the threat manager.

The threat manager immediately switched strategies. He obtained an arrest warrant and began outlining conditions to ask the court to impose should the judge grant bail. Uniformed officers soon had James in custody. The judge granted him bail, but at the threat manager's request included a requirement that James stay away from Jenny's workplace. At trial, James pled guilty. Once again at the request of the threat manager, the judge granted probation with the condition that James keep away from Jenny, not call her at work, and stay sober.

Once again, the threat manager switched strategies, this time to Third Party Control or Monitoring. He worked closely with James' probation officer to monitor James. Jenny's office changed her work number, but left the old one live in order to capture any messages James might leave. The threat manager set up a schedule for reviewing the messages at the old number. He also arranged with the probation officer to violate James' probation immediately if James contacted Jenny again.

Effective threat management requires flexibility and quick responses to changing circumstances.

SOURCE: Authors' personal knowledge.

Principles of Threat Management

When a threat manager uses any threat management strategy, he or she should be constantly mindful of three fundamental principles of threat management. The first principle addresses the transient nature of threat assessments. Any threat assessment conducted at any time during the course of a case is nothing more than a snapshot of what is going on at that particular moment. The assessment includes all that has gone on before, but nothing of what is to come. Consequently, threat assessments rapidly deteriorate from the moment they are completed. Their fast aging is compounded by any new information uncovered by a protective investigation. The new information must be factored into reassessments. That process repeats itself endlessly for as long as the case remains active. Consequently, throughout each case, the threat manager must use the most current assessment to determine which threat management strategy best applies at that precise moment. That decision, in turn, must be continually reevaluated as new assessments are made. In protective investigations, on-going assessments and new investigative leads are intimate partners. Each feeds the other with new directions and new information. These dual tasks make the threat management process lively and anomalous. That, in turn, requires the threat manager to be quick witted and flexible.

A corollary of this principle of threat management prohibits previous assessments from casting too long a shadow over new assessments. Previous assessments give new assessments a case-context and a measuring rod for determining how the case is progressing. Conditions change, sometimes dramatically, sometimes incrementally, sometimes barely noticeably, and sometimes not at all. Initial high-risk assessments should not be taken to mean that all subsequent assessments will be high risk. Too often, law enforcement officers have trouble accepting good news. Naturally, the reverse also holds true. Initial low-risk assessments may become high risk if the subject begins engaging in negative behaviors. The threat manager should ensure that each assessment stands independent of all previous ones. Each assessment needs to account for all the information available at that particular moment in the life of the case.

Case Study:

Changing Information, Changing Assessments

Michael G. liked to volunteer. He volunteered for the reelection campaign of a state senator and he voluntarily protected the women volunteers, especially the candidate's daughter. Michael wrote the campaign manager to report that another volunteer was harassing the daughter. The campaign manager turned the letter over to the threat manager. He also advised that Michael appeared infatuated with the daughter. Michael had asked her out and appeared jealous whenever another man talked to her. He had also left small presents on her desk.

The threat manager did a records check, but found nothing of concern. Michael had no registered firearms. Discretely, he learned that other campaign workers considered Michael a "strange little man" who spoke often of protecting others. The threat manager assessed Michael as low risk.

Still, a subject interview seemed warranted. Using Michael's expressed concern about the other volunteer, the threat manager and his partner listened empathetically, encouraging Michael to talk about his role as protector. Michael confided that he had worked on other campaigns in Minnesota and Florida, always finding someone to protect. He bragged about his martial arts skills and his expertise with edged weapons and firearms. He freely admitted he owned several unregistered guns.

The threat manager began in-depth checks in Minnesota and Florida and reached out to other law enforcement agencies. He learned Michael had been committed to a mental hospital in Minnesota after attempting to board an airplane with a firearm. The U.S. Secret Service reported that their agents had arrested Michael for approaching Mikhail Gorbachev carrying a concealed military knife. They committed him based on a diagnosis of paranoid delusions. Florida records uncovered an incident in which Michael led police on a car chase ending in an accident leaving Michael partially disabled.

The threat manager now assessed Michael as high risk. He arranged for the reelection campaign to notify Michael his services were no longer needed. Separately, the threat manager confiscated the firearms based on his mental health history. The threat manager also arranged to closely monitor Michael and keep in frequent contact with him. That close monitoring continues.

New information necessitates new assessments and possibly new strategies.

SOURCE: Authors' personal knowledge.

The second principle of threat management addresses the interactive nature of applying any of the threat management strategies. At any given time, each strategy triggers a complex interplay between the threat manager and the subject. Any action (or inaction) taken by the threat manager will always result in one of three mutually exclusive outcomes. It will either:

- make the situation better;
- make the situation worse; or
- make no change in the situation.

Which of those outcomes occurs results from the actions of the threat manager and the reactions of the subject *combined.*

Therein lies the challenge. By acting, even by not acting, the threat manager becomes a part of the case, as active an ingredient as yeast in the rising of bread. It is simple chemistry. Actions or inactions by the threat manager cause a reaction by the subject just as actions by the subject prompt the threat manager to react. Defusing the risk requires constant experimentation to determine the perfect mix of action and reaction that will produce a non-violent resolution.

The risk, of course, is that the mixture will become too volatile. It is already unstable before the threat manager gets involved. Some grievance or issue pressed enough on the subject to prompt the Inappropriate Communication or Contact (IC&C). The threat manager, then, must take considerable care to avoid further exciting whatever demons haunt the subject. This can be accomplished simply by remembering that the threat manager is part of the chemistry of the case and therefore must avoid doing anything, including nothing, that might further escalate the risk.

Consequently, when deciding on which threat management strategy to deploy, the threat manager should always measure each strategy in terms of its effect on the subject and the potential risk to the target or others. Safety is the primary consideration, not only for the target, but for everyone else as well – including the subject. The selection of the appropriate strategy must be made with safety always in mind. This means that the subject's attention should not be redirected to someone else, nor should the strategy be employed to incite the subject in hopes of prompting him or her to a criminal act. The strategy must represent the threat manager's firm belief that employing it will lessen, not increase, the risk.

Since the threat manager unavoidably becomes one of the elements of the case, the choice of which option to implement needs to be based strictly on a deliberate risk assessment of the current situation. These strategies are part of the process of threat management, not stand-alone actions. Too often, the choice of strategy is prompted by the emotionally driven demands of the target, the desire of the threat manager to relieve some seemingly petty annoyance, or impatience with the subject's irritating or irrational behaviors. Any actions caused by these motives increase the risk of a volatile reaction. Only an intelligent, objective assessment of the circumstances of the case and the potential reactions of the subject provide any hope of defusing the risk. Each action the threat manager takes must be scaled to the *previous actions* and *potential reactions* of the subject. Only in that way can the threat manager control the chemistry of the case.

Case Illustration:

Managing Love

The day's duty officer assigned to a large threat management unit responds to the call from the city manager's office. Todd L. attracted attention there, which is easy for him to do. He stands six feet, six inches tall, wears a tuxedo, and carries a bouquet of flowers. He wants to give the flowers to Lisa D., the city engineer who had been interviewed on the news last night. Todd belligerently refuses to leave the office until he gives Lisa the flowers.

When the threat manager arrives, she finds three uniformed officers surrounding Todd ready to physically subdue him. She immediately begins to calm the situation down. Todd responds positively to her. She talks him into handcuffs and accompanies him to the mental hospital. A week later, the hospital releases Todd. The threat manager chooses a refocus strategy combined with third party monitoring through Todd's parents.

Todd responds well, frequently writing the threat manager to keep her updated on his progress. His parents advise her that he continues on his medication and seems much better.

After several months, however, the tone of Todd's letters changes. They become much more familiar, then flirtatious, then romantic. Todd also begins dropping the letters off in person at the front desk of the police station. The next time the threat manager calls Todd's mother, the mother tells her how pleased she is that the threat manager and Todd are now "dating."

The threat manager alerts her supervisor to the changed situation. Later that day, another officer notices Todd sitting in his truck across the street from the police parking lot. The supervisor sends two other threat managers to the truck. They discover Todd has a pistol loosely concealed under his coat lying on the seat. Todd explains that he needs to protect the original threat manager. The investigators arrest Todd on weapons charges. With the first threat manager's concurrence, the supervisor assigns Todd's case to another threat manager.

Once a threat manager opens a case, he or she becomes an integral part of the chemistry of that case.

SOURCE: Hypothetical illustration drawn from authors' professional experiences.

On few, though fortunately rare occasions, certain cases require immediate and heroic actions by the threat manager. Learning that a subject is armed and traveling toward the target requires neither much finesse nor long contemplation of the options at hand. Rather, it demands physically intervening to stop the subject. Such cases are easy to assess. The resolution depends more on the promptness of the threat manager's actions than the deliberateness of the assessment. Indeed, if someone starts shooting at the target, do not waste time with the Dietz-10, de Becker's Justification, Alternatives, Consequences, and Ability (JACA) scale, or any other assessment tools. React. But these situations are as rare as they are clear.

The vast majority of threat management cases are neither so clear-cut nor so pressing. Most cases begin almost innocuously, with barely a hint of the ultimate risks involved. The subject complains inappropriately or the target feels some ill-defined sense of danger. In an obvious fit of anger, the subject threatens, then immediately recants and apologizes. An informant may report a strange comment or act by the subject. Or the subject begins planning and preparing in secret, leaving only sporadic, vague clues for the threat manager to assess. These cases – and they are the majority of all threat management cases – have no quick fix or ready solution. They entail, instead, long-term problem solving.

And that, in turn, leads to the third principle of threat management and the greatest challenge facing threat managers: the need to think one's way through the case. Recognizing the need for a threat management program, setting up look-outs for identifying potential risks, deliberately and systematically assessing them as they occur, and conducting thorough protective investigations are relatively straightforward tasks. They are also very familiar techniques for law enforcement officers. Defusing the risk through managing the threat, however, is the hardest part. Its difficulty derives from several sources. It relies on no set rules, no certain standards, no clear directions. Its choices are judgment based and case, even situation, specific. Threat managers frequently employ non-traditional, off-the-wall strategies completely outside most law enforcement officer's training and experience. Contemporary threat management is less about fighting crime and more about solving problems. Good threat managers are good cops, but they are also good social workers, good father-confessors, and, most of all, good thinkers.

Case Illustration:

Solving the General Problem

Stanley W. shows up at the principal's office of his old high school dressed in military fatigues with two stars on each side of his collar. The threat manager responds to the school to interview Stanley. The government, Stanley explains, has assigned him to a special mission. He needs to give his former principal information vital to national security, but a colonel has tried to stop him.

A quick check of Stanley's military records discloses he is a private in the Army Reserve. The threat manager arranges for a mental commitment. Doctors there diagnose him as suffering from a delusion that he is a Major General in the Army and the Secretary of Defense is trying to kill him. After three days of treatment, the hospital releases Stanley.

The threat manager arranges for third party monitoring through Stanley's sister. Several weeks after his release, the sister calls to report that Stanley told her he needs to go to his military reserve base to take over the commandant's office. The threat manager immediately alerts officers at the base.

Military guards prevent Stanley from getting on the base. They also find a loaded rifle lying on the car floor. The threat manager again arranges a mental commitment. After another week, the hospital decides to release him.

The threat manager believes Stanley needs longer, more intense treatment, but the city hospital is overcrowded. The threat manager contacts Stanley's commanding officer. Together, they work with attorneys in the Judge Advocate General's office. They arrange for Stanley's admittance to the local Veteran's Affairs hospital where he receives the treatment he needs.

Threat managers must creatively use all resources available to them, keeping in mind that those resources are case specific.

SOURCE: Hypothetical illustration based on authors' professional experiences.

Strategies for Defusing the Risk

We define the threat management strategies in a particular order, starting with the least intrusive and noxious to the subject and proceeding by degree of intrusiveness to the most confrontational. We use this order quite purposefully. It emphasizes an important process threat managers should always consider. The strategies should be applied proportionately to the behavior of the suspect. The threat manager can always increase the degree of intervention with the subject, but once escalated, it becomes very difficult to go back. Although different strategies will come into play as the case evolves, the opening approach can be crucial in locking in the threat manager's immediate options. The threat manager cannot open a case by arresting the subject, then revert to some non-intervention strategy if the arrest does not stick or the suspect makes bail. In considering which strategy to employ, it is a wise rule of thumb to consider them in order from the least to the most confrontational.

Although each strategy is defined individually, the threat manager should not treat them as exclusive of each other. Flexibility and innovation, both in selecting, combining, and adapting the strategies and in the overall threat management process, hold the keys to success. The threat manager should never get locked into a rigid approach, a single solution, or a myopic view of the problem and ways to solve it.

For each strategy, we first provide a brief description of what that strategy means and the purpose it serves. Then we give some of the pros and cons that result from employing it. Finally, we discuss the various situations in which the strategy is most likely – and least likely – to be effective. This format will help prompt the threat manager to consider the advantages and disadvantages of each strategy within the context of the particular case he or she is managing. The strategies are not panaceas. Their effectiveness can be quite limited. At the first indication that the strategy is not going as planned, the threat manager should immediately reassess and consider other options.

Taking No Further Action At This Time

Taking no further action at this time requires a deliberate, justified decision to assign the case to inactive status. That decision must rest on a clear assessment that both the subject and the situation pose no risk to the target at the time of the assessment. This strategy usually results from a determination by the threat manager that the initial report on the IC&C was wrong or overly exaggerated. The subject might have been misunderstood, speaking in jest, or simply ignorant of the meaning or impact of his or her words or actions. Perhaps the person reporting the IC&C took the circumstances out of context. With IC&Cs reported by informants, the informant often proves to have lied.

In some cases, regardless of how horrific the language of the IC&C, the threat manager determines that the subject does not have the physical or mental ability to cause harm or injury.

Case Illustration:

The Complaint

The governor receives a letter stating: "I told you that you can't keep treating me this way. I'm going to do something that will really hurt you and make you sorry. Leave me alone!"

The governor's staff forwards the letter to the threat manager. The threat manager assesses enough risk to open a protective investigation. The investigation determines that the writer is developmentally disabled and confined to a bed and care home. He has the mental capacity of a 10-year-old and is completely dysfunctional. He wrote the letter because he was angry at his care giver and told her he was going to report her to the government.

Taking no further action means the subject poses no risk to the target and no further action is therefore needed.

SOURCE: Hypothetical illustration drawn from authors' professional experiences.

Making the decision to take no further action can become a very risky choice if the threat manager is not absolutely certain, without doubt or reservation, that the subject does not pose any risk to the target at this time. Choosing this strategy must be a deliberate decision based on assessment and investigation. It is not an alternative to not knowing what to do or throwing one's hands up in frustration. Nor is it an option for threat managers who are busy or distracted or about to go on vacation. Taking no further action at this time is only justified if the threat manager consciously determines that no further action is actually required.

Case Study:

Picture's Worth 1,000 Words

A federal prosecutor involved in a high-profile criminal prosecution reported seeing someone taking photographs of his house. Neighbors confirmed that someone in a late-model, light-colored car had been in the vicinity of the prosecutor's home. Several of them saw the male driver taking pictures.

The protective investigation revealed that a local real estate agent had been taking photographs of houses throughout the development. The agent explained that he was putting together a portfolio of the different house models for use in selling similar models.

The threat manager determined the case needed no further action at this time.

SOURCE: Authors' personal knowledge.

Advantages of Taking No Further Action At This Time

Taking no further action at this time offers several advantages. It saves time and resources better expended on higher risk cases. It does not risk any negative reaction from the subject, such as the confrontational strategies chance. By doing nothing beyond the protective investigation and assessment, the threat manager avoids any possibility that doing something might anger or insult the subject. Individuals who believe what they are doing is well within their rights often become greatly incensed if they perceive law enforcement trying to prevent or punish them for whatever they were doing. Protecting one's innocence can be a strong motivator for drastic actions – or reactions.

Disadvantages of Taking No Further Action At This Time

Taking no further action effectively allows the subject, not the threat manager, to determine the next step in the case. By deferring to the whim of the subject, the threat manager risks having the next case event come as a surprise. The threat manager should take great care to ascertain what the subject likely expected would happen as a result of the IC&C. If the subject hoped – even wanted – some kind of reaction and none occurs, he or she may decide to escalate. Consequently, any threat assessment should address what motivated the IC&C and what the subject expected from it.

When to Take No Further Action At This Time

Taking no further action applies only to those cases positively assessed as no risk and only as a conscious decision based on an assessment of the known facts. In effect, adopting this strategy makes the case inactive. Taking no further action, it bears repeating, is a decision informed by assessment and investigation. It is not the threat manager's default response.

In terms of evaluating this strategy's effectiveness according to the several venues of intended violence, the threat manager will likely find that taking no further action at this time will be used more often in cases involving non-intimate situations or group settings. Often, individuals upset at public officials make statements they do not seriously mean. In addition, they feel better for having made the statement. Ironically, the IC&C, however out of line, actually helps de-escalate the situation because the subject draws satisfaction from having said or done it. Once satisfied, the subject goes on with his or her life, little knowing the reaction caused by the IC&C.

In addition, the chances that a statement or action gets misunderstood, misinterpreted, or exaggerated increases in school or workplace settings because of the effect of group dynamics. Reports of IC&Cs that are not based on eyewitness accounts from someone who knows the subject are probably far more susceptible to distortion. Things easily get misreported. The threat manager may often discover that he or she is investigating a rumor that got out of control. Once the threat manager unearths the truth, the IC&C may look entirely different. It may not even be inappropriate.

Case Study:

Blowing Smoke

Early in the morning, the supervisor at a large manufacturing plant fired an incompetent employee. The employee cleared his personal effects from his locker and carried them to his car where he began loading them into his truck. A group of other employees were taking a smoking break near the parking lot. Several of them began joking that the fired employee was probably arming himself with weapons. As they joked about the fired employee returning to shoot the factory up, another employee walked by and overheard their comments.

That employee did not realize the smokers were joking. He immediately reported to the supervisor that the fired employee was arming himself in preparation to return to the factory and begin shooting. Acting on this information, the supervisor ordered the factory evacuated. Before he fled, he called the police.

Since all the witnesses had gone home, it took investigators the entire day to chase down the source of the rumor.

SOURCE: Authors' personal knowledge.

Conversely, statements or actions by one partner to an intimate relationship are less likely to be misinterpreted by the other partner. We suspect, as well, that intimate partners and non-strangers are far more likely to expect or want a reaction than those who direct IC&Cs at public officials or strangers. In assessing the IC&C, the threat manager should factor in the source of the IC&C and how it made its way to getting reported.

When Not to Take No Further Action At This Time

This strategy should never be used in any case that has the potential to escalate to a higher risk or if there is evidence the subject intends to continue behaving inappropriately. This strategy should not be adopted if the threat manager has any questions about the facts of the case or if any outstanding issues still exist. Subjects with a history of violent behaviors or mental health problems are also not good candidates for this strategy.

Watch & Wait

Watch & Wait means unobtrusively monitoring the subject while waiting to see if he or she will take additional actions in relation to the target. This strategy does not involve any intervention with the subject. In fact, when used as the initial strategy, Watch & Wait depends entirely on the subject not knowing that he or she has now come to the attention of investigators. It requires the threat manager to take great care that the subject remains ignorant of any investigative actions. Otherwise, Watch & Wait can backfire with high-risk results. Should the subject learn that he or she has become of interest to an investigator, the strategy then becomes intrusive from the subject's point of view. This can easily cause resentment at being investigated if the subject takes issue that his or her "innocent" complaint to or about the target prompted a reaction. Watch & Wait only works as an initial strategy if the subject remains completely unaware that the threat manager is watching.

Threat managers usually employ this strategy either with the assessed expectation that nothing further will happen or as a way to monitor the effectiveness of some other strategy. Often, individuals initiate an IC&C toward public figures as a way of blowing off steam. They may not even be aware that they crossed the line to inappropriateness. In other cases, subjects involved in intimate relationships may say things in a fit of anger that they later come to regret or recant. In these type situations, Watch & Wait gives the subject time to calm down. It intentionally allows the subject to decide what happens next, unprovoked by any action of the target or the threat manager.

In addition, threat managers use Watch & Wait in order to evaluate another strategy's effectiveness. Perhaps the threat manager interviewed the subject, arranged some assistance or warned the subject about his or her actions, and now needs to see if that help or warning will resolve the subject's issues. Watch & Wait also allows the threat manager to determine if the subject will obey civil orders. It gives time for the threat manager to determine if any mental health interventions have had a positive effect on the subject.

Giving the subject time is the waiting part. But that does not mean the threat manager does nothing while waiting. Rather, the threat manager should set up alerts with the target for any future contacts from the subject. This involves training the target and any others in reporting future IC&Cs or appropriate contacts by the subject. The threat manager should also collect and assess as much information on the subject and the subject's issues as can be obtained without the subject's knowledge. Much can be learned and assessed from the content and context of the IC&C itself. The target and the target's family, friends, or staff also may be able to shed considerable light on the case. In other words, while waiting, the threat manager continues investigating and assessing.

Case Illustration:

Seeking Respect

A small businessman has a large liability case pending in court. Because so much is at stake, the businessman has been unusually sensitive to the slightest indication that the case is going badly. On several occasions he has grimaced at the judge's rulings and whispered animatedly in his lawyer's ear. The judge has had to admonish the man twice to control himself.

With court in recess one Friday, the man calls the judge's chambers. Told the judge is unavailable, he asks the secretary to tell the judge that he expects to be treated with more respect. "If the judge can't show that respect," the secretary quotes the man saying, "then I might as well be dead."

The threat manager interviews various court personnel who have witnessed the man's behavior in court. Based on the fact that the IC&C was delivered over the telephone and was reasonably understandable based on the stakes to the businessman and his unfamiliarity with court procedures, the threat manager assesses the situation as low risk. Since the businessman's complaint is about respect, the threat manager determines that any interview or intervention strategy might further arouse the man's anger. After arranging for extra security at the next court session, the threat manager settles on a Watch & Wait strategy to see if the telephone call is a one-time outburst by a distraught litigant.

Throughout the remainder of the case, the businessman behaves appropriately. The judge rules in his favor and the man returns to his business. He never contacts the court again.

In the right circumstances, Watch & Wait allows time for the situation to defuse itself.

SOURCE: Hypothetical illustration drawn from the authors' professional experiences.

Watch & Wait has two modes: passive or active. Threat managers adopt the passive mode after completing their protective investigation. This mode requires the threat manager to wait and see if the subject attempts to contact the target again. Obviously, this requires the threat manager to carefully instruct the target and other concerned individuals, such as members of the target's staff or family, to be on the lookout for any subsequent communication or contact from the subject. Since the subject has already made at least one IC&C, any subsequent contact from the subject need not cross the threshold of inappropriateness. The threat manager should arrange for the target to immediately inform the threat manager of any subsequent action by the subject, inappropriate or not.

The threat manager needs to assess subsequent communications or contact within the overall context of the case, not just the particulars of that communication or contact. Naturally, if the new contact is appropriate, that might indicate a de-escalation or diminishment in the risk. It would not, however, on its own support assigning the case to the inactive category. Once a subject makes an IC&C, all subsequent communications or contacts need to be assessed. The fact that the subject continues to make contact indicates that his or her grievance or issue with the target that prompted the initial IC&C has not been resolved. That leaves open the chance that future communications or contacts might escalate the risk.

Case Illustration:

The Angry Constituent

An angry constituent writes his state congressman to complain about the rising price of electricity. The constituent describes his belief that the increased costs result from the congressman's collusion with the power company. He accuses the congressman of accepting campaign contributions from the company in exchange for turning a blind eye to the high rates. The constituent mentions that the cost of electricity is "killing" him and his family.

The congressman's staff recognizes the reference to killing as inappropriate and forwards the letter to the threat manager. The threat manager reads the letter carefully. The tone of the letter suggests that the constituent is outraged over events beyond his or her control and clearly needs someone to whom he can complain. The language of the letter also indicates that the constituent does not expect a response from the congressman.

The threat manager spends one morning discreetly inquiring about the constituent. She determines that the constituent owns a small business, is married, has children, and owns his own home. He is active in his church and the local Rotary Club. These inhibitors suggest that the constituent may have been venting to the congressman with no further intention to take any action toward the congressman.

The threat manager determines to wait to see if the constituent will take any subsequent actions. She briefs the congressman and his staff about reporting any future contacts regardless of whether or not they cross the threshold of inappropriateness.

When nothing further is heard from the constituent after three months, the threat manager assigns the case to inactive status.

Time resolves as many cases as the other strategies do.

SOURCE: Hypothetical illustration drawn from authors' professional experiences.

Active Watch & Wait requires more assertive measures. It combines an ongoing protective investigation with frequent contacts with the target and other concerned individuals to ensure immediate notification if subsequent communications or contacts are received. The active mode also entails more aggressive measures by the threat manager to find out as much as possible about the subject and the subject's issue with the target. Active Watch & Wait might also warrant surveillance activity on the subject to monitor his or her activities and movements.

When the threat manager selects active Watch & Wait as the initial strategy, the trick, of course, is conducting the protective investigation without letting the subject know about it. When the threat manager applies Watch & Wait as a follow-up strategy to an arrest, mental health commitment, or subject interview, further protective investigation need not be secretive. In these circumstances, active Watch & Wait may include occasional visits or subsequent interviews with the subject to ensure the subject obeys any controls that might be in place. For instance, the threat manager may contact a mentally ill subject to confirm that he or she continues to take prescribed medication. Similarly, the threat manager may want to check on subjects released on probation or parole with the restriction that they abstain from alcohol. Depending on the circumstances of the case, Watch & Wait serves well as the initial strategy and as a companion or follow-up to other threat management strategies.

Case Illustration:

The Anti-Abortionist

Roy M. works full-time protesting at a local reproductive health care facility that performs late-term abortions. He writes the doctor an emotionally charged letter accusing the doctor of committing murder. He tells the doctor that he prays daily for the doctor to either quit performing abortions or die. Roy warns the doctor that if he does not repent, he will burn in hell for all eternity. The letter ends with a quote from Genesis: "He who sheds the blood of others shall have his own blood shed."

The doctor's staff turns the letter over to the threat manager. The threat manager carefully reviews the letter. He interviews the doctor and his staff to confirm that nothing unusual or suspicious has come to their attention. Although Roy continues to protest outside the clinic, his recent behavior has been no different from the way he has acted in the past. The threat manager makes the assessment that the case poses some potential risk given how strongly Roy feels about the abortion issue and the fact that his protest activities put he and the doctor in the same proximity.

But the threat manager also understands that Roy's letter did not constitute an illegal threat and that his protest activities remain well within the law. In the past, too, Roy has used every opportunity to get publicity for his cause. The threat manager concludes that any intervention strategy risks further inflaming Roy's feelings, giving him an opportunity to get publicity, and might prompt him to more drastic action.

Consequently, the threat manager settles on an active Watch & Wait. He trains the doctor and the clinic staff on what to report and what security measures they can follow. He also arranges to stop by the clinic regularly to monitor Roy's protests and to check with the staff for any new information.

SOURCE: Hypothetical illustration drawn from the authors' professional experiences.

Advantages of Watch & Wait

Watch & Wait can be very effective in several different types of situations. It works well with subjects who have multiple inhibitors and whose IC&C constitutes an act of emotional venting over a specific issue or action associated with the target. A public figure takes a provocative stance on a particular issue. The subject reacts angrily. Almost on impulse, he or she picks up the telephone, calls the official's office, spouts off, and incidentally makes a vague threat or some other inappropriate statement. Feeling better from the emotional release, the subject rings off with scarcely another thought about what just happened. Two days later, the threat manager knocks on the subject's door. Such an intervention may escalate the case by reminding the subject of what happened and by further incensing the subject since it makes plain that he or she is now under investigation. By not intervening, the threat manager allows the subject to calm down and get past the incident – and the anger. By waiting, the threat manager gives the subject time to prove that the IC&C was a one-time event. In effect, Watch & Wait lets time itself tell what will happen next while avoiding any risk of further provoking the subject.

Watch & Wait also offers an effective management strategy in cases where the subject repeatedly makes low-risk IC&Cs over a long period. Watch & Wait lets the threat manager monitor the IC&Cs for any changes in tone, content, or method of delivery. If the protective investigation determines that the subject is a habitual threatener, Watch & Wait allows the threat manager to monitor all subsequent communications. In these situations, a new strategy would be needed only in response to any change initiated by the subject. In these situations, Watch & Wait saves time, energy, and resources.

Disadvantages of Watch & Wait

Ironically, the chief disadvantage of Watch & Wait as an initial strategy is that it prohibits the threat manager from intervening with the subject. This can be a frustrating posture to take. Waiting can be nerve wracking, particularly since there are no set rules determining how long to wait. As we will discuss later about inactivating a case, how long does one wait for nothing more to happen before deciding that nothing else is going to happen? This question is crucial, but also very difficult to answer except on a case-by-case basis. Since it is predicated on the gamble that the IC&C was a low risk or singular occurrence, how many days or weeks have to pass before that singularity is established?

The strategy also risks emboldening the subject to make additional IC&Cs. If the subject feels better from the first inappropriate telephone call and suffers no consequences for having made it, will that encourage him or her to make a second protest when something else occurs to his or her disliking?

Finally, Watch & Wait as an initial strategy applies only to a very limited range of cases. Its use should be matched only to those.

When to Use Watch & Wait

Watch & Wait applies to three particular ways: as an initial strategy on its own; when the threat manager feels the case has some unresolved issues; or as a follow-on to the other strategies. Watch & Wait works effectively on its own when the threat manager determines that the subject might have used the IC&C to vent. The strategy allows for time to determine if the venting fully relaxed the subject's emotions. Watch & Wait might be effective in those situations when taking no further action does not apply because the assessment suggests some continued potential, but not high, risk. Similarly, if the threat manager still has concerns about the subject or unanswered questions about the case, Watch & Wait might be effective. Used in this way, Watch & Wait is a slightly escalated response compared to taking no further action. It effectively keeps the case active without requiring a lot of time and effort on the part of the threat manager.

Watch & Wait also works well in monitoring the effect of any of the interventionist strategies. The threat manager might try a subject intervention – say an interview and warning – then wait to assess any reaction or change in behavior by the subject. After applying an interventionist strategy, the watching should always be in the active mode. As discreetly as possible, the threat manager should closely monitor the subject's subsequent behaviors and activities. In doing so, the threat manager needs to keep in mind that good news is as acceptable as bad news. If the intervention worked, the subject's behavior will reflect it every bit as much as the subject's behavior will indicate when the intervention failed.

Lastly, Watch & Wait should be used in those cases that cannot be resolved, yet never quite escalate to an approach or an attack. This use essentially allows the threat manager to monitor the subject over the long-term. The case is not being actively investigated, since all necessary investigation has been completed. Yet, enough potential risk remains or additional IC&Cs continue to occur that the case cannot be assigned an inactive status. It is, instead, an on-going or continuing case. This application of Watch & Wait eventually can be done in the passive mode.

In terms of evaluating this strategy's effectiveness according to the several venues of intended violence, the threat manager will usually find that Watch & Wait is less effective in managing cases involving intimate relationships where emotions are volatile and the subject appears intent on getting a response of some sort from the potential target. In those cases, the appearance of not doing anything can be as inflammatory to the subject as doing something. Because other strategies allow the threat manager to control the next action, that action can be chosen based on an assessment of the subject's possible reaction. Watch & Wait surrenders that control to the subject.

The threat manager will usually find that Watch & Wait is more effective in cases involving singular emotional outbursts – most often anger – toward a stranger to the subject, such as a public figure or government official. In workplace and school settings, Watch & Wait should only be used to monitor the impact of an interventionist strategy. In these settings, it is usually not a good choice on its own.

When Not to Use Watch & Wait

The threat manager should never apply Watch and Wait in any case in which the risk might be high or might escalate to high. Nor should it be used if a criminal violation, such as a direct threat, took place. If the IC&C culminates a long-simmering, emotionally charged situation, such as a protracted divorce or domestic dispute, Watch & Wait should not be considered. As with taking no further action at this time, subjects who have a history of violent behavior or mental illness are not good candidates for this strategy. Watch & Wait is also not appropriate as a first-choice strategy in work or school settings where the subjects and the targets are in close and frequent contact. In these situations, the threat manager should exert other strategies and use Watch & Wait only to gain time to assess the effectiveness of the other strategies.

Third Party Control or Monitoring

Third party control or monitoring requires identifying a *reliable* third party. That individual or organization has to have the ability to either control the subject or monitor the subject's activities. In either event, the threat manager needs to keep in close communication with the third party to keep tabs on what is going on with the subject. Usually, reliable third parties are parole or probation officers, correctional or jail personnel, mental health providers, board and home-care providers, physicians, or close relatives of the subject. Whatever the type of third party, the threat manager should continuously confirm that the controlling or monitoring remains reliable. Probation officers can get distracted; psychologists, psychiatrists, and physicians have other patients; and relatives can change their minds about helping. Consequently, third party control or monitoring works only for as long as the third party cooperates. It can be disastrous if the dependability of the third party deteriorates.

In addition, third party control or monitoring is more effective if the subject does not know about the third party's arrangement with the threat manager. Indeed, it works especially well if the subject perceives the control or monitoring as a natural outgrowth of his or her relationship with the third party. Such a perception may keep the risk to the target from escalating. If the subject thinks of it as normal, then the subject is less likely to blame the target for an additional hardship (the control or monitoring). If the subject begins to see the control or monitoring as an outgrowth of his or her IC&C toward the target, he or she may begin to blame the target for the control or monitoring.

Case Illustration:

Control

A prisoner in the state penitentiary spends his days writing threatening letters to public officials throughout the state. The threat manager approaches the warden and asks him to impose some controls on the prisoners access to the mail. The warden agrees and restricts the prisoner's mail to legal correspondence.

In addition, the threat manager arranges with prison officials to flag the prisoner's file to remind them to alert the threat manager if the prisoner's status changes in any way.

SOURCE: Hypothetical illustration drawn from the authors' professional experiences.

The threat manager needs to keep always in mind the difference between third party *control* and third party *monitoring*. Control works best in institutional settings, such as prisons or mental health facilities. In fact, if the control is strict enough, it can defuse the risk enough for the threat manager to inactivate the case. Consequently, in using third party control, the threat manager needs to assess the extent and effectiveness of the control as part of the periodic threat assessments of the situation.

Case Study:

The Landlady

Brad F. made several approaches to the offices of state elected officials, including the governor, the Speaker of the House, and the state Attorney General. Each time, he appeared delusional, acted slightly aggressive, but did not meet the criteria justifying a mental health commitment. Then Brad drove his car onto the lawn in front of a state office building. He ran into the comptroller's office clearly in a psychotic state. The threat manager arranged for a mental commitment and began planning for an aggressive follow-up as soon as the hospital released Brad.

The threat manager contacted the landlady of the rooming house where Brad lived. She agreed to call the threat manager if she noticed Brad acting strangely. The hospital released Brad.

Several months later, the landlady called the threat manager, telling him Brad "was at it again." She explained that recently he had begun talking animatedly about how angry he felt toward the comptroller for wasting the state's money.

This report prompted the threat manager and his partner to visit Brad. When they knocked on his door, Brad jerked it open. Wild-eyed, he immediately accused the two officers of coming to kill him. Brad leapt toward both officers, flailing his arms and fists. The officers tried to restrain him, but Brad continued punching and kicking them. After a protracted struggle, the officers handcuffed him and forced him face down on the hall floor.

The state prosecutor convicted Brad of battery on a police officer. The criminal justice system took over his mental treatment as part of his incarceration. Prison officials now controlled him.

Third-party monitors do not equal third-party controls.

SOURCE: Author's personal knowledge.

Unlike third party control, especially strict control, the monitoring side of the strategy offers no hope for a solution. It simply ensures that the third party keeps the threat manager informed about the subject's activities, especially those related to the target. Monitoring, after all, is simply watching. The third party can intensify the monitoring, but again, the threat manager should not confuse that with resolving the situation. Instead, it gains the threat manager more information to factor into the on-going assessments. In choosing third party control or monitoring, the threat manager needs to identify clearly whether he expects the third party to control or to monitor.

Case Study:

Teacher's Pet

In the fall of 2001, five high school students in New Bedford, Massachusetts, began plotting a Columbine-style attack on their high school. Indeed, their ambition was to make a bigger attack than Dylan Kleibold and Eric Harris had managed. The students planned to sneak longarms and bombs into the school, kill as many teachers and students as they could, then throw a party on the roof of the school.

Although police began picking up clues of the conspiracy, they had insufficient evidence to take much action.

`Fortunately, the only female student involved told her favorite teacher about the plot. She wanted to spare him from any danger. The police were able to use the teacher to monitor the conspiracy until they had sufficient evidence to arrest the students.

Third parties can serve as early warning alerts on individuals with violent intent.

SOURCE: Associated Press, "Fourth Student Charged in Mass. Plot," November 28, 2001.

Advantages of Third Party Control or Monitoring

Third party control offers the threat manager a way to effect an intervention through an established control system which the subject accepts. As the subject understands the situation, the intervention results from his or her relationship with the third party and not as an outgrowth of the subject's IC&C toward the target. Consequently, the subject may be more willing to accept the intervention or, at the least, to see it as some normal part of his or her relationship with the third party.

Case Illustration:

The Drunken Parolee

A subject telephones the judge's chambers and in angry, vulgar terms demands help with his civil rights lawsuit against the prison. The subject's speech is slurred and the judge's secretary reports he sounded intoxicated. She also reports that the subject stated the slow progress of the lawsuit was "driving me crazy."

The threat manager learns that the subject is on parole. He had sued prison authorities for taking away his television privileges three months before his parole. One of the special conditions of the parole is that the subject not drink alcohol.

After assessment, the threat manager settles on a third party strategy using the subject's parole officer. The parole officer agrees to a surprise urinalysis from which to bring up the alcohol problem. Once that is brought before the subject, the parole officer arranges for special counseling in alcoholism and anger management. The threat manager also arranges to contact the parole officer frequently to learn of the subject's progress with the treatment.

Dependable third party intervention can help keep the subject under control and get the subject help.

SOURCE: Hypothetical illustration drawn from the authors' professional experiences.

Third party monitoring provides the threat manager information on the activities, thinking, and attitude of the subject without the subject knowing the threat manager has the information. Such intelligence about the subject is a great boon for the on-going assessments. It helps the threat manager pinpoint where the subject may be along the path to violence. Third party monitoring also assists the threat manager to recognize any changes in the subject's behavior or plans.

Disadvantages of Third Party Control or Monitoring

The major disadvantage of third party control or monitoring centers on the chance that the third party may lose or surrender control or decide to cease monitoring. Even worse, the third party may take the subject's side and tell him or her about the arrangement with the threat manager. If in ignorance the subject accepted the control or monitoring without blaming the target, once enlightened, the subject's anger toward the target may dramatically increase. Not only, in the subject's view, does he or she now learn the target was responsible for the control or monitoring, but the subject was also tricked and bamboozled. At that point, third party control or monitoring has completely backfired and has now escalated the potential risk to the target. That is the worse disadvantage.

Another concern is that the controls or monitoring may begin to relax. Unbeknownst to the threat manager, the third party may not have as much control over the subject as the third party originally had. The information produced by the monitoring may not be complete or it may be inaccurate. These risks require the threat manager to continually verify that the third party's relationship to the subject has not significantly changed or, if it has changed, how does it effect the implementation of the strategy.

When to Use Third Party Control or Monitoring

Third party control or monitoring works only when the third party – whether individual or institution – can reliably exert control over the subject or can reliably monitor the subject's activities. It depends, too, on frequent and open communications between the threat manager and the third party. The strategy is not about the threat manager transferring his or her problem to someone else. Rather, third party control or monitoring uses resources already in place to assist the threat manager in managing problem subjects.

In terms of evaluating this strategy's effectiveness according to the several venues of intended violence, third party control or monitoring is less affected by the different venues than the other strategies because it depends entirely on the availability and reliability of the third party. The threat manager needs to be mindful, though, that in certain settings the third party may take actions that effectively end, frequently abruptly, the ability to control or monitor. In workplaces, for example, a supervisor or manager may have control over a problem employee because of the supervisor's power to fire that employee. Once that power is exercised, however, the supervisor no longer has any control or any ability to monitor the fired employee. Similarly, school officials have disciplinary control over unruly students right up to the moment that they expel the student. In domestic situations, one partner may be able to monitor, even to some extent control, the other partner's behaviors simply by remaining in the relationship. That ability both ends and exacerbates the problem once the partner separates from the other partner.

When Not to Use Third Party Control or Monitoring

Threat managers should avoid using third party control or monitoring if they doubt the third party or have *any* reason to suspect the third party's interest in cooperating or ability to help. Asking a social worker with an overwhelming caseload for help probably will not work. Parents sometimes may refuse to believe their child could do anything wrong, regardless of any evidence to the contrary. As any uniformed officer knows too well, spouses frequently change their minds about their spouse, cooperating with law enforcement one moment and siding with their partner the next. It bears repeating that successfully implementing this strategy hinges entirely on the reliability of the third party. And the threat manager should remember that that reliability can disappear in an instant.

Case Study:

Rifling the Attic

As required by state law, a psychologist reported to a city councilwoman that her patient, Ali M., had made threats to shoot the councilwoman. In turn, the councilwoman contacted the threat manager. The protective investigation revealed that Ali had been committed to a mental hospital, but was due to be released in a few days. He blamed the councilwoman because the city had denied his disability claim for work-related stress.

In preparation for Ali's imminent release, the threat manager contacted Ali's wife, a city schoolteacher. The wife voluntarily surrendered a handgun. She assured the threat manager that she knew of no other weapons in the house.

The psychologist informed the threat manager that Ali fantasized about shooting the councilwoman in the head with a rifle. During the threat manager's interview with Ali prior to the hospital release, Ali assured the threat manager that his medication helped him and he no longer dreamed about shooting the councilwoman.

Acting on a hunch, the threat manager asked Ali where he kept his rifle. Ali admitted that he stored his rifle and scope in the attic of his house. He also confirmed that his fantasy involved shooting that rifle.

The threat manager returned to Ali's house to confront his wife and take custody of the rifle. The wife reluctantly admitted that she knew about the rifle, but thought it was illegal. She did not want to get her husband in any more trouble.

Threat managers should tread carefully with third parties, for their loyalties may lie elsewhere.

SOURCE: Authors' personal knowledge.

Subject Interviews: Refocus or Assist

In the previous chapter, we discussed the efficacy of using subject interviews to gain information on the subject's issues, viewpoint, and intentions. When the threat manager uses an interview to gather information, we strongly recommended taking the time to organize the threat manager's information in order to plan and sequence the questions. However, interviews provide other benefits to effective threat management. Interviews create opportunities to intervene with the subject, either to help or to confront. The interview itself is an intervention since it clearly alerts the subject that he or she is of interest to law enforcement. Even as the threat manager methodically collects information from the subject, he or she should be constantly alert to the possibility of using the interview to explore ways to help the subject resolve his or her problems or to warn the subject that his or her behaviors could result in trouble for the subject. This requires that the interview be organized and planned, yet flexible and responsive.

The dynamic created by the interaction between the subject and the threat managers creates its own momentum. The threat manager needs to be ever sensitive to that impetus in order to take advantage of it. Frequently, simply hearing the issues from the subject's point of view helps the threat manager find ways to resolve the problems. As the dialogue evolves from information gathering to threat management, the level of confrontation between the threat manager and the subject may increase. But that need not be negative. The strategies of refocus or assist are subject interventions, but positive ones. They require the threat manager to empathize with the subject's concerns and, if possible, help the subject to resolve them.

By refocus, we do not suggest or imply substituting one target for another. That is both unethical and risky – and probably immoral and unlawful. By refocus, we mean that the threat manager should present himself or herself as the government or security official with whom the subject should henceforth deal. If successful, the subject will shift his or her attention away from the target and look to the threat manager to resolve whatever his or her issue is. Refocus, then, requires convincing the subject that the threat manager can assist or, at the least, lend a sympathetic ear to the subject's problems.

By assist, we mean actually helping the subject resolve his or her problem. Although this no doubt sounds more like social work than law enforcement, helping the subject can be one of the most effective ways of defusing the risk and inactivating the case. Especially in dealing with institutions, like government agencies, the subject's problem may stem from frustration spawned by ignorance of proper procedures or bureaucratic processes. Simply by cutting through the bureaucracy, the threat manager can help get the subject where the subject wants to be.

Using subject interviews to refocus or assist depends on the threat manager establishing a positive rapport with the subject. Although both strategies involve a confrontation with the subject, both are positive efforts to assist the subject. In the next chapter, we will review ways to use negative confrontations with the subject. When trying to help, the threat manager needs empathy and patience. Refocus or assist requires hearing the subject out, making an honest effort to understand what the subject's problem or issue is, and thinking creatively of how to address that problem or issue.

Advantages of Refocus or Assist

Using a subject interview to refocus the subject's attention allows the threat manager to redirect any future IC&Cs away from the target. By setting up as the recepient of future contacts by the subject, the threat manager essentially arranges to maintain contact with the subject. That will allow the threat manager to monitor the subject, thus gaining valuable information to factor into on-going assessments. By giving the subject access to a sympathetic ear, the threat manager invites the subject to share his or her current and future concerns, frustrations, and anger. When done successfully, refocus provides the subject with someone to gripe to and allows the threat manager to monitor the griping. Consequently, refocusing is best suited to subject's with long-term problems.

Case Study:

Power of Attorney

In a midwestern jurisdiction, a local anti-government militia group constituted its own court. It began issuing pseudo-judicial process toward the local judge. The fake process made various demands for records and explanations of particular court decisions.

After analyzing the documents and investigating the militia group, the threat manager determined that the group intended to use its court primarily as a vehicle to publicize its ideological views. The threat manager drew up his own fake document assigning him the judge's power of attorney for purpose of accepting the pseudo-process. Since the power of attorney essentially accepted the militia group's pretense, the group had to accept it or admit to its own fiction. Thenceforth, the group began serving its process on the threat manager rather than sending it to the judge.

By refocusing the group's attention to the threat manager and away from the target, the threat manager positioned himself to be able to continue monitoring the group's interest in the judge while leaving the judge undisturbed by any more annoyances.

SOURCE: Authors' personal knowledge.

Using a subject interview to find ways to assist the subject is best suited for those subjects with solvable problems. Indeed, it can be counterproductive to effective threat management to raise the subject's hopes for a resolution only later to dash them. Yet, with that caution in mind, the threat manager should consider any way to get the subject some relief.

Threat managers often use these types of solutions:

- obtaining *pro bono* legal advice for a subject;
- arranging proper medication for a mentally ill subject;
- acting as a liaison between a subject and a government agency;

- involving family members to arrange closer supervision for a developmentally disabled subject;
- helping a spouse deal with harassments by the other spouse;
- encouraging plaintiffs and defendants to use alternative dispute resolution resources;
- working with mental health providers to improve treatment of a mentally ill subject;
- arranging with social workers to address a subject's relief and welfare needs.

We chose these examples precisely because they go way beyond the limits most practiced by law enforcement. Threat managers need to think outside the law enforcement box. Threat management requires innovation and creativity. Good threat managers have good imaginations and are able to see solutions to problems in areas well outside their normal work experience.

Case Study:

Getting Paid

A government personnel supervisor contacted the threat manager because of his concerns over the behavior of a recently terminated employee. The subject had been making increasingly angry telephone calls to numerous agency employees regarding the money owed him for accrued vacation hours.

After investigating the situation, the threat manager decided to interview the subject. The goal of the interview was to gather information from the subject's point of view and to exploit any opportunities to assist the subject in getting paid. During the interview, the subject explained that his frustration grew out of the fact that he had a job opportunity in another state, but could not afford the move without the money owed him. The new job would not wait. Although the subject admitted to feeling bitter over being fired, he also felt he was getting the run-around from his former colleagues at the agency.

The threat manager met again with the personnel supervisor, who arrogantly told him that these checks receive low-priority. It could take several more weeks before the subject's check would be cut. The supervisor was upset and angry at the telephone calls and was unreceptive to expediting the check. He demanded the subject's arrest.

Instead, the threat manager went over the supervisor's head to the director of the agency. The director immediately understood the threat manager's plan. With a phone call he arranged for the check to be cut immediately. The threat manager then hand-delivered it to the subject, taking that opportunity to engage in a second interview. The threat manager also kept in touch with the subject during the few days it took him to pack his belongings and move out of state.

Sometimes, the best way to defuse the risk is simply to resolve the subject's problems.

SOURCE: Authors' personal knowledge.

Disadvantages of Refocus or Assist

Refocus or assist require considerable commitment and effort on the part of the threat manager. Refocus in particular depends on the threat manager acting as the government's representative, not just pretending to. The strategem does not work if the threat manager uses it as a ploy to fool or temporarily divert the subject. Such shenanigans risk making the situation worse by further angering the subject.

Instead, the threat manager has to carry through and allow the subject to make contact and then follow-up on the subject's concerns. This, of course, can require a lot of time, which then competes with the threat manager's other cases and responsibilities.

Assist, depending on the complexity of the subject's issue, may not demand as much time, but it still requires effort. Often, the threat manager's greater familiarity with bureaucratic processes make the assistance fairly simple. In these situations, the case can be easily resolved. Other times, the subject has more complicated issues requiring the threat manager's time and energy. It also requires imagination and innovation outside the threat manager's law enforcement background. Assist brings the threat manager that much closer to social work.

When to Use Refocus or Assist

The threat manager should only choose refocus if the subject appears amenable to it and the threat manager can pull it off. Refocus is particularly useful when the case requires long-term management. It works well for those individuals who do not pose a significant threat and whose IC&Cs are more bothersome or annoying than risky. Good candidates for refocusing are subjects who suffer mild mental problems or who have difficulty coping with – much less understanding – the government or private institutions with which they are dealing.

Obviously, assist only works when the subject has a problem with a court, government agency, or business that the threat manager can help resolve.

In terms of evaluating this strategy's effectiveness according to the several venues of intended violence, the decision to use refocus or assist has less to do with the type of situation the threat manager is dealing with and more to do with whether refocusing or assisting the subject will work. Assist works only if the threat manager can help resolve whatever the subject's issues are. Unlike the other strategies, which may be more or less suited to particular venues, the issue for refocus or assist depends on whether refocusing makes sense or assisting can actually help. Both are effective across venues, but only to the degree to which the threat manager can actually achieve the refocusing or achieve the assistance.

When Not to Use Refocus or Assist

Neither refocus nor assist work in situations assessed as high risk. In addition, neither one is effective with subjects who have irrational, outrageous, or unreasonable demands. Threat managers would be ill advised to promise a subject help achieving unrealistic objectives. Refocus does not work if it raises the subject's expectations too high. Indeed, the threat manger should always be extremely careful never to promise the subject anything the threat manager cannot deliver. Creating expectations only to frustrate them increases the risk by further angering the subject.

Summary

This chapter described four non-confrontational strategies threat managers can use to manage individuals of violent intent. The chapter defined *Take No Further Action at This Time, Watch & Wait, Third Party Control or Monitoring*, and subject interviews to *Refocus or Assist.* With each definition, we also discussed the advantages and disadvantages of each strategy and offered suggestions on when and when not to use each. We also pointed out the effect that each venue of intended violence played on each strategy.

CHAPTER NINE

Managing Individuals of Violent Intent: Confrontational Strategies

Law enforcement officers are more comfortable employing the confrontational threat management strategies than the non-confrontational ones. Each entails exerting the full weight and authority of the state. This is, after all, what police officers do. They arrest criminals, commit the mentally ill, enforce court orders, and confront problem people. One does not end a riot by watching and waiting anymore than deterring thieves by assisting them. Police act, sometimes forcibly, but always powerfully. As a result, many officers leap immediately to the confrontational strategies because they are so used to employing them. The non-confrontational strategies we discussed in Chapter 8 are not nearly as familiar.

Unfortunately, confrontational strategies are effective in a limited number of situations. They may solve the problem, but they can just as frequently exacerbate it. Arresting a subject defuses the risk, but only for as long as the subject remains in custody, provided the subject has no allies, outside support, or resources. The risk returns – and possibly with a vengeance – once the subject makes bond, probation, parole, or completes the prison sentence. Arresting the subject may at best merely postpone the problem to a later time. The same holds true for mental health commitments. They work for only as long as the commitment holds, though receiving treatment may help the subject better control his or her delusions or illness.

Stay-away orders work only if the subject obeys them or the issuing authority strictly and immediately retaliates against any infractions. Certain individuals interpret these orders as direct challenges that must be met with disobedience. Confronting or warning may frighten away some individuals, but it may anger others. Other subjects cower before the full weight and authority of the state;

still others rebel against it. Distinguishing between them is hard to do.

That said, however, we recognize that ultimately these strategies are the tools law enforcement uses. In certain situations, some of them may be ineffective. In other situations, they may risk escalating the problem. Some strategies may only postpone the trouble. Nonetheless, these are all the weapons law enforcement can bring to bear. That means that the threat manager needs to recognize the limitations of each strategy, both confrontational and non. Through training and experience, the threat manager will be able to wisely choose which strategy offers the most reasonable hope of reaching goal of the interview. The goal may not always be completely defusing the risk. Many times, the best we can hope to do may well be postponing it.

Subject Interview: Warning or Confronting

Warning or confronting the subject lie at the most confrontational end of the interview approach. Either can occur in one of two ways. The threat manager may plan to use a warning or confrontation prior to the subject interview. Or the threat manager may spontaneously take advantage of any opportunities that may develop during the course of the interview to warn or confront the subject. Either way, threat managers employing these strategies need to remain extremely sensitive to officer safety issues. By their vary nature, warning or confronting spark emotions, especially anger, that may lead to physical reactions on the part of the subject. Whether used intentionally or spontaneously, the threat manager should use them cautiously.

Warnings apply best to individuals engaged in behaviors that have not yet crossed the border into illegality. Frequently, individuals do not understand the gravity of their actions. Because they think of themselves as wronged, they feel perfectly entitled in insisting on the justice of their cause. This blinds them to the repercussions of their own behaviors. Often, subjects do not understand how close their actions come to breaking the law or what the consequences to them might be. Explaining the situation and warning of the potential legal or disciplinary consequences may be enough to induce them to change their tactics.

Case Study:

The Expulsion

Sixteen-year-old Taylor Hess helped his father box up his grandmother's linens, books, and kitchenware to take to the local Goodwill store in Bedford, Texas. They loaded the boxes in their pickup truck and made their delivery.

Taylor also drove the pickup truck to school each day. A security guard patrolling the school parking lot noticed a 10-inch bread knife in the truck bed. Undoubtedly, it had fallen out of the box of the grandmother's kitchenware. Since the state of Texas adopted a zero-tolerance weapons policy, school officials expelled the honor student from L. D. Bell High School. They claimed they had no choice even though no one believed Taylor intentionally put the knife in the truck.

For two weeks, Taylor attended a local alternative school. If the expulsion had held, he would have been transferred to the Tarrant County Juvenile Justice Alternative Education Program. Fortunately, school officials overrode the policy and readmitted Taylor to his high school.

Individuals may not understand or even know they are causing a problem. Warnings offer a flexible way of getting their attention.

SOURCE: Associated Press, March 20 and 21, 2002

Confronting the subject works best in situations where the threat manager has collected sufficient evidence against the subject to support criminal charges. The threat manager should not confuse confronting the subject with provoking him or her. Confrontation involves presenting the subject with evidence of his or her criminal or near-criminal acts. It is not about provoking the subject into committing a crime – such as assault on an officer – during the interview.

Case Study:

The Price of Provoking

An habitual threatener turned his attention to federal and county judicial officials. He sent numerous inappropriate letters, none of which crossed the line into crimes. An aggressive threat manager decided to visit the man at his home. As he and his partner drove out to see the threatener, the threat manager explained his intention to provoke the threatener into taking a swing at him. That would allow the officers to arrest the threatener for assault on a federal officer.

The threat manager introduced himself to the threatener and gave him a business card. The threatener refused to let the officers into his home. The threat manager used the refusal to become aggressive, but the threatener did not respond to any of his taunts. In fact, he remained quite calm.

Several days later, the threat manager received in the mail a box containing human feces. The U.S. Attorneys office refused to prosecute because the threat manager could not prove any link between the box and the threatener.

Confronting subject's with their criminal acts does not mean provoking subjects into committing a crime.

SOURCE: Authors' personal knowledge.

Advantages of Warning or Confronting

Sometimes, warning the subject may actually work. Often, individuals simply cannot recognize their own behavior as inappropriate, much less illegal. In their search for their self-defined justice, they see themselves as just. Hence, their actions in turn must be just as well. An employee fired for what she perceives as unfair reasons may begin harassing her supervisor. She sees that as justified retaliation. Frequently spouses feel if only they could have one last talk with their estranged spouse, then the old magic would work its spell once again. In efforts to cast that spell they do not understand their behavior as stalking. With these type individuals, usually recognized by their accumulated inhibitors and their previous exemplary behavior, a simple, even stern, warning from the threat manager can dissuade them from further Inappropriate Communication or Contacts (IC&C's). In essence, the threat manager educates the subject in distinguishing between appropriate and inappropriate behaviors.

Case Study:

The Chatty Bankruptee – 2

During the interview with C.F., the bankruptee who had researched the personal life of the bankruptcy judge, she stated that she no doubt gave the judge nightmares. The threat manager seized the opportunity to warn her. In a friendly, patient tone, the threat manager explained that he understood she meant no harm, but some other law enforcement officer, such as an FBI agent, might not be so understanding. Since threatening a federal judge is a federal crime, the threat manager advised C.F. to be careful in how she chose her words. She had been through a lot and certainly did not need more problems.

At that point, C.F. realized why the threat managers were interviewing her. They were not there to help her with her case as she had originally thought. She immediately began apologizing and denying any thought or intent of hurting the judge or anyone else. She promised to stay away from the judge and to keep in contact with the threat manager.

Simply pointing out the legal ramifications of a subject's behavior can be sufficient to defusing the risk.

SOURCE: United States Marshals Service, National Sheriffs Association training seminar, Newark, NJ, January 20, 2000.

Confronting the subject might jar a confession. Presenting an individual with evidence of his or her prosecutable behaviors may prompt a full admission of guilt. It may lead the subject to dispute some of the facts while admitting to others. The subject may feel compelled to correct minor details, thus confirming that he or she actually did what the threat manager just accused him or her of doing: "I didn't do that on Tuesday, it was Wednesday." Obviously, either of these reactions constitutes an admission of guilt.

Case Study:

Prompting a Confession

Jackie S. was a confused, troubled person. A transgender, he was undergoing the procedure to change from male to female. While enduring this, Jackie committed a robbery, ending up in the county jail. Deputy sheriffs strongly suspected he suffered some kind of mental problem, but they decided not to seek treatment for him.

Then he wrote an anonymous letter to the governor complaining about the governor's policies on prison sentences, especially the "third strike" provision. In the letter, Jackie explicitly and vividly threatened to kill the governor and the governor's wife. The crime lab lifted Jackie's fingerprints off the letter and the inside of the envelope.

After checking Jackie's criminal history and discussing him with deputies at the county jail, the threat manager arranged an interview with Jackie. Jackie, whose robbery sentence expired in two months, did not request an attorney. After giving Jackie his Miranda rights, the threat manager asked him about the letter.

Jackie proudly admitted authorship, then added that he meant what he said and planned to obtain a gun as soon as he got out of jail. Surprised by Jackie's confession, the threat manager asked him to sign a statement admitting to the letter, then thanked him and left. The threat manager used the confession to file charges against Jackie for terrorist threats. It was Jackie's third felony offense, which meant that he could get a sentence of 24 years to life.

Jackie, however, proved mentally incompetent to stand trial. The state mental hospital admitted him for an extended stay to receive treatment. He will go to trial once he is mentally fit.

SOURCE: Authors' personal knowledge.

Disadvantages of Warning or Confronting

Both warning and confronting the subject effectively reveals to the subject what the threat manager knows or suspects. The subject can use that new knowledge to identify any informants or as additional fuel to feed his or her anger at the potential target. Warnings, in particular, set up behavioral boundaries the subject can use to determine how far he or she can go with the next IC&C. By warning, the threat manager effectively draws a line in the sand. The subject can decide to use that line to limit his or her behavior by henceforth going only up to the line, but never over it. If, in confronting the subject, the threat manager relies on erroneous information, that bit of intelligence strengthens the subject's hand. Obviously, that result simply compounds the problem. It might also embolden the subject to act even more inappropriately.

Consequently, the threat manager should choose this strategy – as with any of the confrontational strategies – only after a very careful assessment of the subject's likeliest reaction to it and only after all the facts and accusations have been doubly verified. If the threat manager has any reason to believe that the reaction will be adverse or there is a question about the facts, then neither should be employed. As we will point out repeatedly in this chapter, all of the confrontational strategies carry grave risks. This does not mean we fear using them, we only urge they be used deliberately and intelligently.

Case Study:

Settled for an Undisclosed Amount of Money

Police officers received a report on a subject who made an angry, vulgar telephone call to a government office regarding a controversial issue in the news. Although not convinced the phone call constituted an IC&C, the officers were pressured by the office staff to do something about the caller. They promised to talk to the subject.

Two uniformed officers responded to the subject's residence situated in a middle-class neighborhood. The officers rather forcefully warned the subject to quit calling the government office or they would arrest him. The subject told the officers that he could call anyone he wanted to. He then ordered the officers off his property. The officers repeated the warning, to which the subject challenged them to arrest him then or leave him alone. The argument escalated into a scuffle on the front lawn. Neighbors watched as the officers used pepper spray to subdue the subject, then arrested him for resisting an officer and took him to jail.

The prosecutor declined prosecution. The subject then filed a civil lawsuit against the officers and the police department. The case was settled for an undisclosed amount of money. The staff at the government office, appalled at how the situation got so out of hand, refused to report any future IC&Cs.

The confrontation strategy only works when the subject has committed a crime before the interview.

SOURCE: Authors' personal knowledge.

When to Use Warning or Confronting

Warnings work most effectively with certain subjects who have not yet committed a crime but who seem headed that way. Subjects who have multiple inhibitors, no criminal record or just minor offenses, no history of mental health problems, and who have only recently begun to act inappropriately make the best candidates for warnings. The threat manager can also combine warnings with the assist strategy. That is, the threat manager can offer his or her assistance to resolve the subject's issue, but only if the subject vows to discontinue his or her inappropriate behaviors. Once the threat manager issues a warning, he or she needs to carefully monitor the subject's future behaviors and be prepared to back up the warning with harsh actions. Empty warnings do more harm than good. They tell the subject that the threat manager is only bluff and bluster.

Confronting, of course, usually works best when the threat manager has sufficient evidence already in hand to support a prosecution. It is also best to get the prosecutor's support beforehand. Nothing can make the situation worse than by either warning or confronting the subject and not be able to carry through with either.

In terms of evaluating this strategy's effectiveness according to the several venues of intended violence, the threat manager should evaluate the potential outcome of the warning or confrontation within the context of what the subject perceives to be at stake. Subject's who worry about losing everything they hold dear hardly pause about the prospects of an arrest. This rule of thumb applies especially to domestic disputes and workplace settings where the subject has already been fired. The *Intimacy Effect* works against the warning strategy because it raises the stakes by throwing in emotional influences. The threat manager may find warnings more effective in non-intimate settings.

When Not to Use Warning or Confronting

Obviously, neither should be used unless the threat manager can make good on the warning or carry through with the confrontation. This strategy simply does not work and has no place with subject's who have not committed a crime or other prosecutable offense. It also becomes detrimental if the prosecutor declines prosecution.

Civil Orders

In a limited number of cases defined by precise and specific conditions, the threat manager or the target acting on the advice of the threat manager can apply to the court to issue civil process ordering the subject to cease and desist his or her threatening behaviors and stay away from the target. These orders are known by different names in different jurisdictions B restraining orders, stay-away orders, or protective orders.

In some jurisdictions, violating such a civil order can carry criminal penalties. In addition, each jurisdiction usually has specific requirements to meet when filing for the order. Each threat manager should confer with his or her legal counsel on the name and scope of civil orders available.

Advantages of Civil Orders

Civil orders offer two contradictory advantages depending on the characteristics of the subject and the circumstances of the case. When the threat manager has reason to believe that the subject will obey the order, civil orders are obviously an effective strategy for defusing the risk and stopping the subject's problematic behaviors. As a very general rule of thumb, restraining orders work best on law-abiding individuals who have significant inhibitors – that is, a lot to lose – in their lives.

Case Illustration:

The County Crusader

A committed anti-abortionist reads in the newspaper that the county judge ordered the local police department to protect an abortion clinic from the efforts of anti-abortionists to blockade the clinic's entrances. Outraged, the subject begins a telephone campaign to the judge's chambers demanding to speak with the judge.

The judge's staff repeatedly tell the subject that the judge is not and will not be available to take this or any other call. The subject responds to these refusals angrily, verbally abusing the staff and warning that God's wrath will descend upon them and the judge. The calls disrupt the office routine and interfere with the staff getting their work done.

The threat manager's protective investigation determines that the subject is a local small businessman with a moderately successful business. The subject feels strongly about the abortion issue and has behaved in the same way toward other officials when he is unhappy with their stance on the issue. The subject never takes any action beyond telephoning in an aggressive and disrupting manner.

The threat manager's assessment is that there is little risk of violence, though clear reason to suspect the subject will continue telephoning. A civil order prohibiting the calls combined with a subject interview is the best strategy. During the interview, the threat manager stresses that the subject's behavior is harassment. If continued, it will result in a criminal violation being filed against the subject.

After the interview, the threat manager continues to monitor the situation. He prepares the necessary paperwork to file a criminal complaint so that he can respond swiftly if the subject calls again.

Civil orders work best if the threat manager has confidence the subject will obey them or if the threat manager is prepared to fully and immediately enforce them.

SOURCE: Hypothetical illustration drawn from the authors' professional experiences.

One particular value of these orders is that they send a clear message to those individuals willing or able to receive it to stop their problem behaviors. That message can help later in the case if more intrusive strategies, such as criminal prosecutions, need to be brought into play. Often, formerly law-abiding subjects will defend their actions by claiming that "no one told me to stop" or "I am just exercising my rights." Serving a restraining order on these individuals clearly lets them know that their behavior is wrong and that they risk criminal penalties if they continue. It robs them of the excuse of ignorance.

Conversely, civil orders can be effective if the threat manager has reason to believe that the subject will violate the order and that the court that issued it will enforce it with criminal sanctions. In effect, the order may open the way for the threat manager to effect an arrest, thus bringing some temporary respite from the subject's threatening behaviors. We caution, however, that this is an extraordinarily risky approach that should be employed either never or only when the target is fully protected and the threat manager can react to the violation instantly. These conditions are hard to meet. Our general advice would be not to take advantage of this peculiar advantage in all but the rarest cases.

Table 9-1 lists some subject characteristics associated with obeying civil orders and a number of subject characteristics common to those with a high chance of violating such orders. The list is neither exhaustive nor comprehensive, merely illustrative.

Table 9-1. Subject Characteristics Associated with Obeying or Violating Civil Orders

OBEYING THE ORDER

- Individuals generally known to be law-abiding
- Individuals with strong inhibitors, such as a good job, good home life, or good reputation in the community
- Individuals who have a lot to lose, such as those on probation or parole or who have a new job

VIOLATING THE ORDER

- History of previous violations
- Few or diminishing inhibitors
- Mental illness, especially command delusions or hallucinations to harm another
- Behavioral pattern of resistance to authority, e.g., warrant arrest, assault on police officer, or failure to appear
- Known alcohol or substance abuse
- History of stalking behavior without a civil order in place
- Dispute is long running
- History of violence
- Provocation or escalation by the target, whether intentional or unintentional

SOURCE: California Highway Patrol Special Investigations Unit practices.

Disadvantages of Civil Orders

Civil orders should not be considered as a solution to the case or problem. They are the start of a process, oftentimes a lengthy process, that requires continuous monitoring. If the threat manager decides on this strategy, he or she must be committed to full and immediate enforcement of the provisions of the order, even small or technical violations. A civil order that is not enforced is worse than no order at all. It proves to the subject that the order does not really apply to him or her and that the threat manager is unwilling or, worse yet, unable to control the subject's behavior.

The threat manager should always approach this strategy with considerable caution and a healthy skepticism about its effectiveness. Among threat management practitioners, civil orders remain very controversial. The field has yet to develop a consensus on if they should be used, much less when or under what conditions. The Threat Management Unit of the Los Angeles Police Department uses restraining orders routinely, almost as a matter of course. Psychologist Reid Meloy concluded from a survey of the research that "protective (restraining) orders are good, most of the time." However, Meloy cautioned that the research supporting that conclusion had some weaknesses. He suggested more research needed to be done. Gavin de Becker, on the other hand, believes such orders frequently prompt violent attacks, especially in situations involving domestic violence or the potential for domestic violence.[1]

As de Becker points out, obtaining civil orders entails considerable risk of escalating the problem. To the subject, the order can seem a highly provocative act on the part of the target. The subject may interpret such a move as an embarrassing public attack on his or her reputation. Unlike arrests or mental health commitments, civil orders leave the subject free in the community immediately after receiving the insult. The subject remains free until he or she violates the order. That leaves the choice of the next step up to a potentially angry, vengeful person. It's a bit like slapping an angry grizzly bear across the snout, then immediately turning one's back to the bear.

The greatest disadvantage of civil orders is that they are a risky way of trying to defuse the risk.

Case Study:

Grinding the Axe

Early Sunday morning, Christopher Howard called 911 from his hotel room in Romulus, Michigan, then hung up the phone. Police responded and found him bleeding from the wrists, though the slashes were not life threatening. An alert officer noticed a protection order for Howard to keep away from Marie M. Irons, dated one week earlier, in the room. The officer called Southfield police to ask them to check on Irons, who was Howard's estranged wife. The police searched Howard's hotel room and found an ax hidden between the mattress and box spring.

Southfield police found a much worse crime scene than the Romulus police encountered. Irons lay in bed, her head nearly severed at the neck, with her two-year-old son asleep beside her.

Protection orders can be more provocative than protective.

SOURCE: Associated Press, December 31, 2002

When to Use Civil Orders

The threat manager should consider civil orders only after he or she is confident four conditions can be fully met.

1. The probable response of the subject will be non-violent, even if it is likely the subject will violate the terms of the order.
2. The court will take a zero-tolerance approach to any violations, even minor ones.
3. The threat manager and his or her agency has the capability to closely monitor the case and to respond immediately to any violation.
4. Reasonable protective measures for the target have been set up.

Threat managers will find the first two of these conditions especially hard to assess. Predicting the subject's reaction is risky business. Depending on a court system overloaded with myriad cases may not be as risky, but it carries its own chances that the court will simply be to busy to want to bother with violations, especially petty violations.

In terms of evaluating this strategy's effectiveness according to the several venues of intended violence, once again the threat manager will find the Intimacy Effect an especially good barometer of the chance of success. The more intimate the relationship between the subject and target, and the more that intimacy is challenged by the situations of the case, the less likely will the subject respond positively to the order. The status of the subject's inhibitors also help assess the potential effectiveness of the order.

When Not to Use Civil Orders

The threat manager should not apply for a civil order if any of the four following conditions apply:

1. When the subject's probable response may be violence.
2. If the threat manager suspects the court may show some leniency to violations, including minor violations.
3. The threat manager and his or her agency cannot adequately monitor the situation or respond quickly to any violation.
4. Reasonable protective measures for the target have not been set up.

Mental Health Commitments

Subjects who display signs of mental illness and engage in dangerous behaviors may be best managed through mental health commitments. This strategy requires the threat manager to present to a mental health professional sufficient, compelling evidence to convince the doctor that the subject requires immediate treatment. Every state has set its own legal requirements regulating commitments. Generally speaking, most states expect proof of probable cause showing that the subject, due to a mental disorder, is now:

- a danger to self;
- a danger to others; or
- gravely disabled.

Every threat manager needs to consult with his or her legal counsel for guidance on the legal standards in the threat manager's jurisdiction. Whatever the regulations, adopting this strategy means emphasizing mental health problems. Commitments, as a threat management strategy, apply only to those subjects who suffer a real and provable mental illness and pose a danger to themselves or others.

Threat managers will find this a difficult strategy to apply successfully, but not because of difficulties proving mental illness or dangerousness. Rather, hospital overcrowding and severe budget shortfalls daunt it. Mental health facilities cannot provide bed space at the threat manager's whim. These days, doctors demand relevant information organized in an intelligible format. The burden thus falls on the threat manager to collect concrete evidence directly bearing on the subject's mental state and potential dangerousness. In some cases, the original IC&C that opened the threat manager's case may not prove relevant. The threat manager needs to seek other behavioral evidence showing mental illness and dangerousness. That evidence should then be fully documented in an affidavit. Good affidavits present precise, detailed, and specific behavioral descriptions, but always in layman's language. Affidavits offering medical diagnoses usually do little more than offend or amuse the doctor.

It will help the threat manager to keep in mind the following guidelines.

- Written, not verbal reports, are more convincing to psychiatric admissions staff.
- The threat manager should describe the subject's specific behavior and relevant background information in as much detail as possible. That description should not include psychological descriptions like "schizophrenic," "manic-depressive," or any other medical jargon. Those terms invite the admissions staff to challenge the threat manager's knowledge of them. Descriptions should be limited to behaviors without a diagnosis.
- The threat manager need not personally observe dangerous or disabling behavior. Probable cause can be legitimately based on information supplied by credible third parties, such as neighbors, paramedics, relatives, or other mental health professionals.
- The affidavit should list the reasons the threat manager decided to take the subject into custody.

Copies of the affidavit should then be presented to all concerned mental health professionals.

Case Illustration:

The Bodyguard

A subject arrives at City Hall demanding to see the mayor. He claims the FBI ordered him to protect the mayor from several assassins. The subject earnestly believes that the mayor will soon be killed without his protection. The subject also produces several documents indicating he has conducted detailed research on the mayor's career and habits. He also admits that he recently purchased a pistol specifically because of the orders he received from the FBI. When pressed, the subject cannot name or describe who supposedly gave him the orders.

The threat manager is summoned to interview the subject. When she tells him that he cannot see the mayor, the subject accuses her and the security officers of being the assassins. The subject becomes increasingly agitated and has to be forcibly restrained.

The threat manager completes an affidavit detailing the suspect's delusions, focus on violence, resistance to restraint, and recent purchase of the pistol. The wording of the affidavit is factual, non-judgmental, and specific. When the threat manager presents it to the duty psychiatrist at the county mental health facility, the psychiatrist quickly agrees that the subject should be admitted for evaluation and probable treatment. The threat manager arranges with facility staff to keep her informed of the subject's status and treatment progress.

Commitments depend on detailed, unbiased, and unemotional descriptions of the subject's behavior.

SOURCE: Hypothetical illustration drawn from the authors' professional experiences.

Threat management does not end with the commitment of the subject. Frequently, initial commitments expire after 48 or 72 hours unless the doctor diagnoses a specific illness and prescribes a treatment regimen requiring a longer commitment. The doctor may determine further commitment unnecessary or that the treatment program requires only outpatient care. Consequently, the threat manager must arrange to follow-up on the subject's progression through the mental health system. This requires arranging with the staff to alert the threat manager to any change in the subject's status, including release back into the community or transfer to another facility. In sum, commitments do not inactivate threat management cases. At best, they allow the threat manager to adopt the Watch & Wait strategy to monitor the subject's response to treatment.

Case Study:

Slicing Through the Evil Voices

Even with the telephone receiver on the hook, Chad E. heard the evil voices yelling at him. Clearly, he concluded, the telephone company had given the voices special access to his phone. He held out as long as he could, but by summer he could stand the yelling no longer. He went to the local phone company headquarters to angrily express his frustrations about the voices. Phone company staff called the police.

When the uniformed officers arrived, Chad threatened them. They detained him until the threat manager arranged his admittance to the city mental health facility based on his paranoid, violent behavior. After three days, facility staff convinced Chad to remain voluntarily for further treatment. Chad asked to get out for just a few hours to pick up some personal belongings.

He never came back. The next day, a staff member contacted the threat manager to report Chad as missing. The threat manager went by Chad's house. No one answered the doorbell and the house appeared vacant. The threat manager left.

Three days later, neighbors reported a foul odor emanating from Chad's house. Since Chad's address was linked to the threat manager's case file, he was notified of the complaints along with the uniform division. Together, they found Chad's body in the living room of his house. The knife he used to kill himself lay beside him.

Mental health treatment succeeds only as long as the subject accepts it.

SOURCE: Authors' personal knowledge.

Nor can the threat manager assume a successful treatment once the doctor releases the subject. Often, that release includes a prescription for the subject to take medication. That assumes that the subject will now self-administer the drugs. As long as that continues, the subject's behavior may remain appropriate. All too often, however, subjects discontinue their medicine. When that happens, they revert to the original behaviors that brought them to the threat manager's attention. In effect, the process starts over again.

Case Study:

The Vicious Cycle

Russell R. called the CIA in Washington, D.C. to tell them he planned to load his van with explosives and drive to a specific city and blow up a government building there, just like Timothy McVeigh. The Agency passed word of the call to the city's police, which turned the case over to the threat manager.

The threat manager's protective investigation revealed that Russell lives outdoors down by the river, though he usually visited his mother every three or four days to bathe and get something to eat. Russell's mother helped the threat manager find Russell for an interview. Russell talked irrationally about death and murder. He also claimed he received messages from billboards and street signs. His behavior so frightened his mother that she refused to let him live with her and allowed his visits only because she feared he would react violently to a refusal.

The threat manager arranged for a three-day commitment at the city mental hospital. Once psychiatrists stabilized his behavior with medications, the facility released him. A few weeks later, Russell stopped taking his medicine. Russell's mother contacted the threat manager, who arranged another commitment.

This cycle continued for several months. Then Russell broke into his mother's house and threatened her. She obtained a restraining order against him. Russell quickly violated it, so the threat manager arrested him. The judge sentenced him to a week in jail, after which the new cycle of jail and release began.

Eventually, the mother quit reporting the restraining order violations. Occasionally, uniformed officers pick Russell up for minor crimes, like disturbing the peace or drug use. These result in short-term jail stays or occasional mental health commitments on "bad" days.

When the threat manager contacted the mental health staff to see if the cycle could be broken, they claimed they could only hold Russell as long as his mental illness made him dangerous. After they stabilized him with medication, he no longer posed a danger to himself or others, so the law required them to release him. Once released, Russell dropped off his medication and his mental illness – and dangerousness returned. The cycle seemed endless.

Threat managers must understand that medication controls a mentally ill person's behavior only as long as the person takes the medicine.

SOURCE: Authors' personal knowledge.

Advantages of Mental Health Commitment

Mental health commitments treat the subject's illness and offer the advantage of a possible cure or long-term regulation of his or her problematic behaviors. In the short term, it gives the target and the threat manager a respite from dealing with the subject's menacing behaviors. In the long term, psychiatric treatment may succeed in helping the subject gain control over himself or herself. At a more practical level for the threat manager, many states prohibit subjects who have been involuntarily committed from possessing a firearm. The threat manager should research the laws governing his or her jurisdiction to determine if this advantage exists. If so, the threat manager should always enforce that law as part of the mental health commitment strategy.

Case Illustration:

Taxing the Clerks

A subject repeatedly calls the county tax clerk's office asking for help. The subject believes that her house is bugged. She also hears voices. The tax clerks have tolerated the situation, but begin to grow concerned when the calls increase in frequency and the woman talks about violent themes. She also begins accusing the Chief Clerk of planting the bugs and telling the voices what to say. Each call now disrupts the office routine as the staff waits to hear what she says.

After the Chief Clerk notifies the threat manager of the problem, the threat manager opens a protective investigation. He learns that the subject has two firearms and recently purchased a third one. The threat manager confers with the county mental health provider, who informs him that the subject has not been showing up for her scheduled voluntary treatment. The threat manager reaches out to two other law enforcement agencies in whose jurisdiction the woman once lived and finds out that she had engaged in problem behaviors in both places. The threat manager prepares an affidavit seeking involuntary commitment.

The court grants the commitment and the threat manager takes her into custody. The threat manager uses the state's law on involuntary commitments to confiscate the three firearms and to search for any others. Working together, the threat manager and the mental health providers convince the judge to order a long-term commitment. The threat manager then arranges to be kept informed of the treatment's progress and of any change in the subject's status.

SOURCE: Hypothetical illustration drawn from the authors' professional experiences.

Disadvantages of Mental Health Commitment

Even if a mental health commitment succeeds in helping the subject, that success does not necessarily or automatically translate into inactivating the case. For one thing, time alone will tell if the treatment worked as measured by the subject's attitude toward the target. Successful treatment often involves behavioral modifications, not a true medical cure such as seen in physical ailments. Treating mental illnesses cannot be as simply done as removing an appendix or patching a hernia. Often, doctors achieve the behavioral modifications through drug and other therapies. Obviously, these modifications disappear whenever the subject quits taking his or her medicine for several weeks. We have seen cases in which the subject dutifully followed the prescribed treatment regimen for years before suddenly dropping off the program and reverting back to the IC&Cs that first opened the case. The threat manager will be well advised to consider mental health commitments less a solution to the problem and more the beginning of a process that can be complex and time consuming.

At a more practical level for the threat manger, too, getting a long-term commitment requires a lot of work gathering evidence and preparing its presentation. Longer commitments beyond the initial involuntary 48 or 72 hours can only be ordered by a judge after a probable-cause hearing. The threat manager will have to work with the state's attorney to present the state's case as compellingly as possible. Any failure risks having the subject released, but now with even more motive for anger at the target.

Case Study:

The Longbow

Shawn C. fled to the safety of the county government building. Although still out of breath, he began raving to the woman in the Information Booth about an FBI conspiracy to kill him. He spoke frantically about the violence they would commit, suicide, and the weapons he had collected. Security officers detained him until the threat manager could arrive.

During the threat manager's interview with Shawn, Shawn admitted that he kept a gun in his car. With Shawn's permission, the threat manager searched the car. He discovered a .44 magnum pistol and a flak vest, military helmet, and three knives. Shawn explained that he needed all of them to protect him from the rogue FBI agents.

The threat manager arranged for a mental health commitment. He also initiated the process for seizing Shawn's firearm due to the mental commitment. He also arranged for a third party monitoring through Shawn's sister. The facility released Shawn after three days.

The threat manager maintained close contact with Shawn, who expressed even greater fear of the FBI now that he no longer had a gun to protect himself. Three weeks later, Shawn's sister informed the threat manager that Shawn was pressing her to buy a gun for him. The threat manager warned Shawn about the weapons' restrictions on him. Shawn spoke only vaguely of his intentions, though he clearly exhibited continued fear of the FBI.

Two weeks later, the threat manager checked on Shawn, who proudly showed him the hunting bow and arrows he now owned. Unfortunately, the law prohibited only firearms, not other weapons. Shawn refused the threat manager's request to give up the bow.

The staff at the mental facility explained to the threat manager that without an overt act, Shawn cannot be committed again. The threat manager began closely monitoring Shawn through visits and contacts with the sister, but he was powerless to get the bow and arrow away from him. And Shawn remained deeply afraid of those rogue agents.

Sometimes, the mentally ill can find their way around the law.

SOURCE: Authors' personal knowledge.

When to Use Mental Health Commitment

Table 9-2 lists relevant behaviors for suggesting the need for mental help. The threat manager should consider the commitment strategy if the subject displays any of these behaviors.

The threat manager should learn the mental health laws in his or her jurisdiction. He or she should also take the time to visit local mental health clinics to meet the administrators and find out about the process for voluntary and involuntary commitments prior to a crisis situation. Many mental health providers offer training for law enforcement in when and how to apply for a commitment. In addition, prior to making a decision about seeking a commitment, the threat manager should consider consulting with the doctors about the case.

In terms of evaluating this strategy's effectiveness according to the several venues of intended violence, the threat manager should be alert to symptoms of mental illness in every case. Delusions, schizophrenia, paranoia, and every other type of mental illness can inject itself into any relationship, whether intimate, business related, or public official to constituent. Treating such illnesses can go a long way toward resolving the problem, even though it may take a long time to actually see the resolution. Indeed, if the threat manager sees evidence that some mental illness prompts the subject's inappropriate or problematic behavior, mental health commitment and treatment offers the only realistic threat management strategy, both in the short and the long term.

Table 9-2. Relevant Behaviors for Mental Health Commitments

Due to a mental condition:

Danger to Others

- Assaultive behaviors
- Threatening behavior with immediate intent to harm
- Subject admits to "hearing voices" instructing him or her to hurt someone
- Fire setting or leaving gas turned on in the home
- Engaging in dangerous behavior without regard for the safety of others, such as throwing objects, reckless driving, brandishing or random discharge of a weapon, or breaking windows

Danger to Self

- Actual suicide attempt
- Threat to commit suicide with available means (a formulated plan increases the risk)
- Hearing voices instructing the subject to injure himself or herself
- Self-mutilation, burning or cutting self, or banging head
- Refusing medical treatment for a life-threatening medical problem
- Walking in front of cars
- Leaving gas on or setting fires

Gravely Disabled

- Unable to provide food for himself or herself
  – refuses to eat or claims that food is poisoned or altered
  – claims that subject does not need to eat
  – too depressed to eat, claims of no appetite
  – afraid to leave room to obtain food
- Unable to provide clothing
  – nude or semi-nude in a public area
  – person has disposed of his or her own clothing
  – paranoid ideation that clothing is contaminated
  – clothing is dirty, tattered, or inappropriate for weather conditions
- Unable to provide shelter for himself or herself
  – living on the streets, but cannot explain why
  – has history of evictions without understanding why
  – living conditions are uninhabitable or pose fire/health hazards

SOURCE: California Highway Patrol Special Investigations Unit practices

Case Study:

Meeting Ron and Nancy

Jeff M. explained to the traffic clerk at the metropolitan courthouse that voices ordered him there to meet Ronald Reagan and his wife Nancy. Jeff then began describing the various violent acts the voices commanded him to do. Summoned by the clerk, the threat manager intervenes. A quick records check showed that Jeff had a past history of violence and alcohol abuse.

The threat manager arranged for a mental health commitment. The facility agreed to hold him three days, which gave the threat manager time to prepare a detailed affidavit describing Jeff's past behaviors. This results in a 14 day commitment.

During that fortnight, the threat manager arranged for Jeff to live in a half-way house specializing in mental illness and substance abuse. Once released from the mental facility, Jeff lived at the half-way house for six months.

When he moved from the half-way house, the threat manager set up procedures to monitor his progress and encouraged Jeff to call him regularly. Several years later, Jeff continued clean and sober. Occasionally, he thanked the threat manager for helping him.

Mental health commitments can work if the threat manager is committed to making them work.

SOURCE: Authors' personal knowledge.

When Not to Use Mental Health Commitments

Mental health commitments depend on the full determination of every official involved to see the strategy applied successfully. If the threat manager has any reason to suspect a lack of such determination on the part of anyone involved, then the process should not be relied on. Nor should the threat manager initiate the process simply to get a problem individual off the streets. Commitments cannot be seen as a vehicle for transferring the threat manager's problems to another agency. Finally, commitments should not be attempted in the expectation that they will resolve or end the case. Simply put, as a threat management strategy, the threat manager should turn to mental health commitments only in those cases in which the subject shows clear signs of suffering from a real mental illness. It has no place or application in any other situation requiring threat management.

Criminal Prosecutions

Throughout this book, we have used the concept of inappropriate communications or contacts as the trigger for opening a threat management case. Now, we must emphatically reiterate that inappropriate is not synonymous with illegal. Law enforcement officers new to the field of threat management find arrest and prosecution the most tempting strategy to apply. They forget that they cannot sustain an arrest or prosecution unless the suspect actually commits a crime and the threat manager can prove it. It takes most officers a considerable time to realize that this threshold, proving a crime, actually makes this strategy a very risky one to attempt. Despite its natural allure, threat managers will find they rarely have sufficient grounds for arrest and prosecution. Rarer still will they successfully defuse the risk through criminal prosecution alone.

Threat managers deciding whether or not to employ arrest and prosecution as a threat management strategy (as opposed to simply enforcing the law) must factor into their deliberations four particular considerations that weigh heavily on the ability of this strategy to work. First, a crime has to have been committed. Assessing this consideration requires the threat manager to have a sound understanding of his or her jurisdictions' criminal definition of threatening or stalking. This is the crossroads between criminal acts and First Amendment rights. The Constitution protects American citizens who express their anger, dismay, or opposition to their company's business practices, the actions of government officials, or the policies of their schools. It even protects them in describing individuals negatively, provided that such descriptions are rooted in fact and not intentionally distorted. Does the law prohibit a spouse from following an estranged spouse home once, twice, or multiple times? Does the threat manager understand the legal definition of harassment, especially as it applies to the unique circumstances of the case at hand? When does a comment cross the line to become a prosecutable threat? What behaviors have to occur before the threat manager can arrest a subject for stalking?

Consequently, law enforcement should take note of a subject's letter, telephone call, or contact only if it crosses recognized and clearly delineated guidelines for being inappropriate or if the context in which the action was made is sufficiently disturbing or ominous to raise legitimate safety concerns. Usually, the applicable laws address only threatening communications or behaviors, things like terrorist threats, stalking, criminal trespass, or threatening telephone calls. In most jurisdictions, convictions depend on proving the suspect made a credible threat, intended to cause fear, and actually did instill fear in the intended victim. Some jurisdictions also require proof that the suspect has the apparent ability to carry out the threat. Proving that threatening words are in fact a prosecutable threat is a technical legal point that can sometimes be difficult to determine. Other jurisdictions recognize implied threats through a pattern of conduct or a totality of circumstances.[2]

Although each threat manager should consult with his or her legal advisor or prosecuting authority, the following guidelines apply to what legally is a true or credible threat.

- Language conveying a direct threat – "I'm going to kill you" – is usually a crime.
- Language conveying a conditional threat – "If you don't rule in my favor, I'm going to kill you" – is usually a crime.
- Language conveying a veiled threat – "Now I know why people blow up buildings like in Oklahoma City. The same thing could happen here the way you treat people" – would be considered by most jurisdictions as rhetorical and not a crime without other conduct.
- Language conveying an oblique threat – "Watch your back" or "You'll regret messing with me" – would be considered by most jurisdictions as rhetorical and not a crime without other conduct.

Threat managers who rush to file a criminal complaint frequently find out that the words actually spoken or written did not constitute a prosecutable threat. The charges are then dropped, thus leaving the subject free and angrier than before.

The second consideration involves going beyond proving a crime occurred to proving the subject committed it. Simply because a threatening letter is signed John Jones or a telephone caller claims to be John Jones or an hysterical target claims to have seen John Jones stalking does not mean the threat manager does not have to prove that the John Jones under suspicion wrote the letter, made the call, or actually stalked. Obviously, establishing this proof requires the threat manager to conduct a plain, old-fashioned criminal investigation. The evidence, then, is the same as in any such investigation – fingerprints; handwriting analysis; witness testimony; or, most commonly, by the suspect's own admission. In the rush to resolve a seemingly threatening situation, this fundamental investigative step can be overlooked. The threat manager should ensure that it is not.

Case Study:

The Frame-Up

The governor's office of a large western state received a letter containing a direct threat to kill the governor. The writer signed the letter with both name and address. Through his contacts with other law enforcement agencies, the threat manager learned that a similar letter with a threat to kill the president had been referred to the United States Secret Service for investigation.

Working together, the threat manager and the Secret Service agent contacted the individual whose signature closed the letter. Their investigation determined that she was a recently divorced woman with two children living in a middle-class suburb of the state capital. Their visit surprised her. She adamantly denied any knowledge of the letter. She also told them that since her divorce several strange things had occurred. She received unwanted magazines, her utilities had been canceled, and she had been subjected to a series of hang-up calls.

Further investigation proved that the ex-husband was responsible for the harassment and the threatening letters. He had signed her name to both letters because he knew law enforcement would have to react, thus exposing her to possible arrest.

The threat manager should always prove the identity of the suspect who wrote the threatening letter or made the threatening phone call.

SOURCE: Authors' personal knowledge.

The third consideration requires a more subtle judgment call by the threat manager. Will the arrest actually result in confinement or will the subject obtain a prompt release on bail. The threat manager can best counter this possibility by working with the prosecutor to prepare an exhaustive affidavit for the judge or magistrate that presents all the relevant evidence, with particular emphasis on the risk of danger posed by the subject. This information can be used to convince a judge to increase the bail or, in rare cases, deny any bail to the subject. The threat manager's worst nightmare is to affect an arrest, then learn that the subject made bail and dropped out of sight. Once the suspect is in custody, the threat manager should make arrangements to have any change in the suspect's status reported immediately to the threat manager.

If bail remains a possibility, the threat manager must try to convince the judge or magistrate to impose strict conditions on the bail. This will allow the threat manager to exercise third party control over any future problematic behavior until the trial. These conditions can include mental health treatment, a ban on drugs and alcohol, confiscation of all weapons, authority to search the subject and the subject's residence, and a requirement for the subject to stay away from the target.

Case Study:

Making Bail

Eric Keifer posted bail one last time. He had been arrested numerous times for harassing his ex-wife and daughter after following them from San Antonio, Texas, to Laguna Hills, California. On Sunday, October 27, 2002, Kiefer again broke into his ex-wife's house and attacked her and their daughter. Police arrested him for violating a restraining order she had take out against him. Keifer posted $25,000 bail.

About 1:00 a.m. Thursday morning, Keifer broke into the house again. He tried to force his daughter to drink a caustic liquid, but her grandparents rescued her. Keifer kept them at bay by swinging a hatchet at them. The grandfather got a handgun, but his shot missed. A friend staying at the house got a shotgun and shot Keifer in the neck. Kiefer died at the scene. The friend and grandparents suffered deep cuts to their heads and arms.

Arrests do little good if the subject can quickly make bail.

SOURCE: Associated Press, October 31, 2002

The fourth consideration that the threat manager should assess before engaging the arrest and prosecution strategy requires evaluating the chances of the subject pleading to a lesser offense and receiving a short jail term or – worse – a fine or suspended sentence. Heavy caseloads tempt prosecutors to cut deals with defendants all the time. In this regard, threat management cases carry no immunity from such wheeling and dealing, especially if the degree of risk appears low. If this happens, the threat manager should work closely with the prosecutor to require strict conditions on any probation as part of the ultimate plea bargain agreement.

Case Study:

The Caller

A subject called the office of a government agency and stated he intended to arm himself, go to the office lobby, and hurt someone. He also threatened to commit suicide in the lobby. The subject's telephone number appeared on the agency's caller identification.

The threat manager contacted the subject, who admitted he made the call. However, the subject disputed the quotes noted by the agency secretary. He agreed to meet with the threat manager to discuss the situation.

At the appointed place, the threat manager arrested the subject for making terrorist threats. A search of his house uncovered four firearms, including a semi-automatic assault rifle. The threat manager confiscated the weapons.

The suspect pled guilty to the felony charge and received a short county jail sentence. When he became eligible for probation, the threat manager arranged that it be conditioned on the suspect receiving mandatory mental health treatment, periodic drug and alcohol testing, and that he subject himself to being searched. The threat manager also arranged for his probation officer to maintain very close supervision. The threat manager closely monitored the suspect's progress while on probation.

Arrests do not guarantee long-term incarceration. The threat manager needs to arrange for other threat management strategies to take over once the subject's incarceration ends.

SOURCE: Authors' personal knowledge.

These four considerations, all realities of the judicial system, make the rush to arrest and prosecute far less tempting for the threat manager who pauses long enough to account for them. Experienced threat managers determine beforehand if prosecuting the suspect will be a successful intervention strategy for defusing the risk. As with deciding to apply any strategy, the threat manager always asks, "Will it make the situation better or worse?"

As with a mental health commitment, arrest and prosecution does not of its own end a threat management case. Even a conviction and lengthy sentence does not ensure the risk has truly been defused. The threat manager has to ensure that the suspect does not have any outside contacts or resources to carry out any harm. The threat manager will have to notify the correctional facility, and any other facilities, whenever the prisoner is transferred, to inform the threat manager of any change in the prisoner's status, such as escape, parole, or unrestricted release.

Advantages of Arrest and Prosecution

Successful criminal prosecutions put the subject behind bars, thus hampering his or her ability to harm the target. Incarceration does not guarantee the target's safety, but it certainly goes a long way toward making that goal. At the least, a criminal conviction and sentence to prison gives the threat manager a way to physically control the subject. When dealing with individuals who have no criminal history, but who now find themselves caught up in some highly emotional risk, such as losing their job or their spouse, an arrest can serve as a blunt, forceful notice that the system will not tolerate his or her behaviors. For those subjects already familiar with prison life, another arrest may result in a longer prison sentence.

Case Study:

Strike Three

A prison inmate wrote a series of letters to the district attorney, his trial judge, and members of the last jury that convicted him. The letters complained about his treatment in prison, which prompted the inmate to threaten to kill all of the recipients once he was released.

The threat manager went to the prison and interviewed the prisoner. The inmate admitted writing the letters. He expressed considerable bitterness at his treatment and repeated his belief that the individuals he wrote were responsible and should be held to account for his sufferings.

The protective investigation convinced the threat manager that the prisoner had no outside support or contacts to carry out the threats. He would only become a risk once he was free from prison. The threat manager also learned that the prisoner was scheduled for release in 18 months.

The threat manager took the case to the district attorney's office and pointed out that the prisoner already had two prior felony convictions. The threats thus constituted a "3rd Strike" offense. The prosecutor proved the case and the new judge sentenced the prisoner to three consecutive 24-to-life terms.

Arrest and conviction can be an effective threat management strategy if the threat manager is sure that the suspect has no outside support or resources, the incarceration is lengthy, and the correctional institution knows to alert the threat manager of any changes in the inmate's status.

SOURCE: Authors' personal knowledge.

Arrest and prosecution has another distinct advantage. Law enforcement officers know how to do it. They know how to make a case, affect an arrest, and work the case through the system. This strategy provides a very high comfort level for most police officers, especially compared to several of the other strategies. We caution, however, that an officer's comfort with the strategy should never be the reason for using it. Simply knowing how to do it does not equate with whether or not arrest and prosecution offers the best way to manage the case.

Perhaps the main advantage of arrest and prosecution derives from society's interest in punishing individuals who commit crimes. Law enforcement officers cannot turn a blind eye to the commission of a felony, even if they believe it may have a negative impact on their management of the threat. In effect, then, threat managers may have less choice in deciding on arrest and prosecution as a threat management strategy. Enforcing the law takes precedence.

Disadvantages of Arrest and Prosecution

From the subject's point of view, arrest and prosecution constitutes the most confrontational strategy of them all. A failure to obtain a conviction therefore has a number of adverse consequences. It might embolden the subject to more aggressive actions toward the target. Arrest and prosecution, after all, are the biggest guns in the threat manager's arsenal. The subject can easily conclude from any failure to use them effectively that he or she has triumphed over the judicial system. Such a victory for the subject invites greater aggression.

In addition, making the arrest rather bluntly puts the subject on notice that law enforcement has an interest in him or her. Subtlety and finesse go out the window every time handcuffs come out. Once this strategy comes into play, it becomes very difficult for the threat manager to revert to less confrontational strategies.

Finally, because law enforcement officers must enforce the law, the need to arrest and prosecute actually limits the options available to the threat manager. If a crime occurs, the threat manager cannot debate whether or not Watch & Wait would work better than Refocus & Assist. As we mentioned above, enforcing the law takes precedence. But that principle effectively ties the hands of the threat manager. Indeed, it may very well put the threat manager's law enforcement responsibilities at odds with his or her ability to manage the threat.

Case Study:

Flight of the SEAL

Edward T. bragged to the security guard at City Hall that he was a Navy SEAL. Impressed, the guard struck up a conversation with him until Edward told him about his mission to assassinate the mayor because the city owed him 33 million dollars. Uniformed officers took Edward to the mental health clinic, which held him for treatment. The treatment succeeded in ridding Edward of his delusions. Once released, he resumed a normal life with his wife and two children.

Four years later, Edward suddenly began making repeated phone calls to various city and county offices. He laced his language with profanity and made references to mobsters intent on killing him. The threat manager's protective investigation uncovered the earlier commitment through the police reports. This information helped the threat manager arrange for a second commitment. Once again, the treatment worked and the hospital released Edward back to his wife and children.

Unknown to the threat manager, while making his phone calls to government offices, Edward had also made 38 calls in one day to a Harley Davidson dealership in the neighboring county where he lived. That constituted a misdemeanor violation. When he arrived home, sheriff's deputies greeted him with an arrest warrant.

Although the county prosecutor subsequently dropped the charges for lack of evidence Edward made the calls, that decision came too late. Once released on bail, Edward abandoned his wife and children and fled. Some think to Texas, but no one knows since he remains at large.

Sometimes, arrests have a negative impact on threat management strategies.

SOURCE: Authors' personal knowledge.

When to Arrest and Prosecute

The decision on when to arrest and prosecute depends solely on the threat manager finding enough evidence that the subject committed a crime. To the extent that the threat manager can integrate his or her threat management responsibilities with his or her law enforcement obligations, the threat manager should slow down the timing of the arrest until the chances of a successful prosecution and incarceration are high. Arrest and prosecution works best in cases where the threat manager can prove the subject committed a felony serious enough to result in a significant prison sentence.

Prosecuting lesser crimes still leave the threat manager some maneuvering room by working within the system. Misdemeanor charges offer the threat manager the ability to arrange conditions of probation to use in long-term case management. However, these type charges, of themselves, do not constitute effective strategies for managing the risk.

Although not the optimal solution, the threat manager can opt for arrest when he or she can arrange for conditions on a suspended sentence. Such conditions provide some systematic controls on the suspect's future behaviors. They also allow a quick way to get the suspect back into custody should he or she do anything to escalate the risk to the target. In addition, criminal charges can be quite effective against those subjects who are already on parole or probation. Parole or probation searches, drug and alcohol testing, or other controls empowered to the supervising officer can be useful for controlling subjects currently engaged in IC&Cs toward a target. In some cases, new criminal charges or violations of the parole or probation can be used to bring the subject back into custody.

Case Study:

The Probationer

Goodwin D. hated his father that day because his father would not let him use the family car. In revenge, he called the car dealership where his father worked and claimed a bomb would soon go off. Police linked the crime to Goodwin through phone records. Since his history showed past emotional problems and his mental state did not match his age of 22 years, the threat manager was called in to help on the case.

During a subject interview, Goodwin confessed to the threat manager that he made the call. He added that he intended to kill his father with a knife when the father came home that day.

The threat manager used the confession to work with the courts on setting up conditions of probation. The conditions included no weapons, no drugs or alcohol as proved by urine testing, and regular psychiatric counseling. In addition, the threat manager arranged for Goodwin to be placed in a special probation program for individuals with emotional or mental problems. This program offered close supervision by a probation officer who had a lower than average caseload. Since Goodwin's entire family worked with the threat manager in designing and supporting these probation conditions, the judge agreed to give him a four-year suspended sentence, based on his living up to the prescribed conditions.

Used intelligently and with a keen eye to the unique aspects of each case, threat managers can use conditions on probation as a successful threat management strategy.

SOURCE: Authors' personal knowledge.

In terms of evaluating this strategy's effectiveness according to the several venues of intended violence, the law must be enforced wherever a violation occurs. The different venues, however, can complicate the ability to prosecute. In domestic disputes, for example, spouses frequently agree to file charges of abuse only to later change their minds when the case comes to trial. Businesses often choose not to go through the hassle of prosecuting current or former employees because of the time and expense. They then start pushing for a deal.

When Not to Prosecute

Arrest and prosecution should not be considered if the threat manager has insufficient evidence to support a successful prosecution. It is also ineffective in cases involving nuisance-type violations resulting only in fines. The threat manager should also consider delaying prosecution when such a delay gives a tactical advantage to use later if the problematic behavior continues. In any event, the threat manager should implement measures to immediately increase the protective response should the criminal prosecution strategy for any reason fail and the suspect regain his or her freedom unfettered by any conditions of bail or other controls.

Managing the Risk

Throughout our discussion of the four confrontational threat management strategies, a certain hesitancy or concern about employing them may have been detected. We confess to both. Confrontational strategies, by their very nature, escalate the risk because they bring the threat manager and the subject into an adverse relationship. This injects the threat manager even farther into the chemistry of the case. Threat managers should never take that step lightly and without fully considering the potential repercussions.

Yet, our concern and hesitancy should not be interpreted as opposition to the use of any of these strategies. We wish, instead, merely to underscore that given the right situation, the right time, and the right place, each strategy can be an effective instrument to use in managing the threat. Our hesitation and concern derives more from the issue of accurately identifying the right time and place than from the strategies themselves. Threat management is risky business whatever the strategies employed – confrontational or not. Threat managers can only diminish that risk by thoughtfully, deliberately, and intelligently choosing the best strategy for this situation, time, and place. Doing that alleviates our hesitancy and concern entirely.

We have described some of the advantages and disadvantages of each of the eight threat management strategies. We also tried to give some guidance on when each can be effective or not. But in doing so, we want no pretense to making hard and fast rules – indeed, we offered no rules at all. Threat management cases cannot be so easily bound.

At best, we can merely describe each strategy, illustrate it with realistic examples, and give its pros and cons. The threat manager must determine which one offers the best chance for managing the risk in the particular case at that particular moment. Once a strategy is played, the threat manager should immediately recognize that the situation has now changed *precisely because a strategy has been employed.* The change requires a re-evaluation of the case, the assessment, and the strategy. This may result in using yet another strategy or combination of strategies which, in turn, require yet another re-evaluation and assessment leading to the same or another strategy. The process, we assure you, is not endless – but it often enough seems like it is.

Summary

This chapter described the four confrontational strategies threat managers can use to manage a threatening situation. It discussed the pros and cons of using subject interviews to warn or confront the subject about his or her problematic behavior. It reviewed the advantages and disadvantages of using civil orders to manage the threat. The chapter also identified when and when not to use mental health commitments. Finally, the chapter summarized the issues revolving around arrest and prosecution. Combined with the previous chapter, which went over the four non-confrontational threat management strategies, these two chapters provided an in-depth analysis of all the threat management strategies a threat manager can use to manage a potentially dangerous subject.

Reference Notes Chapter 9

[1] Meloy, *Violence Risk and Threat Assessment,* 185-6; Gavin de Becker, "Intervention Decisions: The Value of Flexibility," Address before the Central Intelligence Agency Threat Management Conference, 1994, 14-9.

[2] For a discussion of threats and stalking from a legal and psychological point of view, see Meloy, *Violence Risk and Threat Assessment,* 167-92.

PART III. IMPLEMENTING THE CONTEMPORARY THREAT MANAGEMENT PROCESS

CHAPTER TEN

Establishing a Threat Management Process

We purposefully use the term process rather than program in order to avoid any implication that threat management requires dedicating significant resources and personnel full time. That depends on the size of the department and the potential number of cases that will need managing. Consequently, the threat management process can require a fully staffed, full-time unit or a part-time collateral duty. Workload alone determines the requirements.

Further, the process requires training whoever takes the responsibility for managing the cases. Although a relatively new field of law enforcement, contemporary threat management has already fully established itself as a specialty. As such, specialists should take primary responsibility for it. That means getting threat managers training, including refresher courses. Threat managers should also be encouraged to establish professional contacts and networks in order to keep abreast of new ideas and emerging techniques. Contemporary threat management attracts a wide variety of specialists, including law enforcement officers, psychologists, private security companies, social science researchers, behaviorists, and analysts. In addition, contemporary threat management has been spawning a growing body of scholarship. Threat managers should make use of these studies.

The first task of any newly assigned threat manager requires contacting and training anyone within the department's jurisdiction who may be aware of Inappropriate Communications or Contacts (IC&Cs) in the future. For city police, that means training city agency staffs, the mayor's staff, officers assigned to local precincts, and local business managers and employees in the concept of IC&Cs and how to report them. Deputy sheriffs should reach out to county government agencies and courts to train them on identifying and reporting IC&Cs.

Threat managers also need to reach out beyond their department's jurisdiction to contact other law enforcement agencies and private security firms providing protective services. Opening and maintaining lines of communication with these individuals and agencies will provide intelligence information on problem individuals. The threat manager should arrange to attend interagency intelligence meetings. Local task forces, such as those sponsored by the FBI focusing on domestic terrorism, are also valuable sources for identifying problem individuals and situations.

The threat manager will no doubt find that individuals of interest to him or her have also come to the attention of other agencies and threat managers. With Howlers in particular, frequently those who commit one IC&C will compound their activities by addressing numerous targets across jurisdictional and geographic areas. People with good manners generally maintain that decorum wherever they may be. The same holds true of people who behave inappropriately – they act that way wherever they may be.

It is crucial for the threat manager to have information flowing from all sources. Both threat assessments and protective investigations feed on facts; both are voracious eaters. But only through information can the threat manager begin to fill in pieces of the puzzle. Information from disparate sources can link one IC&C to another, it can reveal relationships, motives, past behaviors, and previous actions of the subject.

Controlling the flow of information requires information management. Depending, again, on workload, managing the information can be as simple as an index card system or as sophisticated as a computer database. The threat manager should design the system so that it retrieves information quickly and efficiently. The data collected should include not only demographics on the subject, but also key words or topics used by or of known interest to the subject. The latter may prove crucial in identifying anonymous subjects. Table 10-1 lists the variables that should be captured for each IC&C.

Table 10-1. Variables for a Threat Management Data Base

Case Synopsis

Explanation: Provide a brief description of the circumstances of the case.

Case Specifics

Explanation: Date, time, place IC&C received, who received it.

Method of Delivery

Explanation: Was IC&C delivered through suspicious activity, verbally, telephone, written, or through an informant.

Content

Explanation: Explicit or intangible threat, direct to target or veiled, immediate or deferred, key words and topics.

Suspect Demographics

Explanation: Age, race, sex, incarcerated or not, group member or not, other suspects or not, subject's height, weight, eye color, known numeric identifiers (Social Security Number, Driver's License number, NCIC number).

Target Demographics

Explanation: Age, race, sex, title, other victims.

Motive

Explanation: Case related, unknown motive, irrational, habitual, ideological, unrelated to target's official duties.

Case Study:

The Graffiti Fire-Starter

A subject became incensed at the official acts of a local prosecutor in the capitol city of a large western state. He wrote several letters of complaint about the prosecutor to various officials in different government agencies. Each letter crossed the threshold of inappropriateness and were duly reported to the respective threat managers for each agency. The threat managers routinely shared information.

Unsatisfied with the letter-writing campaign, the subject began setting fires near the capitol building. Each time, he left cryptic graffiti near the scene. The threat manager used several key words and topics in the graffiti to search his database. That search identified a likely suspect. The protective investigation put the suspect under surveillance. Officers arrested him as he prepared to set another fire.

Information is the coin of the realm in contemporary threat management.

SOURCE: Authors' personal knowledge.

Managing Threat Management Cases

Criminal investigators can manage their caseloads in a fairly simple and straightforward manner. They *open* their investigation by uncovering evidence someone has committed a crime. They *clear* the case upon the arrest and conviction of the perpetrator. In between, the case remains *ongoing*, although, perhaps, growing increasingly cold. Thus, criminal cases usually can be catalogued as open, ongoing, or cleared.

Not so threat management cases and their protective investigations. Threat managers rarely enjoy such an open and shut approach that criminal investigators have. Threat management cases usually open because someone receives an IC&C or reports their suspicions about an individual's behavior to the threat manager. Neither need be a crime. Nor will the case necessarily end with a climactic point of closing, what the movies always portray as the cell door slamming shut. Threat managers may have frequent opportunities to arrest their suspects, but neither the arrest nor the conviction diminishes the need to keep managing the threat. Slamming the cell door does not restrain the threat, however much it confines the threatener. Subjects can continue sending IC&Cs to the target from jail or prison. Worse, they can plot to take action, all the while behind bars. In other cases, anonymous subjects may deliver an IC&C to a target, then drop completely out of sight. The threat manager has no clear benchmark as to when to clear those type cases. Neither the subject's arrest and confinement nor continued silence offer threat managers much comfort.

As we have said repeatedly throughout this book, threat management cases are not about investigating or solving crimes. Instead, they center on managing the behavior of an individual whose previous inappropriate behaviors suggest some potential for risk. The threat manager does not have a caseload of crimes assigned to him or her to investigate. Rather, the threat manager's caseload consists of problem individuals. Consequently, threat managers can best understand their caseload as a hybrid mix of a criminal caseload and a parole or probation officer's caseload.

Thus, we avoid such traditional law enforcement case management terms as open, ongoing, or cleared. Instead, we prefer the terms active, inactive, chronic or habitual, and long-term. These best describe the stages involved in contemporary threat management. We define them (and give case studies) as follows:

- **Active Cases**. Cases remain active as long as the subject's behaviors indicate an escalating or potentially escalating risk to the target. The threat manager may have employed various threat management strategies, but they have yet to have an effect. In the active case stage, the circumstances of the case press the threat manager to make ongoing assessments, conduct protective investigations, and apply threat management strategies.
- **Inactive Cases.** Threat managers can designate a case inactive only if the threat manager can confidently document that the subject does not pose a risk to the target at this time. The threat manager no longer needs to conduct ongoing assessments, pursue leads in the protective investigation, or apply any threat management strategies, including passive Watch & Wait. We discuss in a subsequent section some of the issues and ramifications surrounding the decision to inactivate a case.

Case Study:

Skating into the 21st Century

The mayor forayed into the twenty-first century with a web site inviting e-mails on city issues. The threat manager knew immediately that it would bring him new business. Three days after the city established the site, a message came in addressed to the mayor reading, "You are so gay. I am going to kill you."

The threat manager obtained search warrants for the subscriber information from the Internet provider that relayed the message. The subscriber was a city police Sergeant, who was also the president of the Police Officers Association. The threat manager got a new warrant to seize the computer. When he interviewed the Sergeant, he learned that the Sergeant's 13-year-old son also had access to the computer.

With the Sergeant's permission, the threat manager interviewed the son. He readily admitted that he and a friend had been looking at a skateboard web site when they noticed a link to the city web site and an invitation to comment on the Mayor's proposal to restrict skateboard use in city parks. The son wrote the e-mail as a joke, but adamantly claimed he never sent it. The threat manager tracked down the friend. He admitted that, as a prank, he hit the "send" button after the son briefly left the study.

The threat manager, with the Sergeant's full cooperation, arranged for an informal adjudication of the threat through the Juvenile Justice system. The threat manager also concluded from the protective investigation that neither the son nor his friend posed a risk to the mayor at this time. He assigned the case to inactive status.

Inactive cases consist of subjects who clearly pose no risk to the target at this time.

SOURCE: Authors' personal knowledge.

- **Chronic or Habitual Cases.** Chronic or habitual cases involve subjects who repeatedly direct IC&Cs toward targets, frequently multiple targets, over extended periods of time, but never escalate the risk by taking any steps beyond their preferred choice of IC&C. The IC&Cs may be fixed on one particular target or they may be diversified among many targets, crossing jurisdictions and geographic divides. Many habitual or chronic subjects (the terms are interchangeable) reside in mental hospitals or prisons. The threat manager still has to review and assess each new IC&C, but he or she no longer has to initiate a protective investigation or apply any threat management strategies beyond passive Watch & Wait because the IC&Cs do not change in tone or circumstance.

Case Study:

The Hobbyist

R.F., a federal prisoner confined to the Bureau of Prison's Springfield, Missouri, mental health facility, for many years spent most of his days composing lengthy letters to judges, federal and local, all across the country. He mailed the letters – all filled with threats and recriminations and angry, irrational ramblings – to any judge of any jurisdiction that he could think of or for whom he could get an address. The overwhelming majority of the judges never met or heard a case involving R.F; he did not know them or their caseloads or even their decisions.

After investigating R.F., deputy marshals concluded that R.F. threatened judges solely because they were judges. At the deputies' request, R.F.'s psychiatrist asked him why he wrote so many letters to so many judges whom he did not know and had nothing personal against. R.F. seemed surprised by the question, but then explained to the doctor that if he did not have his letters to write, he would simply not know what to do with himself all day. Writing threat letters was his hobby.

Based on the protective investigation, the deputies categorized R.F. as an habitual threatener. Although future letters would be assessed for changes in tone or situation, the habitual assessment allowed the deputies to reassure recipients of R.F.'s communications that he was well known and that the deputies had arranged for him to be closely monitored by the Bureau of Prisons.

Some subjects like to harass public officials, often over long periods of time. Once the threat manager can determine that the subject does not pose a risk to the target, the threat manager can classify these subjects as chronic or habitual threateners.

SOURCE: Calhoun, Hunters and Howlers, xix.

- **Long-Term Cases.** Threat managers use the long-term case designation for those situations in which the risk, though low, remains steady and all appropriate threat management strategies have been applied with limited success. A Watch & Wait strategy, either passive or active, or third party monitoring or control has been implemented because the subject remains of protective interest. Although both chronic and long-term cases can extend over significant stretches of time, long-term cases do not necessarily involve IC&Cs repeatedly directed toward the target. Indeed, the case may be based on only one IC&C, but its significance or the circumstances of the case prohibit the threat manager from inactivating the case because the subject cannot be assessed as not posing a risk to the target at this time.

Case Study:

Keeping the Controllers at Bay

Fourteen years ago, Larry B. first tried to smuggle a gun into City Hall. His arrest led to a mental health commitment. Over the years, police arrested him a second time for trying to take a gun into City Hall. He spent two years in the state mental hospital and did a couple of short stints at city facilities. Since his first arrest, the threat manager had been managing Larry's case.

The threat manager knew that Larry did well as long as he maintained the drug regimen prescribed by his doctors. Without the medication, Larry believed that "controllers" radiated his body causing burns and great pain. Larry could only stop the pain by doing the controllers' bidding. They ordered him to take a gun to City Hall.

The threat manager oversaw Larry through regular contacts with him, mental health prescriptions, and third party monitoring through his parents. For the past two years, Larry had stayed on his medication. The threat manager knew Larry did not pose a threat at this time, but he also knew that Larry sometimes neglected to take his pills. Although his parents helped keep him on the medicine, they had aged visibly over the last decade.

The threat manager assigned the case to long-term status. He had to be ready for any time Larry might drop off his medication. He also had to be prepared for the time when Larry's parents would no longer monitor Larry's behavior. Consequently, the threat manager continues to schedule regular meetings with Larry and his parents. He knows keeping the controllers at bay will always be part of his caseload.

Long-term cases consist of subjects who, though generally posing only a low risk, have the potential to escalate to high risk.

SOURCE: Author's personal knowledge.

When Is When?

The decision to designate a case inactive harbors some profound challenges. Philosophically, this decision requires the threat manager to reach two extraordinarily difficult questions. When has enough time passed with nothing further occurring to confidently say that nothing more will occur? How does the threat manager prove the negative, that the subject did not do something and therefore will not do anything further in respect to the target? Threat managers will find answering these two questions impossibly difficult, yet absolutely essential in order to manage their caseloads properly and efficiently.

The milestones law enforcement officers normally use to measure success simply do not apply with threat management. Arrests, the culminating event of a criminal investigation, make things more difficult for the subject of a protective investigation, but it does not make it impossible for him or her to harm the target. Consequently, threat managers cannot use incarceration as the sole measure for determining the subject no longer poses a risk to the target at this time. The case has to remain active until the threat manager can answer either of the two questions. Measuring the success of any threat management strategy can be illusory because it depends so much on nothing additional happening. The subject has not done this or has not done that. The target is safe because no violence occurred – yet.

Therein lies the rub. When does the *yet* become a permanent state?

Case Study:

The Unforgiven

Marin County, California, District Attorney William Weissich convicted Malcolm Schlette of arson in the late 1950s. Schlette took the conviction personally and vowed revenge. While serving his sentence, Schlette talked about killing Weissich once he got out. Reports of those threats were passed on to the prosecutor. He took them seriously enough to install a steel door in his office, stash a gun in his desk drawer, and take other security precautions.

Unfortunately, when Weissich left office for private practice, the reports on Schlette's continued threats quit coming to him. Time passed and Weissich relaxed his guard.

But Schlette never forgot. Even after his release from prison in the 1980s, Schlette talked about revenge. Even worse, he collected an arsenal. Police arrested him for having the weapons, which violated the terms of his probation. The court, however, released him back on probation. No one thought to warn Weissich.

On November 18, 1986, Schlette went to Weissich's office and shot him to death. Later, Schlette swallowed poison to commit suicide.

While incarcerated, Schlette could not act out his threat to Weissich. Law enforcement confused the length of his sentence with nothing happening, so the threat appeared to decrease.

When is when? Some subjects can hold a grudge for decades before taking action or being able to take action.

SOURCE: San Francisco Examiner, October 10, 1992.

These are the philosophical issues. In reality, the pressure from other cases will compel a practical inactivation of those cases that appear to the threat manager less serious. The most experienced threat managers can handle only a dozen or so active cases at a time. As a result, managing threat management cases is best modeled on crisis management. Threat managers will – of necessity – put more energy and attention on their most serious cases, letting the others languish until the subject does something that raises the seriousness of that case above others in the caseload.

Threat managers will develop their own personal techniques for managing their caseload. We can only recommend being creative and intelligent about it. For example, effective threat management factors in such intangibles as anniversaries or significant upcoming events affecting the subject. Clearly, Schlette's release from prison should have been recognized as an increase in the seriousness of the risk toward his target. Some subjects time their IC&Cs around certain holidays or anniversaries. Workplace violence, for example, frequently occurs on the anniversary of the employee's termination. Violence toward abortion providers tends to increase around Christmas and New Year, Easter, and Mother's Day.

After the threat manager has inactivated a case, he or she can set up a suspense system to schedule follow-up actions at designated dates over the course of the year – say once a quarter or every six months or just before specific dates, holidays, or anniversaries known to be of importance to the subject. For example, after a mental health commitment and subsequent outpatient treatment that appears to have successfully resolved the subject's problems, the threat manager can use the suspense system to contact the outpatient clinic about the subject's status in four months. This approach conserves the threat manager's time while acting as a margin of safety in cases involving subjects who respond positively to the management strategy, but who may possibly revert once time wears down the effects of the strategy.

Case Study:

That Time of Year

A mentally ill subject aggressively attempted to contact an elected official at an annual Christmas event. After a threat management strategy was effected, the case was designated inactive. The following year, the subject again attempted contact at the Christmas event.

As a result, the threat manager now schedules time just prior to Christmas to check on the subject, confer with his doctors, and develop a strategy to prevent an approach.

Sometimes subjects follow patterns. The threat manager can use those to help manage the case and the caseload.

SOURCE: Authors' personal knowledge.

Documenting the Cases

As with any law enforcement investigation, threat managers should carefully document all aspects of each threat management case. Such documentation helps justify what the threat manager did, what the assessments concluded, what the protective investigation uncovered, why the threat manager selected the particular management strategy or strategies, and when and why the threat manager inactivated the case. Since some cases remain in long-term status for years, the documentation helps remind the threat manager of events that happened early in the case. It also supports any trade-off in cases as new threat managers take over. A detailed record also helps in presenting the case to a court or in any effort to have the suspect committed to a mental health facility or to support a request for a restraining order. It also supports training programs by opening the threat manager's case experiences to others.

Managing the Targets

Many targets, with considerable justification, fear for their lives. They look to the threat manager not only to allay those fears throughout the duration of the case, but also to make those fears baseless by stopping the subject from acting violently. Consequently, threat managers need to constantly project an image of themselves as professional problem solvers. At the same time, the threat manager should strive to keep the target calm, compliant to instructions, and willing to follow the threat manager's lead. In many situations involving high-ranking government officials, business executives, doctors, and other targets, the target is someone used to being in charge; used to making decisions, even life and death decisions, and not accustomed to taking orders, however politely given. The threat manager should prevent any effort by the target to take over control of the case or choose the threat management strategy or otherwise exert operational control over the case.

Always offering some degree of protective response allows the threat manager to keep control over the case. Protective responses range from providing a security briefing at the minimum to a full-fledged protective detail or target relocation at the maximum. The threat manager should select the appropriate protective response in direct proportion to the assessment and to the findings of any protective investigation. Simply by giving the target and his or her family and associates a security briefing gives the threat manager the opportunity to project an image of control and reassurance. The briefing tells the target that the threat manager cares for his or her security and is taking measures to ensure it. Enhanced security measures, if needed by the circumstances of the situation, send an even stronger message.

Always providing some level of protective response serves two important purposes. First, it enhances the target's security. Even a security briefing helps remind the target to take simple precautions and to be aware – and immediately report – any suspicious incidents. Obviously, going up the scale of protective responses adds even more security. The threat manager needs to constantly balance each protective response with the most current assessment, the findings of the protective investigation, and the success of the threat management strategies. That will ensure that the threat manager's limited resources are applied the most efficiently and effectively. Secondly, always implementing some degree of protective response sends a positive signal to the target. It helps underscore the threat manager's professionalism, competence, and concern. That signal will allay the target's fears and give him or her the reassurance that everything necessary is being done.

At the same time, the threat manager should diplomatically and gently remind the target that he or she ultimately bears the responsibility for his or her safety. Although many public officials, especially the president, vice-president, and governors, receive full-time protection, the majority of a threat manager's targets will not be afforded that luxury. Consequently, threat managers face severe limits on the degree and amount of physical protection they can offer the target. Although contemporary threat management works hand in hand with protective responses, the threat manager needs to work carefully with the target to ensure that the target sets up the proper physical measures.

Case Study:

Panic Attack

An experienced staff assistant to an elected official contacted the threat manager to report a serious threat situation. The two were well acquainted from having worked together on several previous IC&Cs. They shared an excellent rapport. Hearing the assistant's report, the threat manager immediately implemented an aggressive management strategy, which brought the situation quickly under control.

Later, the staff assistant told the threat manager that this time she had been really frightened, but not so much by the incident as by the threat manager's response to it. She explained that in previous cases, the threat manager was very reassuring and calm. This time, he became very abrupt. She could sense that his reaction was different by the way he became almost demanding in his requests for information and written statements. She confessed that his attitude scared her much more than the assertive protective actions taking place around her and the fast pace of the investigation.

Targets and their staffs often gauge how they should react to a situation by the way the threat manager reacts to it. Visibly shifting into a crisis mode may panic the targets.

SOURCE: Authors' personal knowledge.

Although always implementing some protective response sends a positive signal to the target, it can also send an unnerving one at the same time. However relieved the target feels because the threat manager has arranged some security, it can also make the target even more nervous precisely because the threat manager considered a protective response necessary. The logic flows like this: "Why is this officer telling me to alter my commuting habits unless I'm really in danger." By its very nature, establishing a protective detail on a target tells the target that this case is dangerous, even frightening. Consequently, if the threat manager determines that the risk requires physical protection, the threat manager should take the time to explain to the target that the protection is in response to a *temporary* concern that will be relieved once certain information is obtained or certain, and specific things, such as the arrest of the subject, happen. By stressing the transient aspect of the protective detail that has clearly defined end points, the threat manager also prepares the target for when the time comes to bring down the detail.

In addition, the threat manager should take care when divulging information about the case to the target. Although we do not recommend withholding information since any new piece of information may jog more memories from the target, we do believe that the threat manager should disclose the information in its full context, complete with the threat manager's reasoned interpretation of its significance. An old assault charge that may not appear serious to a seasoned law enforcement officer may nonetheless scare the target. Presenting the information in its larger context and explaining how it was factored into the assessment will help alleviate much of the target's concerns.

Keeping the target to the facts and keeping those facts in their proper assessment context will also help combat the natural tendency of the target to play the *What If?* game. We discussed in an earlier chapter the importance of the threat manager controlling his or her imagination. A far greater challenge is presented by the target's imagination. In these situations, the target has a natural concern for his or her safety and for the safety of family members and staff. The What If? game plays extraordinarily well off those safety concerns.

Taking and keeping charge of the case provides the threat manager the best antidote to the *What If?* game. By sticking to the known facts and fully briefing the target on the known information and how the threat manager assesses its significance, the threat manager becomes a model for the target to follow. Earlier we pointed out that facts alone fuel assessments. They also have a soothing effect on the target's worries and concerns. By keeping the target fully informed and fully apprised of how the threat manager intends to respond and why, the target will feel a greater respect for the threat manager's abilities in general and handling of this case in particular. Targets with unanswered questions frequently begin to question the threat manager and the threat manager's competence in handling the case. Targets with unanswered questions also begin getting answers themselves through the *What If?* game. Both tendencies eat away at the threat manager's relationship with the target.

Summary

This chapter described how the threat management process can be developed at any level, whether from an officer or individual doing it part-time or a fully staffed, organized unit doing it full-time. We discussed managing cases by designating cases active, habitual or chronic, long-term, or inactive. Every case should be fully documented in order to justify what the threat manager did and serve as a references in managing long-term cases, developing training, and passing cases from one threat manager to the next. Finally, the chapter discussed managing the target, and the target's fears and worries, as well as the threat.

In closing, we suggest that a successful threat management process consists of ten basic elements, each integral to all the others. They are:

1. Recognizing the need for a threat management process.
2. Assigning responsibility and authority to manage cases to specific individuals, who are then trained and their training maintained with on-going updates.
3. Providing training and liaison with potential targets, their key staff members or associates, and family members.
4. Establishing liaison with other agencies as sources of threat information.
5. Creating an incident tracking system and well-documented files that can be cross-checked.
6. Using consistent and valid assessment methods.
7. Conducting thorough, progressive protective investigations.
8. Applying threat management strategies flexibly and intelligently.
9. Dealing with the target and other interested parties professionally, confidently, and competently.
10. Managing cases appropriately.

These are the golden rules of effective contemporary threat management. Following them, and keeping them close to heart, will guide the threat manager through the entire threat management process.

Recommended Resources

The authors recommend the following books and organizations as resources for those working in threat management.

Books

The Gift of Fear: Survival Signals That Protect Us From Violence, by Gavin de Becker, 1997, Little, Brown and Company

Hunters and Howlers: Threats and Assaults Against Federal Judicial Officials in the United States, by Frederick S. Calhoun, 1789-1993, (Arlington, VA: United States Marshals Service, 1998) Copies can be obtained from the United States Marshals Service, Printing and Distribution Division, U.S. Department of Justice, Washington, D.C.

The Psychology of Stalking, by Reid Meloy, Ph.D., 1998, Academic Press (www.academicpress.com)

School Violence Threat Management, by Kris Mohandie, Ph.D., 2002, Specialized Training Services (www.specializedtraining.com)

Threat Assessment: A Risk Management Approach, by James Turner, Ph.D. and Michael Gelles, Psy.D., 2003, The Haworth Press (www.HaworthPress.com)

Violence Risk and Threat Assessment, by Reid Meloy, Ph.D., 2000, Specialized Training Services (www.specializedtraining.com)

Violence Assessment and Intervention: The Practitioner's Handbook by Michael Corcoran, Ph.D. and James Cawood, CPP, 2003, CRC Press (www.crcpress.com)

Organizations

The Association of Threat Assessment Professionals (ATAP)

Specialized Training Services, Inc. (www.specializedtraining.com), *books, tapes, videos and staff training*